Black Civil Rights
During the Johnson Administration

Black Civil Rights During the Johnson Administration

James C. Harvey

UNIVERSITY AND COLLEGE PRESS
OF MISSISSIPPI
JACKSON

ISBN 0–87805–021–3
Library of Congress Catalog Card Number: 73–00000
Copyright © 1973 by
The University & College Press of Mississippi
Manufactured in the United States of America
Printed by The TJM Corporation, Baton Rouge, Louisiana
Designed by J. Barney McKee

THIS BOOK IS AUTHORIZED
AND SPONSORED BY
JACKSON STATE COLLEGE
JACKSON, MISSISSIPPI

In memory of
Dr. Martin Luther King, Jr.,
who died struggling for the cause
he believed in so deeply.

CONTENTS

This is an important book. It matters not whether you are an historian or a political scientist or even a layman with an abiding interest in civil rights, *Black Civil Rights During the Johnson Administration* is toned to satisfy all intellectual and emotional appetites.

During the 1950s and early 1960s, few advances were achieved in the political arena, at least with respect to policy pronouncements, in the vain attempts to foster civil rights. Interest groups had access to the presidency and Congress, but little leverage. The courts always stood ready and willing to render decisions, but the cost and energy involved in promoting civil rights through the judicial system was staggering. And all too often the pronouncements of the courts were too late, too modest, and too easily circumvented. Discrimination was still an abstraction to middle-class America in the fifties, and policies are seldom formulated on the basis of abstract notions of equality. The dreams for a better tomorrow remained dreams, and the future looked almost as black as the past. Langston Hughes saw what was coming when he wrote:

> What happens to a dream deferred
> Does it dry up like a raisin in the sun
> Or fester like a sore and then run
> Or does it explode

The patience of many black Americans had been strained. They took to the streets to protest, demonstrate, cajole, indeed, even riot in order to break down the abstraction of discrimination so that governmental policy-makers could at least vicariously feel and understand the enormity of the problems of discrimination. From the Montgomery bus boycott to the freedom rides and the sit-ins, to the tragic deaths of Medgar Evers and three civil rights workers, the abstraction was broken down. The last four years of the Eisenhower administration and the three short years when John Kennedy was president might be characterized as years of public agitation—an agitation designed to break down the abstract notion that discrimination was just another political issue.

By the time that Lyndon Johnson became President, the years of public agitation had run their course. The foundation had been laid and it was time to make policy. When it came to understanding and mastering the policy-making process, there was no one who could match Lyndon Johnson. While Johnson was not a great innovator of policy, he possessed the necessary skill and cunning for bringing it into effect. Indeed, it may be that one of Johnson's greatest contributions as president can be measured in terms of policy output in the field of civil rights. Unfortunately, much of the policy only touched the lives of the talented and the middle classes; still it constituted a significant step forward.

It is through this sensitive period of history that James Harvey has documented his chronology of events which have had such a great impact upon civil rights. To call this just a chronology of events, however, is really to do a great disservice to the enormous contribution that this book makes. It is the finest respository, explanation, and analysis of the laws, executive orders, administrative regulations and governmental statistics that can be found today. If this were all there was to the book, one might perceive it as a meticulously researched document that could serve for resource material, but otherwise too academic to be interesting. On the contrary, Harvey has integrated this great fund of data and statistics into a fascinating and perceptive analysis of the politics surrounding the controversial Johnson years. He brings keen insights into the delicate relationships existing between Johnson and the variety of interest groups seeking to promote civil rights. Political issues don't just hang abstractly in the air. They are well crystallized and cloaked in the excitement of dynamic political combat that so characterized the presidency of Lyndon Johnson. And all of this is set off by some of Johnson's best rhetoric. Johnson never laid claim to being a great orator, but on several occasions he did rise to the occasion with moving appeals to the nation. On each of these occasions the president was talking about civil rights. While Harvey has obviously been unable to capture the tone of this rhetoric, the substance is there in all its splendor.

Perhaps one of the most gratifying aspects of *Black Civil Rights During the Johnson Administration* is the objectivity with which Harvey has handled the Johnson years. Too often we are prone either to glorify or to damn a president for his accomplishments or lack thereof. This book tells it as it is. When progress advanced, it has been noted; where frustration levels increased because of a lack of progress, this assumes an equally prominent role.

You are about to embark upon an enriching experience. Read the following pages with care. They place the problems and advances of civil rights during the Johnson years into a very real perspective.

CLIFFORD M. LYTLE

This study serves as a sequel to the earlier volume, *Civil Rights During the Kennedy Administration*. It deals broadly with the conditions endured by black people in America during the period from 1963 to 1969 and the efforts made by the Johnson administration to ameliorate them.

In terms of methodology the approach is descriptive and analytical. In Chapter I the major civil rights accomplishments of the Roosevelt, Truman, Eisenhower, and Kennedy administrations are reviewed. In addition, there is a brief discussion of President Johnson's succession after the tragic assassination of President Kennedy. Chapter II deals with the passage of the Civil Rights Act of 1964 and President Johnson's election victory over Barry Goldwater. Chapter III contains a summary of events leading up to the enactment of the Voting Rights Act of 1965 and the Civil Rights Act of 1968, as well as the major provisions of those laws. In Chapter IV there is an analysis and description of efforts made during the Johnson administration to coordinate federal civil rights activities and to expand the employment of blacks in the federal bureaucracy. In addition, the handicaps faced by blacks in the various armed services are examined. In Chapter V, conditions for blacks in the areas of housing and private employment are investigated along with attempts made by the Johnson administration to improve them. Chapter VI contains an analysis of the obstacles faced by blacks in the areas of voting and education in the South and the actions taken by the Johnson administration to overcome them. Chapter VII analyzes efforts made by the federal government to desegregate health and welfare services in the South. In the epilogue, an evaluation is made of President Johnson's civil rights accomplishments.

As with the Kennedy book, I do not pretend that this volume constitutes an exhaustive study of the subject matter dealt with. I hope that some of those who read it will be encouraged to delve into the topics more deeply now that the civil rights section of the Lyndon

Baines Johnson Library in Austin, Texas, has been opened to scholars. The failure of the American people and government to accord full citizenship to and recognize the human dignity of black people remains our most pressing domestic problem.

Shortly after preparing this manuscript I attended the Civil Rights Symposium sponsored by the Lyndon Baines Johnson Library on December 11–12, 1972. While there, I heard the former president deliver his last public address. He made it clear that much of the task in civil rights remained unfinished. He died in January, 1973.

In preparing this study I wish to thank the librarians at Jackson State College, Millsaps College, and the University of Texas at Austin. In addition, I want to give my special thanks to Jackson State College and the University & College Press of Mississippi for making this publication possible. Finally, I am grateful to my friend and former instructor, Dr. Clifford M. Lytle, chairman of the government department at the University of Arizona, Tucson, Arizona, for writing the foreword.

JAMES C. HARVEY

Black Civil Rights
During the Johnson Administration

CHAPTER I

Introduction

Recognition by the federal government of the cruelly harsh conditions under which most black people have been forced to live has been slow in coming in this country. Yet, recognition at the federal level has been badly needed, since state and local governments have attempted little in improving the lot of blacks. The states' rights argument has usually served as a rhetorical guise for the maintenance of the status quo as far as blacks are concerned. It would be more accurate to hold that all levels of government, including the federal government, have done much to retard the advancement of black people. However, since the state and local governments have proven to be the most unresponsive and recalcitrant, particularly in the South, blacks have had to rely largely on pressure on the federal government. As a result of the electoral college situation, the presidency has generally been more amenable to black needs than congress where white southerners have dominated many of the committees much of the time.

There was scarcely any concern about blacks in the twentieth century until the Franklin Roosevelt administration. Even then, blacks benefited for the most part only because most of them were among the poor who were helped by the New Deal programs. The emphasis was on economic and social class rather than color of skin, but societal institutions, including the "breadlines," remained segregated. The federal government made no concerted effort to lift the barriers that surrounded blacks at every turn. During World War II, as the result of a threatened march on Washington by black leaders, President Roosevelt issued an executive order banning discrimination in employment in defense industries and established a Fair Employment Practices Committee (FEPC) to deal with government contract employment.[1]

---

[1] See Harold C. Fleming, "The Federal Executive and Civil Rights: 1961–1965," *Daedalus*, 94 (Fall, 1965), 923.

President Roosevelt's successor, Harry S. Truman, initiated desegregation in the nation's armed forces; and as a result of pressure from black leaders and white liberals, he recommended what was then regarded as a very far-reaching civil rights program. It was considered significant at the time that a president would make such proposals even though they were not enacted into law. Truman also created a Fair Employment Practices Board (FEPB) in the Civil Service Commission, since the FEPC had been discontinued by Congress.[2]

President Dwight Eisenhower continued Truman's attempts to desegregate the armed forces, promoted desegregation in the nation's capital, and established committees to deal with discrimination against blacks in both government and government contract employment. However, Eisenhower disliked the use of executive power to deal with what he considered basically local problems. He never publicly committed himself when it came to school desegregation cases, including *Brown* I and *Brown* II, and his silence seemed to indicate neutrality at best on this sensitive matter.[3] Though Eisenhower's own role was ambiguous, it was during his administration that Congress enacted into law the first civil rights laws passed since Reconstruction, the Civil Rights Acts of 1957 and 1960, both of which dealt largely with voting rights for blacks. However reluctantly, Eisenhower set an important precedent when he sent in federal troops and federalized the Arkansas National Guard in order to enforce a federal court order calling for limited school desegregation in Little Rock.

During the 1960 elections there were some signs of change as the platforms of both major political parties took relatively strong stands on civil rights.[4] Blacks played a major role in the election results with some 60 percent voting for Kennedy. As a result of his narrow victory over Richard Nixon and the tight situation in Congress, Presi-

[2] See William C. Berman, *The Politics of Civil Rights in the Truman Administration* (Columbus, Ohio: Ohio State University Press, 1970), for a good discussion of the subject.

[3] See John Emmet Hughes, *The Ordeal of Power: A Political Memoir of the Eisenhower Years* (New York: Atheneum Publishers, Inc., 1963), 201. See also Dwight D. Eisenhower, *The White House Years: Waging Peace, 1956–1961* (Garden City, N.Y.: Doubleday & Co., Inc., 1965), 51.

[4] This discussion of the Kennedy administration is a brief summary of James C. Harvey, *Civil Rights During the Kennedy Administration* (Hattiesburg, Miss.: University & College Press of Mississippi, 1971).

dent John Kennedy decided to shelve any plans for additional legislation and to emphasize executive action instead. In 1961 and 1962 the primary methods employed were negotiation and litigation. However, in 1962, when confronted with defiance of a federal court at the University of Mississippi, Kennedy followed the precedent established by Eisenhower in resorting to force so that James Meredith could attend classes there.

In spite of his caution, Kennedy did make proposals in 1962 for the abolition of the poll tax for federal primaries and elections and the substitution of a sixth grade literacy test for voting purposes. The anti-poll tax measure was adopted as an amendment to the United States Constitution but not the other proposal. The year 1963 proved to be a turning point, however. Deciding that relatively little progress was being made through the use of executive levers, Kennedy made stronger legislative proposals, though, initially, even the new proposals were too mild. The public image of the civil rights cause was strengthened by a devastating report about conditions in Mississippi issued by the United States Commission on Civil Rights; by the tragic murder of NAACP leader Medger Evers in Jackson, Mississippi; and by the abuses which blacks suffered in Birmingham, Alabama. By the time of Kennedy's death in November, 1963, a stronger civil rights bill was on its way through Congress.

What kind of man was Kennedy's successor, Lyndon B. Johnson? A southerner by upbringing, could he be counted on to build upon the foundation laid by his predecessor? His previous career in both houses of Congress and as vice-president seemed to provide at least a partial answer.

Theodore White claims that, in his early years in Congress as a representative and senator, Johnson voted as a white southerner thirty-nine times on matters of civil rights. Among these votes were: six times against proposals to abolish the poll tax; six times against efforts to eliminate discrimination in federal programs; twice against bills to prohibit and punish lynching; twice to support segregation in the military; once against the FEPC; and once to maintain segregation in Washington, D.C.[5] Lyndon Johnson, however, claims that he only voted against six civil rights bills that came up on the House and

[5] Theodore H. White, *The Making of the President, 1964* (New York: Atheneum Publishers, 1965) 252–53.

Senate floors. He insists that those bills were designed more to humiliate the South than to help blacks, and that was the reason he opposed them.[6] In any case, Johnson played a major role in the passage of the Civil Rights Acts of 1957 and 1960.

Even though the last two acts were weak and Johnson bore a large part of the responsibility for their inadequacy, he had changed his stance from earlier days. It would be difficult to prove just why that had happened. The most obvious reason might have been that after he became the Democratic leader in the Senate, he set his sights on a higher office, which meant cultivating a national constituency. By this time, it was well known that black votes in northern cities could be crucial to the outcome of close presidential elections as in 1948. However, it was also possible that Johnson might have developed more sensitivity toward the handicaps suffered by black people. Whatever the reason, he became even more associated with the cause of civil rights during his service as vice-president and chairman of President Kennedy's Committee on Equal Employment Opportunity.

Immediately after the assassination of President Kennedy in November, 1963, Anthony Lewis wrote: "In spite of President Johnson's southern background, no experienced observer doubted he would push the passage of the civil rights bill started by his predecessor." [7] Lewis predicted that history would judge President Johnson on the basis of what he accomplished in the face of a revolution in race relations.[8]

President Johnson was not unaware of the situation as he assumed the reins of power. He knew that there was a great deal of apprehension in the black community. As he noted later: "Just when the blacks had had their hopes for equality and justice raised, after centuries of misery and despair, they awoke one morning to discover that their future was in the hands of a President born in the South." [9]

Some of the black leaders such as Whitney Young, Jr.,and Roy Wilkins tended to place their trust in the new president. They felt that he might be more successful than Kennedy in the civil rights field,

[6] Lyndon Baines Johnson, *The Vantage Point: Perspectives of the Presidency, 1963–1969* (New York: Holt, Rinehart and Winston, 1971), 155.

[7] New York *Times*, November 23, 1963, p. 12.

[8] *Ibid.*, November 24, 1963, IV, p. 5.

[9] Johnson, *The Vantage Point*, 18.

particularly in pushing bills through Congress. Johnson had more experience and was more skilled in legislative matters than Kennedy. Furthermore, being a southerner, Johnson would be extremely sensitive to charges that he was dragging his feet on civil rights. Finally, Young and Wilkins contended that the national revulsion over Kennedy's assassination might shame Congress into enacting the civil rights bill started by him in 1963.[10]

On November 25, 1963, a group of civil rights leaders met in New York City and urged Congress to enact strong civil rights legislation as the unfinished business of President Kennedy. Among those taking part were: Dr. Martin Luther King, Jr., James Farmer, James Foreman, Roy Wilkins, Jack Greenberg, Dorothy Height, and Whitney Young, Jr.[11]

Two days later, President Johnson appeared before a joint session of Congress to declare:

> No memorial or eulogy could more eloquently honor President Kennedy's memory than the earliest possible passage of the civil rights bill for which he fought so hard. We have talked long enough in this country about equal rights. We have talked 100 years or more. It is time now to write the next chapter—and to write it in the books of law.
>
> I urge you again, as I did in 1957, and again in 1960, to enact a civil rights law so that we can move forward to eliminate from this nation every trace of discrimination and oppression that is based upon race or color. There can be no greater source of strength to this nation both at home and abroad.[12]

Through this initial statement to Congress President Johnson informed that body and the nation that he intended to press for passage of the civil rights bill proposed by President Kennedy. Though this step seemed to justify the confidence placed in Johnson by some of the civil rights leaders, it would require time and preseverance to determine whether his actions would be equated with his words.

---

[10] New York *Times*, November 25, 1963, p. 12. See also Lerone Bennett, Jr., "What Negroes Can Expect from President Lyndon Johnson," *Ebony*, 19 (January, 1964), 81–84.

[11] New York *Times*, November 26, 1963, p. 20.

[12] "Johnson Urges Congress to Act. Emphasizes Civil Rights," *Congressional Quarterly Weekly Report*, 21 (November 29, 1963), 2089; New York *Times*, November 28, 1963, p. 20.

CHAPTER II

The Civil Rights Act of 1964 and the Presidential Election

A few days after his succession, President Johnson informed Congress and the nation that he intended to push for the passage of the omnibus civil rights bill already introduced by the previous administration. The bill had been reported out of the House Judiciary Committee on November 20, 1963, and was sent to the House Rules Committee to await a rule governing floor debate in the House of Representatives. In anticipation that Howard Smith of Virginia, chairman of the House Rules Committee, would attempt to delay action by the committee, Richard Bolling of Missouri, a committee member, began proceedings to discharge the bill from the committee. Approving Bolling's move, House Speaker McCormack of Massachusetts declared that every effort would be made to pass the measure before the end of 1963. In addition, President Johnson met with Charles Halleck, the Republican floor leader in the House, to urge his assistance in "unfreezing" the anticipated blocked bill.[1] In the meantime, the strategy in the Senate called for delay in awaiting passage of the House bill. The civil rights forces in the Senate intended to bypass the Senate Judiciary Committee, chaired by James Eastland of Mississippi, and to act directly on the House version.

President Johnson undertook a series of meetings with black leaders such as Roy Wilkins of the National Association for the Advancement of Colored People (NAACP), Whitney Young, Jr., of the National Urban League, Dr. Martin Luther King, Jr., of the Southern Christian Leadership Conference (SCLC), James Farmer of the Congress of Racial Equality (CORE), Clarence Mitchell of the NAACP, and A. Philip Randolph. He assured them that John Kennedy's dream of equality had not died with him.[2] After his meeting with the president, Roy Wilkins told newspaper reporters, "We have very great faith in the new President's attitude on civil rights." [3]

[1] White, *The Making of the President, 1964*, 44.
[2] Johnson, *The Vantage Point*, 29; White, *The Making of the President, 1964*, 44.
[3] New York *Times*, November 30, 1963, p. 1.

On December 1, 1963, the NAACP announced that it would open a drive to purge from office all congressmen opposed to civil rights legislation. Roy Wilkins, the executive secretary, warned that the organization would discontinue its practice of listing a candidate's record on civil rights without any recommendation as to how a voter should cast his ballot.[4]

Concurrently, at meetings on Long Island, James Farmer and Bayard Rustin praised President Johnson for his recent speech to Congress on civil rights.[5] Following a meeting with President Johnson, Dr. Martin Luther King, Jr., expressed his approval of the President's awareness and deep concern about civil rights. Dr. King stated: "As a Southerner, I am happy to know that a fellow Southerner is in the White House who is concerned about civil rights." [6] Dr. King also declared that he would assist in the acceleration of the voter registration drive for blacks, and that demonstrations which had been suspended with the death of Kennedy would be resumed until the injustices causing the demonstrations had been eliminated.

While Dr. King was enunciating his plans, Howard Smith, chairman of the House Rules Committee, as anticipated, announced that he planned to hold no committee meetings on the civil rights measure. However, by December 5, Smith declared that he would schedule hearings in January, 1964. Why had Smith changed his mind? President Johnson had announced that he would lend full support to a discharge petition. Furthermore, the Leadership Conference on Civil Rights met on December 4 to plan a campaign for discharge petition signatures. Roy Wilkins warned that he would work for the defeat of any congressman who voted against the bill. Finally, George Meany and Walter Reuther, labor leaders, issued a statement that organized labor would undertake a letter-writing campaign urging support of the discharge petition. Faced with this array of political power, Smith decided to hold the hearings rather than face up to an inevitable personal embarrassment.[7]

The bill appeared to be on its way through the House when Presi-

---

[4] *Ibid.*, December 2, 1963, p. 1.
[5] *Ibid.*, p. 40.
[6] *Ibid.*, December 4, 1963, p. 39.
[7] *Congressional Quarterly Almanac*, XX (1964), 343–44.

dent Johnson declared in his State of the Union message on January 8, 1964:

> Let me make one principle of the Administration abundantly clear: all of these increased opportunities—in employment, in education, in housing and in every field—must be open to Americans of every color.
>
> As far as the writ of Federal law will run, we must abolish not some but all racial discrimination. For this is not merely an economic issue—or a social, political or international issue. It is a moral issue—and it must be met by the passage of the bill now pending in the House. All members of the public should have equal access to the facilities open to the public. All members of the public should have an equal chance to vote for public officials—and to send their children to good public schools—and to contribute their talents to the public good.
>
> Today Americans of all races stand side by side in Berlin and in Viet Nam. They died side by side in Korea. Surely they can work and eat and travel side by side in their own country.[8]

At long last, on January 30, 1964, the House Rules Committee voted 11–4 to clear the bipartisan civil rights bill for floor debate. The debate on the House floor lasted nine days, and on February 10, 1964, the House passed the bill by a vote of 290–130. Among Democrats 152 voted for the measure and 96 voted against it. As for northern Democrats, the margin was 141–4 in favor of the bill. The southern Democrats voted 92–11 against the bill. Among Republicans 138 supported the bill and 34 were opposed to it.[9] On the same day, the Senate Commerce Committee cleared a public accommodations bill.[10]

Two weeks later, the Senate voted 54–37 to place the House bill directly on the Senate calendar rather than to refer it to the Judiciary Committee chaired by Eastland. This was done to bypass Eastland, an ardent foe of civil rights legislation, to prevent him from delaying indefinitely any consideration of the bill. Senate Majority Leader Mike Mansfield of Montana appointed Senators Hubert Humphrey of Minnesota, Warren Magnuson of Washington, Philip Hart of Michigan, and Joseph Clark of Pennsylvania as floor managers to

[8] State of the Union Message, January 8, 1964, *Congressional Quarterly Almanac* (Washington, D.C.: Congressional Quarterly Inc., 1965), 863. See also *Public Papers of the Presidents: Lyndon B. Johnson, 1964* (2 books; Washington, D.C.: U.S. Government Printing Office, 1965), I, 116.

[9] "House Passes Comprehensive Civil Rights Bill," *Congressional Quarterly Weekly Report*, 22 (February 14, 1964), 293–301.

[10] Clifford M. Lytle, "The History of the Civil Rights Bill of 1964," *Journal of Negro History*, 51 (October, 1966), 291.

conduct the bill through the Senate.[11] The bill was soon faced by a long filibuster.

The overall coordinator of the civil rights forces in the Senate was Humphrey who was assisted by Thomas Kuchel of California for the Republicans. Humphrey assigned six teams of six senators each to maintain a quorum at all times on the Senate floor. The leader of the filibuster, Richard Russell of Georgia, had three platoons (six Democrats for two platoons and six Democrats and one Republican for the other one). The only Republican who was engaged in the filibuster was John Tower of Texas.

At the same time, negotiations were conducted between Humphrey, Everett Dirksen of Illinois, and Attorney General Robert Kennedy concerning a possible cloture vote.[12] Dirksen, whose support was crucial to achieve a favorable vote on cloture, had serious reservations about the public accommodations and fair employment practices sections of the bill. The southerners apparently hoped to delay the bill at least until after the Republican national convention in July.

The president worked closely with Humphrey, Mansfield, and others in the Senate at this time. Johnson let it be known that he would take steps necessary to counter Senator Russell's strategy, even if it meant sacrificing all other legislation. If necessary, the president hinted that he would call a special session should the delay last down to the conventions.[13] At the same time, the president took into account the fact that the southern senators would need to be given time to oppose the bill in order to appease their constituents.

Meanwhile, in anticipation that the bill would become law, the president made a number of well-publicized statements to various groups, including church leaders. On March 25, 1964, President Johnson made the following remarks to members of the Southern Baptist Christian Leadership Seminar:

[11] "Senate Bypasses Judiciary on Civil Rights," *Congressional Quarterly Weekly Report,* 22 (February 28, 1964), 385.
[12] John T. Manley, "The U.S. Civil Rights Act of 1964," *Contemporary Review,* 206 (January, 1965), 11; Lytle, "The History of the Civil Rights Bill of 1964," 293.
[13] Sam Houston Johnson, *My Brother Lyndon* (New York: Cowles Book Co., Inc., 1969), 142–43; Rowland Evans and Robert Novak, *Lyndon B. Johnson: The Exercise of Power* (New York: The New American Library, 1966), 378.

We are going to pass the civil rights bill, but our efforts alone are not enough. I am proud to say that in this cause some of our strongest allies are religious leaders who are encouraging elected officials to do what is right.

But more must be done, and no group of Christians has a greater responsibility than Southern Baptists. Your people are part of the power structure in many communities of our land. The leaders of states and cities and towns are in your congregations and they sit there on your boards. Their attitudes are confirmed or changed by the sermons you preach and by the lessons you write and the examples you set.[14]

He also spoke of their special interest in dealing with distrust and injustice. He said: "Help us to answer them with truth and action. Help us to pass this civil rights bill and establish a foundation upon which we can build a house of freedom where all men can dwell. Help us, when this bill has been passed, to lead all of our people in this great land into a new fellowship." [15]

The president also spoke before a session of the Georgia legislature on May 8, 1964. He declared:

Because the Constitution requires it, because justice demands it, we must protect the Constitutional rights of all our citizens, regardless of race, religion, or the color of their skin. I would remind you that we are a very small minority, living in a world of 3 billion people, where we are outnumbered by 17 to 1, and no one of us are fully free until all of us are truly free, and the rights of no single American are truly secure until the rights of all Americans are secure.

Democratic order rests on faithfulness to law. Those who deny the protection of the Constitution to others imperil the safety of their own desires. So we now move forward under the Constitution to give every man his right to work at a job and the great program that is now going on in this Nation for equal employment opportunity was initiated, conceived, and born here in the great state of Georgia at the Lockheed plant, and it is a model for more than 7 million workers in all the states of this Union.

Finally, he stated, "We must elect our officials, we must educate our children, we must prepare full and equal participation in the American society." [16]

In the meantime, throughout the legislative course of the civil rights bill the Leadership Conference on Civil Rights played a promi-

[14] *Public Papers of the Presidents*, I, 421; Johnson, *My Brother Lyndon*, 144.
[15] *Public Papers of the Presidents*, I, 421.
[16] *Ibid.*, 649.

nent role. Its lobbying activities were under the direction of Clarence Mitchell of the NAACP. The National Council of Churches was a part of this coalition trying to persuade Congress to pass the bill. Aside from the white southerners in Congress, intense opposition to the measure was provided by the Coordinating Committee for Fundamental American Freedoms headed by William Loeb of the Manchester *News Leader* (New Hampshire). The secretary-treasurer of the organization was John C. Satterfield, former president of the American Bar Association and former advisor to ex-Governor Ross Barnett of Mississippi. Much of the funds for this pressure group was provided by the Mississippi State Sovereignty Commission which had been established in 1956. This commission operated with taxpayers' money,[17] although in this instance it was claimed that most of the funds came from private sources.

An editorial in a leading religious journal noted prophetically:

> We have no illusion that this legislation will solve our racial problems. Whatever happens times of trial are ahead. The enforcement of the law will require even greater, more sustained efforts than its passage. Healthy racial relations, although they cannot be attained without legislation, will require far more than legislation alone can do.
>
> Yet the passage of the civil rights bill is essential. It will be at least a token of faith toward those who have long been abused, both by the law and custom.[18]

The future Republican candidate for president, Senator Barry Goldwater of Arizona, attacked certain parts of the civil rights bill, particularly the public accommodations and equal employment sections, as interfering with property rights. Indeed, he insisted legislation could not deal with problems of discrimination against black people. Goldwater claimed to take this stand on moral grounds, although a number of his staff members were counting on white resentment against what were considered black "advancements" to bolster the senator's political strength.[19]

---

[17] Lytle, "The History of the Civil Rights Bill of 1964," 290. See also Allan Wolk, *The Presidency and Black Civil Rights* (Cranbury, N.J.: Fairleigh Dickinson University Press, 1971), 58–59.

[18] "The Time for Pretending is Past," *Christianity and Crisis,* 24 (June 8, 1964), 109.

[19] Murray Kempton, "Senator Goldwater Dissents," *The Spectator,* 212 (June 26, 1964), 843.

One famous black man, Ralph Bunche, Undersecretary of the United Nations, accused Goldwater of "talking utter humbug" about the pending civil rights measure. He declared:

> The Negro is fully aware that the pending civil rights bill, as imperative as its passage is, or any other law, is not likely to change the established attitudes on race or color of very many individuals.
>
> But, since the Negro struggle is for rights and is conducted largely in the courts, what gets into law is of tremendous importance.
>
> Besides this, individual attitudes on questions of race and religion do not change; of course, prejudice can be discarded.
>
> The acid test comes when the individual, who may think right, comes face to face with the problem: when the problem becomes your neighbor, rubs up against you, touches your children.[20]

At long last help came from Senator Dirksen, and it proved to be crucial in the showdown over cloture. Dirksen controlled the votes of uncommitted Republicans needed for the cloture move.[21] The Republican leader had received pressure from William McCulloch, Republican representative from Ohio, and from liberal Republicans in the Senate; he had been "courted" by Attorney General Robert Kennedy and President Johnson. According to the former president's brother, President Johnson had appealed to Dirksen's patriotism, ego, and self-interest as the Senator from a state with a large black population.[22]

While the filibuster had been going on, moreover, modifications were agreed upon between the administration and Dirksen concerning the public accommodations and employment sections. Apparently, "The main change was to restrict government intervention in the field of public accommodations and employment to situations where there was a definite pattern of discrimination rather than just isolaed instances. For the latter, individual and local agencies had to work at their own solutions within a fixed period." [23] With the con-

[20] New York *Times*, June 6, 1964, p. 8; Lytle, "The History of the Civil Rights Bill of 1964," 293.

[21] Neil MacNeil, *Dirksen: Portrait of the Public Man* (New York and Cleveland: World Publishing Co., 1970), 234.

[22] Johnson, *My Brother Lyndon*, 145.

[23] Keith Hindell, "Civil Rights Breaks the Cloture Barrier," *Political Quarterly*, 36 (April–June 1965), 149; "Dirksen Amendments," *New Republic*, 150 (June 6, 1964) 3–4.

cessions, Dirksen became a proponent of the bill. In alluding to his change of attitude, Dirksen was said to have borrowed from Victor Hugo in saying, "Stronger than all the armies is an idea whose time has come, America grows, America changes. In all the history of mankind there is an inexorable moral force that carries us forward." [24]

On June 10, 1964, after some seventy-five days of discussion and some six million words had been uttered, the Senate for the first time successfully voted cloture on a civil rights filibuster, thus ending the debate. The first eleven attempts dating back to 1938 had failed. Apparently, President Johnson did some private "arm twisting" to persuade some reluctant Democrats to vote for cloture.[25] The vote to end the debate was 71 to 29. While 44 Democrats and 27 Republicans voted for cloture, 23 Democrats and 6 Republicans voted against it.

At this point, Senator Russell referred to the bill as "an unbridled grant of power to appointed officers of the Government" and declared that questions raised by the bill "go to the very heart of our constitutional system." [26] In addition, Russell insisted that the bill would have a "tremendous impact on our social system . . . our economic system . . . and what we call the American way of life." [27]

On June 17, 1964, the Senate substitute for the House bill was passed by a 76–18 margin on roll call. The substitute was cosponsored by Mansfield, Dirksen, Humphrey, and Kuchel. Only southern Democrats voted against the substitute, but several Republicans, including Goldwater, warned that they would vote against final passage. This version contained only minor changes beyond those worked out with Senator Dirksen.[28]

A few days later, the final passage of the bill took place in the Senate by a vote of 73–27 (6 Republicans and 21 Democrats against).

[24] MacNeil, *Dirksen*, 234.

[25] See James L. Sundquist, *Politics and Policy: The Eisenhower, Kennedy and Johnson Years* (Washington, D.C.: The Brookings Institution, 1968), 270.

[26] "Cloture on Civil Rights Breaks a 26–Year Precedent," *Congressional Quarterly Weekly Report*, 22 (June 12, 1964), 1169. This was the first time in its history that the Senate successfully voted cloture to end a civil rights debate.

[27] *Ibid.*

[28] "Senate Wraps Up Final Version of the Civil Rights Act," *Congressional Quarterly Weekly Report*, 22 (June 19, 1964), 1199.

Senator Goldwater denounced the bill, arguing that it would require the creation of a "police state" to be enforced and would encourage an "informer psychology." Moreover, he said that he could find "no constitutional basis for federal regulation of public accommodations or equal employment opportunities," while at the same time he insisted that he was "unalterably opposed to discrimination or segregation on the basis of race, color, or creed, or any other basis." [29]

The bill then had to return to the House since the Senate-passed bill was different from the earlier one voted by the House. Representatives Celler and McCulloch immediately announced that they would support the Senate bill although it contained some amendments not to their liking.[30]

Meanwhile, on June 19, 1964, the president congratulated the senators for passing the bill. He referred to the bill as a challenge to men of good will in every part of the country to transform the commands of our law into the customs of our land.[31] While he recognized that no single bill could eliminate all injustice, discrimination, hatred, and prejudice, he insisted that it had gone further in doing so than any other previous legislation in the twentieth century. He pointed out:

> First, it will provide a carefully designed code to test and enforce the right of every American to go to school, to get a job, to vote, and to pursue his life unhampered by the barriers of racial discrimination.
> Second, it will in itself, help educate all Americans to their responsibility to give equal treatment to their fellow citizens.
> Third, it will enlist one of the most powerful moral forces of American society on the side of civil rights—the moral obligations to respect and obey the law of the land.
> Fourth, and perhaps most important, this bill is a renewal and a reinforcement, a symbol and a strengthening of that abiding commitment to human dignity and the equality of man which has been the guiding purpose of the American Nation for almost 200 years.[32]

Within a few days, on July 2, 1964, the House voted to approve

[29] "Final House Action on Civil Rights Bill Scheduled," *Congressional Quarterly Weekly Report*, 22 (June 27, 1964), 1273.
[30] *Ibid.*
[31] New York *Times*, June 20, 1964, p. 1.
[32] *Public Papers of the Presidents*, I, 787.

the Senate version of the civil rights bill by a vote of 289–126.[33] Voting for the bill were 153 Democrats and 136 Republicans, while 35 Republicans and 91 Democrats voted against it. Most of those opposed to the bill were from the South.[34]

The bill was signed into law on the same day by the president. Unquestionably, the president wished to dramatize the event as he told a nationwide television audience:

> We believe that all men have certain unalienable rights, yet many Americans do not enjoy those rights. We believe all men are entitled to the blessings of liberty. Yet millions are being deprived of those blessings—not because of their own failures, but because of the color of their skin.
>
> The reasons are deeply embedded in history and tradition and the nature of man. We can understand—without rancor or hatred—how this happened. But it cannot continue.
>
> Our Constitution, the foundation of our republic forbids it. The principles of our freedom forbid it. Morality forbids it and the law I will sign tonight forbids it.

He then called on all Americans "to join in this effort to bring justice and hope to all our people—and peace to our land." [35]

The major provisions of the act were as follows:

> Title I—Voting Rights—Local officials were forbidden to apply different standards in administering literacy tests to black and white applicants for registration as voters in federal elections, or to disqualify applicants because of minor errors in filling out registration forms. Literacy tests had to be in writing, except under special arrangements for blind persons. Proof of a sixth grade education would be considered a presumption of the applicant's literacy. The Attorney General might initiate court action if he found that "a pattern of discrimination" existed to prevent citizens from exercising their right to vote. Either the attorney general or the defendant state officials in a voting suit could request a trial by a three-judge federal court.
>
> Title II—Public Accommodations—Hotels, restaurants, petrol stations, and places of amusement were forbidden to discriminate or re-

[33] The governors of some southern states, including Mississippi, Alabama, Virginia, and Arkansas, announced that they would not enforce the act until it had been tested in the courts.

[34] "Civil Rights Act Signed Into Law," *Congressional Quarterly Weekly Report*, 22 (July 3, 1964), 1331.

[35] *Ibid.*

fuse service because of race, colour, religion, or national origin if their operations affected Interstate Commerce or if their discrimination "was supported by State action." Private clubs or owner-occupied boarding houses letting five or fewer rooms were excluded from the scope of the Act. An individual who believed himself discriminated against might file a suit in the Federal Court, and if the judge found that discrimination existed, he might apply punitive action and order an end to discrimination. Where the Attorney General believed that any person or group was engaging in "a pattern or practice of resistance" to the rights laid down in this section, he might join in the suit on behalf of the aggrieved person or initiate remedial proceedings, bearing the cost of litigation.

Title III—Public Facilities—Racial discrimination was forbidden in publicly owned and operated facilities such as libraries, parks, swimming pools, golf courses, and stadia. The Attorney General might sue for enforcement of these rights if private persons were unable to do so effectively.

Title IV—Public Education—The Attorney General might file school desegregation suits under the same condition as in Title III. The Federal Office of Education was authorized to survey the state-operated public educational system and to offer technical and financial assistance to school districts in implementing desegregation plans. The title did not cover the transport or assignment of pupils in order to correct "racial imbalance in schools."

Title V—Civil Rights Commission—The life of the Civil Rights Commission was extended until the end of 1967, and it was empowered to subpoena witnesses in investigations of alleged discriminatory practices in voting, education, housing, employment, use of public facilities, transportation, and the administration of justice.

Title VI—Federally Assisted Programs—No person shall be subjected to discrimination on the ground of race, colour, or national origin under any programme receiving Federal financial assistance, e.g., public building projects, agricultural programmes, vocational training, and social security and welfare programmes. Federal agencies might take steps against discrimination, including as a last resort the withholding of Federal funds from State or local agencies practicing discrimination.

Title VII—Equal Employment Opportunity—Employers were forbidden to practise discrimination on grounds of race, colour, religion, sex, or national origin in engaging, paying, promoting, or dismissing workers, and employment agencies in referring workers to employers. Trade unions were similarly forbidden to exclude qualified persons from membership because of their race, religion, sex, or national origin. This section would come into operation one year after the President signed the Bill and would initially apply only to companies or unions with 100 or more employees or members; this figure would be reduced to 75 in the second year, 50 in the third, 25 in the fourth. A five-member Federal Equal Employment Opportunity Commission would be established, which would be empowered to investigate allegations of discrimination. If the Commission failed to bring about voluntary compliance with the law, the person discriminated against might file a suit in a Federal court. The Attorney General was also empowered to seek legal remedies if he found that a "pattern or practice of discrimination" existed in a firm's employment policy or a union's membership, and to ask for a trial by a three-judge court.

Title VIII—Registration and Voting Statistics—The Federal Commerce Department was directed to compile statistics of the number of eligible voters and the number of persons registered and voting in areas recommended by the Civil Rights Commission.

Title IX—Revision of Legal Codes—A defendant in a criminal case who alleged that his civil rights would be denied in a trial before a State Court might appeal to a higher Federal Court if a Federal judge refused to take jurisdiction. The Attorney General might intervene in a suit filed by a private person alleging that he had been denied the equal protection of the laws, if the case was of "general public importance."

Title X—The Community Relations Service—A Community Relations Service with a director appointed by the President, would be established under the Commerce Department. The service, which would conduct its activities in confidence and without publicity, would assist communities in pursuit of peaceful desegregation, and was authorized to offer its assistance in the settlement of racial disputes which threatened the peace.

Title XI—Miscellaneous—Trial by jury was guaranteed for charges of criminal contempt under any part of the Act except Title I. The Act would not invalidate State laws with consistent purposes, and would not impair any existing powers of Federal officials.[36]

One writer optimistically predicted that the most immediate and long-ranged effects of the 1964 act would be the following: it would provide more flexibility to blacks and whites for a just and peaceful solution to the civil rights crisis; and it would serve as a "certification

[36] *Race Relations in the USA, 1954–68* (New York: Charles Scribner's Sons, 1970), 138–39. See also *The Civil Rights Act of 1964* (Washington, D.C.: Bureau of National Affairs, 1964), for the detailed provisions and legislative history of the act.

of faith" by all Americans in their black brethren. He insisted that all the black individual really wanted was to be a full partner in American society.[37]

Just what was the president's role in the passage of the Civil Rights Act of 1964? Most accounts indicate that his role, though significant, was carried on largely behind the scenes. Apparently he was concerned about white southern support for other parts of this program and thus did not want to be too visible. Moreover, there was not a sufficient crisis in Congress to warrant the full exercise of presidential powers.[38] Nevertheless, Johnson was able to see the bill through with less dilution or need for horsetrading than might have been anticipated.[39] There is no doubt also that he applied considerable pressure on some senators in order to achieve a favorable vote on cloture.[40]

As far as the Senate had been concerned, much of the work was done by Humphrey, Johnson's running mate in the November elections, who knew that his chances for the vice-presidential nomination hinged in large part on his ability to get the bill through the Senate. Senator Dirksen, who also played a leading role, realized that the issue of civil rights could have a significant bearing on the presidential election. Thus, both parties' leaders had their eyes on November 3 as they dealt with civil rights.[41]

In the meantime, from a constitutional standpoint the public accommodations section of the Civil Rights Act of 1964 was the most controversial part, and it was soon challenged. At first the question was very much in doubt. A three-judge federal panel in Birmingham, Alabama, ruled that the public accommodations section was unconstitutional when applied to restaurants not involved in interstate commerce. The then Acting Attorney General Nicholas Katzenbach was ordered not to enforce the act against Ollie's Barbecue of Birmingham.[42] However, this decision was reversed when the United States

---

[37] Harold R. Tyler, "The Meaning of the Civil Rights Act," *New South*, 19 (May, 1964), 6

[38] *Congressional Quarterly Almanac*, XXII (1964), 155.

[39] Evans and Novak, *Lyndon B. Johnson*, 378.

[40] Johnson, *My Brother Lyndon*, 145; Hindell, "Civil Rights Breaks the Cloture Barrier," 150; Frederick W. Wirt, *Politics of Southern Equality: Law and Change in a Mississippi County* (Chicago: Aldine Publishing Co., 1970), 67.

[41] Manley, "The U.S. Civil Rights Act of 1964," 13.

[42] New York *Times*, September 18, 1964, p. 1.

Supreme Court in *Katzenbach* v. *McClung*, 379 U.S. 294 (1964), unanimously upheld the constitutionality of the public accommodations section of the act and included Ollie's Barbecue in its coverage. In addition, the Supreme Court in *Heart of Atlanta Motel, Inc.* v. *United States*, 379 U.S. 241, once more unanimously upheld its constitutionality under the commerce clause of the United States Constitution and held that the law applied to this clause involving sleeping quarters.

Meanwhile, Lyndon Johnson had an election to win in 1964. His opponent in November was to be Barry Goldwater of Arizona who had voted against the Civil Rights Act of 1964. This particular vote was to endear Goldwater to many white voters and political leaders in the South.

The Republicans held their national convention first in San Francisco. The platform committee draft pledged "full implementation and faithful execution of the Civil Rights Act of 1964 . . . to assure equal rights and opportunities guaranteed by the Constitution to every citizen." [43] In addition, it expressed "continued opposition to discrimination based on race, creed, national origin or sex," but at the same time noted that "the elimination of any such discrimination is a matter of heart, conscience and education, as well as of equal rights under the law." [44]

This was a much weaker civil rights plank than the one adopted in 1960. It did, however, conform to the Goldwater strategy of polling well in the South, West, and Midwest in order to offset losses in the more highly rights-conscious North.

Moderate Republicans attempted to strengthen the platform stand on civil rights on the floor of the convention but were defeated in their efforts. Governor Scranton of Pennsylvania, for instance, tried to add some specific items such as pride in the Republican support for the 1964 Civil Rights Act, a call for more manpower for the Civil Rights Division of the Justice Department, and pledges to end job bias. Governor Romney of Michigan had also failed in his attempt to pledge actions at the state, local, and private levels to end dis-

---

[43] "1964 Platform Turns GOP Sharply to the Right," *Congressional Quarterly Weekly Report*, 22 (July 17, 1964), 1488.
[44] *Ibid.*

crimination in all fields.[45] The draft plank had remained intact, and it was in accord with the presidential candidate's position on civil rights.

Following the Republican national convention, and preceding that of the Democrats, major civil rights leaders held a meeting. Those present were Dr. Martin Luther King, Jr., Roy Wilkins, A. Philip Randolph, John Lewis, Whitney Young, Jr., and James Farmer. All except Lewis and Farmer signed a statement to the effect that the Goldwater forces were injecting racism into the presidential campaign and were a threat to the "whole climate of liberal democracy in the United States" and to "the implementation of the Civil Rights Act and to subsequent expansion of civil rights gains." Those who signed the statement regarded the situation as so serious that they called upon members of civil rights organizations "to observe a broad curtailment, if not total moratorium, of all mass marches, mass picketing, and mass demonstrations until after election day next Nov. 3." Blacks were urged to concentrate on registration and voting.[46] In part at least, there is little doubt that these black leaders were responding to pressure from the president who was concerned above all else with his reelection.

When the Democrats met in Atlantic City, New Jersey to renominate Johnson they adopted a civil rights plank that was barely distinguishable from that of the Republicans in spite of appeals made by Wilkins, King, and Farmer that a stronger stand be taken. Indeed one word, enforcement, seemed to symbolize the choice between the two major parties on this crucial issue. The Democrats declared that the law "deserves and requires full observance by every American and fair, effective enforcement if there is any default." The promise of enforcement apparently helped to persuade civil rights leaders to accept a Democratic civil rights plank that was no more specific in dealing with black demands than the Republican one had been. White southerners accepted the plank with no open protest, which seemed to support the president's effort to project a unifying image

[45] "Moderate Forces Defeated in Disputes Over Party Platform," *Congressional Quarterly Weekly Report*, 22 (July 17, 1964), 1485.

[46] See Eric F. Goldman, *The Tragedy of Lyndon Johnson* (New York: Alfred A. Knopf, 1969), 175. See also *The New York Times*, July 30, 1964, p. 1.

to the country.[47] "Consensus" had carried the day, at least on the surface.

Something else happened at the convention which was to have an effect on the future. The Mississippi Freedom Democratic Party (MFDP) contended that it represented 450,000 blacks who had been systematically prevented from voting, and that it should be seated instead of the regular Democratic delegation from the state. The MFDP was given only two at-large seats under the general provision that delegates at future conventions were to be selected on a democratic basis to represent all segments of the party.[48] Most MFDP delegates found this decision unsatisfactory; the regulars did also.

In spite of the squabble over the seating of Mississippi delegates, President Johnson had everything going his way in the election of 1964. In October, the president spoke to an audience of 2,500 people in New Orleans about the new civil rights act: "Whatever your views are we have a Constitution and we have a Bill of Rights, and we have the law of the land, and two-thirds of the Democrats in the Senate voted for it and three-fourths of the Republicans, I signed it, I am going to enforce it, and I think that any man that is worthy of the high office is going to do the same thing." [49]

Senator Goldwater appeared to believe that the white backlash against black militancy would help him in the election. In large cities such as New York, Chicago, Cleveland, and Pittsburgh he stressed his opposition to the Civil Rights Act of 1964. Goldwater also argued that compulsory integration was just as bad as compulsory segregation and declared that freedom of association meant the freedom not to associate also.[50]

As it turned out, Lyndon Johnson and his running mate, Hubert Humphrey, won the election by a landslide with over 60 percent of the popular votes. The white backlash had not yet reached the level that it would by 1966 and 1967. In addition, Johnson benefited from

[47] "Democratic Platform Seeks Wide Voter Appeal," *Congressional Quarterly Weekly Report*, 22 (August 28, 1964), 1964.

[48] Edward Peeks, *The Long Struggle for Black Power* (New York: Charles Scribner's Sons, 1971), 358–59; Stokeley Carmichael, "Toward Black Liberation," *The Massachusetts Review*, 7 (Autumn, 1966), 640.

[49] Johnson, *The Vantage Point*, 109.

[50] *The New York Times*, November 1, 1964, p. 75.

public response to the martyrdom of President Kennedy the previous year.

Senator Goldwater won only six states, all of which were in the Deep South except for his own state of Arizona. The southern states he carried were Mississippi, Louisiana, South Carolina, Georgia, and Alabama. Through his "southern strategy" he did not have a white southern third party candidate to contend with as Nixon did in 1968. As a leading study of the election showed, the racial issue cut across class lines to be the dominant factor in the heavy white vote cast for Goldwater in the Deep South.[51]

In general, the Johnson victory had brought in its wake a Democratic upsurge. The Democrats gained 38 seats in the House which gave them a 295–140 margin; they also gained two seats in the Senate giving them a 68–32 edge.[52] It was estimated that 90 percent of the blacks had voted for Johnson, whereas only 60 percent had voted for Kennedy in 1960.[53]

Mississippi had a rather unique type of general election. Most blacks were barred from voting in the state; therefore, the Mississippi Freedom Democratic Party held a "mock" election in which Johnson received 63,000 votes and Goldwater 17. This result was in marked contrast to the regular balloting in the state in which Goldwater received some 360,000 votes and Johnson some 53,000.[54] Indeed Goldwater received 87 percent of the votes cast, which was the highest percentage he received in any state. In addition, MFDP voters selected Aaron Henry, Annie Devine, Fannie Lou Hamer, and Victoria Gray for Congress. The three women and the MFDP attempted to challenge the seating of the regular Democrats in Congress early in 1965, but they were turned down. This episode, like the one at the Democratic convention, led to disenchantment among many blacks about trying to bring about change through the "system." [55] It also

[51] See Bernard Cosman, *Five States for Goldwater* (University, Alabama: University of Alabama Press, 1966), for an excellent analysis of voting patterns in southern states and the significance of the race issue in the South.

[52] "Johnson Defeats Goldwater by 15 Million: GOP Loses 38 House Seats, State Legislatures," *Congressional Quarterly Weekly Report*, 22 (November 6, 1964), 2625.

[53] New York *Times*, November 6, 1964, p. 26.

[54] *Ibid.*, p. 1.

[55] Robert L. Zangrando, "From Civil Rights to Black Liberation: The Unsettled 1960's," *Current History*, 57 (November, 1969), 282–83; Carmichael,

had a lot to do with the development of the "black power" movement in Mississippi in 1966.

In spite of the tragic situation in Mississippi, all seemed on the surface to be going well for President Johnson. Afterall, he had been elected on his own as president and had helped to guide the civil rights bill begun by Kennedy into law. True, the Civil Rights Act had some weaknesses and much depended upon its enforcement, but nevertheless it was the law of the land. Many whites, even liberals, did not understand that it meant little to be able to eat at or sleep at the Holiday Inn to those blacks who could not afford it.

"Toward Black Liberation," 640. See also Leslie Burl McLemore, "The Effect of Political Participation Upon a Closed Society. A State in Transition: The Changing Political Climate in Mississippi," *Negro Educational Review*, 23 (January, 1972), 6–7.

CHAPTER III

The Voting Rights Act of 1965 and the Civil Rights Act of 1968

The Civil Rights Act of 1964 had been the most significant step taken in the field of civil rights during the first year of the Johnson administration. The next major civil rights bill was to deal with voting, although the acts of 1957, 1960, and 1964 had already done so. Blacks were still systematically prevented from voting in much of the South. An incredible array of public and private obstacles still confronted blacks in their efforts to register and vote. As one authority has noted:

> The vote merits attention because it is one of the most widely distributed of all political resources, because all decisions in a democratic form of government rest ultimately on votes, and perhaps because it is the major mechanism for translating popular preferences into governmental decisions. Various groups, from the propertyless to women, have sought the vote on grounds that it is an important resource in the implementation of their preferences and the recognition of their interests, as well as their worth as persons. The Negro struggle for political rights fits into this same context.[1]

President Johnson had only briefly alluded to civil rights and the vote in his State of the Union address on January 4, 1965. He stressed the enforcement of existing laws and urged the elimination of "every remaining obstacle to the right and opportunity to vote." [2] Several weeks later in his inaugural address, the president made no direct reference to the vote. He did, however, condemn the practice of treating American citizens of any skin color differently from the way other citizens were treated.[3]

However, events centered in Alabama would cause the president to decide on a more vigorous course of action with regard to the en-

[1] William R. Keech, *The Impact of Negro Voting: The Role of the Vote in the Quest for Equality* (Chicago: Rand McNally, 1968), 3.

[2] "Text of President Johnson's State of the Union Message, January 4, 1965," *Congressional Quarterly Weekly Report*, 23 (January 8, 1965), 52.

[3] Inaugural Address, January 20, 1965, *Public Papers of the Presidents: Lyndon B. Johnson* (2 books; Washington, D.C.: U.S. Government Printing Office, 1966), I, 72.

Table 1

BLACK AND WHITE VOTERS IN THE SOUTH

State	Total Negro Voters as of 11/1/64 (1)	Increase Since 4/1/62 (2)	% of Eligible Negroes Registered (3)	% of Eligible Whites Registered (4)	% Negro of Total Registered (5)	% Negro of Voting Age Population (6)
Ala.	111,000	42,700	23.0	70.7	10.4	26.2
Ark.[a]	105,000	36,000	54.4	71.7	14.6	18.4
Fla.	300,000	117,500	63.7	84.0	12.0	15.2
Ga.[b]	270,000	94,500	44.0	74.5	16.8	25.4
La.	164,700	13,000	32.0	80.4	13.7	28.5
Miss.	28,500	4,500	6.7	70.1	5.2	36.0
N.C.	258,000	47,500	46.8	92.5	11.7	21.5
S.C.	144,000	53,100	38.8	78.5	17.0	29.3
Tenn.	218,000	67,100	69.4	72.9	14.4	14.9
Tex.	375,000	133,000	57.7	53.2	12.5	11.7
Va.	200,000	89,900	45.7	55.9	16.0	18.8
Total	2,174,200	698,000	43.3	73.2	13.0	22.4

[a] voting figures as of 1/1/65
[b] voting age 18

franchisement of blacks. Statistics indicated how relatively few blacks had the vote in Alabama, or in the South in general. Figures taken from the Voter Education Project of the Southern Regional Council are shown in Table 1.[4]

To show how difficult registration and voting was for blacks in parts of the South, the U.S. Commission on Civil Rights conducted hearings in Jackson, Mississippi, from February 16 to 20, 1965, and fully documented the depth of the problem in Mississippi. Among other things, discrimination was shown in the use of tests. For example, blacks were ordinarily given more difficult sections of the Mississippi Constitution to interpret than were whites. Moreover, violence was perpetrated on those who encouraged blacks to register.[5] The commission later transmitted its findings and recommendations about the situation in Mississippi to President Johnson.[6] It determined:

1. Mississippi had enacted laws providing for a constitutional interpretation test, "and other tests for registration, and has vested broad discretion in county registrars to administer the requirements. The stringency of these tests was increased at a time when most whites were already registered and few Negroes were registered." [7]

2. Registration records indicated that many county registrars had discriminated against blacks through a number of devices such as: (a) more difficult constitutional sections to interpret; (b) insufficiencies in the completion of application forms; and (c) affording assistance to white applicants but not blacks.

3. The state poll tax was established to prevent blacks from voting.

In its recommendations the commission held that: (1) all literacy tests should be abolished; (2) requirements that applicants complete any form should be abolished; (3) wherever federal examiners had been appointed, applicants should be free to seek registration with examiners without first going through the state registration process;

---

[4] "Southern Negro Voter Statistics By State," *Congressional Quarterly Weekly Report*, 23 (March 23, 1965), 557.

[5] See U.S. Commission on Civil Rights, *Hearings before the U.S. Commission on Civil Rights, Jackson, Mississippi, February 16–20, 1965* (2 vols.; Washington, D.C.: U.S. Government Printing Office, 1965).

[6] See U.S. Commission on Civil Rights, *Voting in Mississippi* (Washington, D.C.: U.S. Government Printing Office, 1965).

[7] *Ibid.*, 60.

(4) the poll tax should be abolished; (5) federal poll watchers should be assigned in areas where federal examiners were appointed.[8] Moreover, the commission recommended an affirmative program in order to assure the more effective dissemination of information about registration and voting, as well as training and education programs for a better understanding of rights, including voting.[9]

In the meantime, in January, 1965, a concerted effort was begun by blacks in Selma, Alabama, to acquire the right to register and to vote. Selma was picked as the focal point of the voting rights offensive. Two organizations, the SCLC and SNCC, planned to dramatize the fact that many blacks were being deprived of the vote there.[10]

Typically, as in the rest of the South where blacks were the most numerous, they were least likely to be able to register and to vote in Selma. Selma was considered the unofficial "capital" of the black belt in Alabama. It was the county seat of Dallas County. Voter registration in Selma took place only two days per week. An applicant was required to fill in more than fifty blanks, write from dictation a part of the constitution, answer four questions about the governmental process, read four passages from the constitution and answer four questions on them, and sign an oath of loyalty to the United States and Alabama. At the time of the 1960 census the population in the county was 57.6 percent black. As for the voting age population, there were 14,400 whites and 15,115 blacks. However, when the demonstrations began, of the 9,877 registered to vote, there were 9,542 whites and the rest were blacks. Between May, 1962, and August, 1964, 93 blacks out of 795 who applied were accepted for registration; however, 945 whites out of 1.232 were accepted.[11]

Dr. Martin Luther King, Jr., became the leader of demonstrations in Selma which had as their purpose arousing the conscience of the nation. Before long, violence erupted. Many blacks and some whites supporting them were arrested, beaten, and a few were killed, including Jimmie Lee Jackson, a black man, in Marion County, Alabama.

[8] *Ibid.*, 62.
[9] *Ibid.*
[10] New York *Times*, January 4, 1965, p. 58.
[11] "Sweeping Voting Rights Bill Introduced in Congress," *Congressional Quarterly Weekly Report*, 24 (March 19, 1965), 428.

Civil rights leaders strongly urged the president to intervene as they decided to march on Montgomery, the capital of Alabama, as a protest against the happenings at Selma.[12]

The president reacted cautiously to demands for federal protection for the marchers and was heavily criticized for his failure to act. He later claimed that if he had acted strongly, the voting rights bill might have been defeated.[13] Within his framework of caution, on March 9, 1965, Johnson announced:

> Ever since the events of Sunday afternoon in Selma, Ala., the administration has been in close touch with the situation and has made every effort to prevent a repetition. I am certain Americans everywhere join me in deploring the brutality with which a number of Negro citizens were treated when they sought to dramatize their deep and sincere interest in attaining the precious right to vote.
>
> The best legal talent in the Federal Government is engaged in preparing legislation which will secure the right for every American. I expect to complete work on my recommendations this weekend and shall dispatch a special message to Congress as soon as the drafting of the legislation is finished.[14]

As violence continued at Selma the president continued to deplore the situation there. Civil rights leaders continued their demand for federal intervention. A meeting took place at the instigation of Governor George Wallace between himself and Johnson. The president indicated to Wallace that he would send in troops if necessary to protect the marchers.[15] On March 13, Johnson announced that more than seventy United States government officials were in Selma, including FBI agents, Justice Department lawyers lead by John Doar of the CRD, and Leroy Collins, director of the Community Relations Service. The president announced that he had met with Alabama Governor George Wallace to discuss conditions in Selma as the governor had ordered state troopers in to hamper the demonstrators.[16]

[12] "It Looks Like a 'Hot Summer' with Selma the Beginning," *U.S. News & World Report*, 58 (March 22, 1965), 32; New York *Times*, February 27, 1965, p. 1.

[13] Johnson, *The Vantage Point*, 162.

[14] Statement by the President on the Situation in Selma, Alabama, March 9, 1965, *Public Papers of the Presidents: Lyndon B. Johnson, 1965* (2 books; Washington, D.C.: U.S. Government Printing Office, 1966), I, 272.

[15] Johnson, *The Vantage Point*, 163.

[16] "Text of President Johnson's March 13 News Conference," *Congressional Quarterly Weekly Report*, 23 March 19, 1965), 450.

At last the president was ready to push for a new bill. He went before Congress on March 15, 1965, and roundly condemned the brutality against blacks at Selma and spoke of voting as a basic right. Johnson declared:

> Every device of which human ingenuity is capable has been used to deny this right. The Negro citizen may go to register only to be told that the day is wrong, or the hour is late, or the official in charge is absent. And if he persists, and if he manages to present himself to the registrar, he may be disqualified because he did not spell out his middle name or he abbreviated a word in the application. And if he manages to fill out the application he is given a test. The registrar is the sole judge of whether he passed this test. He may be asked to recite the entire Constitution, or explain the most complex provisions of state laws and even a college degree cannot be used to prove that he can read and write.[17]

He concluded: "For the fact is the only way to pass these barriers is to show a white face." [18] Then he outlined the bill he intended to present to Congress as follows:

> This bill will strike down restrictions to voting in all elections—Federal, state and local—which have been used to deny Negroes the right to vote.
> This bill will establish a simple, uniform standard which cannot be abused however ingenious the effort to flout our Constitution.
> It will provide for citizens to be registered by officials of the United States Government if the state officials refuse to register them.
> It will eliminate tedious, unnecessary law suits which delay the right to vote.
> Finally, this legislation will ensure that properly registered individuals are not prohibited from voting.[19]

President Johnson concluded by declaring that it was a human rights issue and that:

> Even if we pass this bill, the battle will not be over. What happened at Selma is part of a far larger movement which reaches every section and state of America. It is the effort of American Negroes to secure for themselves the full blessings of American life.

[17] "Text of the President's Voting Rights Speech to Congress, March 15, 1965," *Congressional Weekly Report*, 23 (March 19, 1965), 445; *Public Papers of the Presidents*, I, 281–87.
[18] "Text of the President's Voting Rights Speech to Congress, March 15, 1965," *Congressional Quarterly Weekly Report*, 23 (March 19, 1965), 445.
[19] *Ibid.*

Their cause must be our cause too. Because it is not just Negroes, but really it is all of us who must overcome the crippling legacy of bigotry and injustices. And . . . we . . . shall . . . overcome.[20]

On March 17 the president formally presented the voting rights bill to Congress with a statement that it was designed "to strike down restrictions in all elections—Federal, state, and local—which have been used to deny Negroes the right to vote." [21] Based on the Fifteenth Amendment, the bill was the product of negotiations by Senators Mansfield, Dirksen, and Kuchel; Representatives McCulloch, Albert, and Boggs; and Attorney General Nicholas Katzenbach and his Deputy Attorney General, Ramsey Clark. They did not anticipate a long filibuster in the Senate, but reaction in the House was regarded as uncertain. Even though Roy Wilkins and Dr. Martin Luther King, Jr., praised the bill as proposed, Dr. King promised that demonstrations would continue until the bill had become law.[22]

The march from Selma to Montgomery was completed on March 25 under federal protection. Governor Wallace had notified the president that he would be unable to bear the financial burden of protecting the marchers.[23] The most probable reason was that he did not want to seem to be cooperating with the march which would not have endeared him to the people he claimed to represent. In any case, Johnson had sent 3,000 troops to protect the marchers, including 1,863 federalized Alabama National Guardsmen. Although the rally in Montgomery had taken place without incident, a white civil rights worker, Mrs. Viola Luizzo, was slain shortly thereafter in her car. On March 26 the president announced that four members of the Ku Klux Klan had been arrested in connection with Mrs. Luizzo's murder. They were charged with conspiracy to violate her civil rights since murder was not subject to federal punishment.[24]

At the same time, the president declared war on the Ku Klux Klan. He warned members to leave the organization before it was too late. He promised that he would offer legislation to bring the Klan under

[20] *Ibid.*; Johnson, *The Vantage Point*, 165.

[21] "Sweeping Civil Rights Bill Introduced in Congress," *Congressional Quarterly Weekly Report*, 23 (March 19, 1965), 427.

[22] *Ibid.*, 435.

[23] Johnson, *The Vantage Point*, 163.

[24] "After Alabama . . . Negro's Next Battleground," *U.S. News & World Report*, 58 (April 5, 1965), 37.

"effective control of law" and suggested that Congress should undertake an investigation of this "hooded society of bigots." [25]

Civil rights leaders now indicated that Cleveland, Ohio, in the North and Mississippi and Louisiana in the South would be their next targets of great concern. Strenuous voter registration drives had been going on in Mississippi since 1964. In the process civil rights groups had suffered many arrests and much brutality.[26] In June, 1965, while the voting rights bill was still being debated in Congress, some 675 civil rights pickets and marchers were arrested in Jackson, Mississippi, and many were placed in makeshift stockades on the fairgrounds. There were numerous charges of brutality in the stockyards. The civil rights proponents were demonstrating against a special session of the Mississippi legislature which was considering changes in registration and voting requirements in the state. Among those arrested were John Lewis of SNCC and Charles Evers, state field secretary of the NAACP. All of the demonstrators were charged with parading without a permit.[27]

Congress, while debating the voting rights bill, was greatly influenced by events in the South, especially those in Selma. However, the then attorney general, Nicholas Katzenbach, noted later that contrary to the Civil Rights Act of 1964: "Civil rights groups were not so badly needed for this bill and thus had little effect on its outcome." He said that the "Justice Department embarrassed Southerners with facts showing voting deprivation," because, he believed, "Southerners were not against giving blacks the vote, but rather the way it was done—taking states rights, with this clearly regional legislation." [28] What Katzenbach overlooked, of course, was the propensity of many white southerners to use the language of states' rights to cover their desire to maintain segregation and white control of political institutions.

After a considerable delay in the Senate as a result of a filibuster, on May 25, 1965, the senators approved a cloture motion by a vote of 70–30. On the next day, they overwhelmingly approved the voter

[25] New York *Times,* March 27, 1965, p. 1.
[26] See Pat Watters, *Encounter with the Future* (Atlanta, Ga.: Southern Regional Council, 1965).
[27] New York *Times,* June 16, 1965, p. 1.
[28] Wolk, *The Presidency and Black Civil Rights,* 60.

rights bill by a vote of 77–19. Thirty Republicans joined 47 Democrats in favor of the bill. Two Republicans, Tower and Thurmond, joined 17 southern Democrats in voting against its passage.[29] It was not until July 9, 1965, that the House passed a somewhat different version, by a vote of 333–85. Virtually all of the representatives casting negative votes were from the South. The bill was then sent to a conference committee made up of some members from each house.[30]

The major difference between the two versions had to do with a poll tax ban with the House taking a stronger stand against the poll tax. Civil rights groups, wanting to end the stalemate that had developed, helped to persuade the House conferees to drop plans for a flat ban on the poll tax. After that, the conferees were able to work out an agreement, and the bill was returned to both houses. On August 3, 1965, the House passed the bill by a vote of 328–70, and the Senate did so on August 4, 1965, by a vote of 79–18. A minority of southerners voted to adopt the conference report in both houses.[31]

Shortly thereafter, on August 6, 1965, President Johnson went through a signing ceremony before a nationwide television audience. The president declared that the act would "strike away the last major shackle" of the black's "ancient bonds." [32]

In general, the new Voting Rights Act of 1965 suspended literacy tests and gave the attorney general the power to appoint federal examiners to supervise voter registration in states or political subdivisions where a test or similar qualifying device was in force as of November 1, 1964, and where fewer than 50 percent of voting age residents who were registered on that date actually voted in the 1964 presidential election.[33]

In addition, the act stipulated criminal penalties

for interference with voter rights, outlined a judicial recourse for de-

[29] "Senate Passes Voting Rights Bill, 77–19," *Congressional Quarterly Weekly Report*, 23 (May 28, 1965), 1007–1009.

[30] "House Passes Voting Rights Bill," *ibid.*, 23 (July 16, 1965), 1361–63.

[31] "Voting Rights Bill Sent to the President," *ibid.*, 23 (August 6, 1965), 1539–40.

[32] "Voting Rights," *ibid.*, 23 (August 13, 1965), 1595.

[33] *Congressional Quarterly Almanac, 1965* (Washington, D.C.: Congressional Quarterly Inc., 1966) XXI, 533. See also L. Thorne McCarty and Russell B. Stevenson, "The Voting Rights Act of 1965: An Evaluation," *Harvard Civil Rights—Civil Liberties Review,* 3 (Spring, 1968), 357–69.

linquent state and local governments (through a three-judge federal district court in the District of Columbia) which needed to determine that no racial discrimination in registration and voting practices had occurred for five years, and directed the Attorney General "forthwith" to institute proceedings against the use of state and local taxes as a qualification for voting.[34]

Almost immediately the administration proceeded to implement the Voting Rights Act of 1965. As was anticipated, there was a challenge to the constitutionality of the new law. The state of South Carolina filed suit before the United States Supreme Court on September 29, 1965, to enjoin Attorney General Katzenbach from enforcing the act on the grounds that the law had unconstitutionally invaded states' rights to establish voter qualifications.[35] Soliciter General Thurgood Marshall answered the complaint by insisting that Congress had acted within its constitutional powers.[36]

Nevertheless, even before the Supreme Court ruled, a three-judge federal panel in Montgomery, Alabama, held that the Voting Rights Act of 1965 had to be presumed to be constitutional. Furthermore, state court injunctions against the enrollment of federally registered voters in six Alabama counties were ruled "null, void and of no effect." Early in February, 1966, however, E. Gordon West, a federal judge in New Orleans, Louisiana, termed the law "flagrantly violative of the Constitution" in dismissing a Justice Department suit testing the voter intimidation section of the act. He cited a number of Supreme Court decisions to show that the Fifteenth Amendment was not directed at action taken by individual citizens.[37]

Finally in *South Carolina v. Katzenbach*[38] the United States Supreme Court unanimously upheld the constitutionality of the entire Voting Rights Act of 1965 on the grounds that it was within the power of Congress to take affirmative measures to implement the Fifteenth Amendment to the Constitution. Chief Justice Warren wrote that "against the reserve powers of the states Congress may use any rational means to effectuate the constitutional prohibition against racial discrimination."

[34] *Congressional Quarterly Almanac*, XXI (1965), 533.
[35] *Ibid.*, 564.
[36] New York *Times*, November 24, 1965, p. 1.
[37] *Ibid.*, February 5, 1966, p. 14.
[38] 383 U.S. 301 (1966).

In the meantime, on June 4, 1965, President Johnson had made one of his best-known civil rights speeches in a commencement address at Howard University in Washington, D.C. In addressing himself to the needs of those in the audience he declared:

> Freedom is the right to share fully and equally, in American society—to vote, to hold a job, to enter a public place, to go to school. It is the right to be treated, in every part of our national life, as a man in dignity and promise to all others.
>
> But freedom is not enough. You do not wipe away the scars of centuries by saying: Now you are free to go where you want, do as you desire, and choose the leaders you please.
>
> You do not take a man, who for years, has been hobbled by chains, liberate him, bring him to the starting line of a race, saying "You are free to compete with all the others," and still justly believe you have been fair.
>
> Thus it is not enough to open the gates of opportunity. All our citizens must have the ability to walk through those gates.
>
> This is the next and most profound stage of the battle for civil rights. We seek not just freedom but opportunity—not just legal equity but human equity—not just equality as a right and a theory, but equality as a fact and a result.[39]

Faced with the continued negative news about the treatment of blacks in the South and racial discrimination in the nation as a whole, President Johnson made his next major move in his State of the Union address in 1966. He proposed new civil rights legislation that would require: nondiscriminatory jury selection for federal and state courts; stronger authority of federal courts to try those who attack, intimidate, or murder civil rights workers or other persons exercising their constitutional rights; and prohibition of racial discrimination in the sale or rental of housing.[40]

"Open" housing was to prove the major stumbling block. A number of civil rights leaders realized that strong opposition was likely to develop in Congress against "open" housing, and urged the president to extend the coverage under the executive order issued by President Kennedy in 1962. President Johnson, however, rejected this

---

[39] Albert P. Blaustein and Robert L. Zangrando, *Civil Rights and the American Negro* (New York: Trident Press, 1968), 560–61.

[40] State of the Union Message, January 12, 1966, *Public Papers of the Presidents: Lyndon B. Johnson, 1966* (2 books; Washington, D.C.: U.S. Government Printing Office, 1967), I, 5.

approach allegedly on the grounds that it might raise serious constitutional questions. Many of the civil rights leaders never accepted this explanation given by the president. One writer, Robert Sherill, claimed that an extension of the executive order would have been much easier from a political standpoint, by including bank loans backed by federal guarantees and savings and loan companies with funds secured by a federal agency.[41] Such organizations as the Americans for Democratic Action and the National Committee Against Discrimination in Housing communicated to the president their concern that federal funds and credit were perpetuating and even increasing the amount of racially segregated housing.[42]

Several civil rights bills languished in Congress during the early months of 1966. Once more, however, on April 28, 1966, President Johnson urged action from Congress. He requested that legislation be passed that dealt with the following:

> First, to reform our criminal statutes to provide Negroes and all who labor or speak for racial justice the protection of stronger and more effective criminal laws against interference with the exercise of long established rights.
>
> Second, to establish detailed procedures of jury selection in federal courts so that discrimination may be banished—and to create forceful guarantees that state court juries also will be selected without discrimination of any kind.
>
> Third, to broaden the Attorney General's authority to bring suit for the desegregation of schools and public facilities—enabling him to commit the government's legal resources where they are most critically needed.
>
> Fourth, to declare national policy against racial discrimination in the sale or rental of housing, and to create remedies against that discrimination in every part of America.[43]

Moreover, he stated that "the first year's experience of the Equal Employment Opportunity Commission suggests that it should be endowed with enforcement power and that its coverage should be broadened." [44]

[41] Robert Sherill, *The Accidental President* (New York: Grossman Publishers, 1967), 195–96.

[42] *Congressional Quarterly Almanac, 1966* (Washington, D.C.: Congressional Quarterly Inc., 1967), 195–96.

[43] "Text of President Johnson's Message on Civil Rights, April 28, 1966," *Congressional Quarterly Weekly Report*, 24 (May 6, 1966), 943.

[44] *Ibid.*, 945.

Soon after the president spoke a new movement was born in Mississippi: "black power." The disappointment over the treatment of the MFDP at the national convention of the Democratic party in 1964 and the failure to unseat the regular Democrats in Congress early in 1965 were not the only reasons for the "black power" movement beginning in Mississippi. Dr. Martin Luther King, Jr., who was not a supporter, wrote that "black power" was a cry of disappointment and was a reaction against the failure of white power to alleviate conditions of blacks. Indeed, he noted:

> It is no accident that the birth of this slogan in the civil rights movement took place in Mississippi—the state symbolizing the most blatant abuse of white power. In Mississippi the murder of civil rights workers is still a popular pastime. In that state more than forty Negroes and whites have been lynched or murdered over the last three years, and not a single man has been punished for these crimes. More than fifty Negro churches have been burned or bombed in Mississippi in the last two years, yet the bombers still walk the streets surrounded by the halo of adoration. This is white power in its most brutal, cold-blooded and vicious form.[45]

The bill soon was considered in both houses although the Senate waited on the House to act first on the Civil Rights Bill of 1966. It contained all four provisions mentioned in the president's speech, but nothing about the strengthening of the authority of the Equal Employment Opportunity Commission. The bill faced certain stiff opposition on the Senate floor.

In the House a key vote occurred on August 3, 1966. Title IV (housing coverage) was limited by a vote of 180–179. This was the so-called Mathias amendment which limited the applicability of the title to large apartment buildings and developments and to certain classes of new construction in the housing field.[46] As amended, Title IV covered about 40 percent of the nation's housing. With this change the house passed the civil rights package by a 259–157 roll

[45] Martin Luther King, Jr., *Where Do We Go From Here: Chaos or Community?* (New York: Harper & Row Publishers, 1967), 33. See also Stokeley Carmichael and Charles V. Hamilton, *Black Power* (New York: Random House, 1967) for an explanation of the meaning of "black power."

[46] "Controversy Over Public Housing: Pro and Con," *Congressional Digest,* 45 (November, 1966), 257; "Civil Rights," *Congressional Quarterly Weekly Report,* 24 (August 5, 1966), 1687.

call vote on August 9. The bill was scheduled to go before the Senate in September.[47]

As expected, when the House-passed bill reached the Senate, a filibuster took place. It was, however, supported as usual by the Leadership Conference on Civil Rights. Roy Wilkins let it be known that he opposed the Mathias amendment in the House which severely watered down the section dealing with housing; the AFL-CIO, however, decided to go along in order to obtain the rest of the package.[48]

In the midst of the congressional deliberations on the civil rights bill the annual conference of CORE was held at Baltimore. On July 1, 1966, Fannie Lou Hamer (MFDP) and Stokeley Carmichael (SNCC) spoke at the gathering and both referred to the bill as a useless sham. They insisted that President Johnson was trying to take himself off the spot once more. Carmichael also declared that the attorney general already had the authority to place blacks on southern juries and that the president could end 80 percent of the housing segregation with an executive order.[49]

On September 14 the senators rejected a cloture motion on an amended version of the Civil Rights Bill of 1966 by a vote of 54–42. Senator Dirksen was a key influence in the outcome just as he had been earlier. This time, however, he was against cloture. Dirksen objected strongly to Title IV (housing) on constitutional grounds. Apparently heartened by the outcome of the cloture vote, Senator Eastland of Mississippi spoke of a revival of the Republican-Southern Democratic Coalition. Eastland also indicated that before long a beginning could be made toward the repeal of the earlier civil rights laws. Like Dirksen, the southerners held that Title IV was unconstitutional. In addition, the other senator from Mississippi, John Stennis, insisted that the whole bill was politically motivated.[50]

The senators had been deluged with mail attacking the civil rights bill, particularly Title IV. An article in *Newsweek* indicated that behind everything could be heard "the ominous snap of the back-

[47] "House Passes Civil Rights Bill," *Congressional Quarterly Weekly Report,* 24 (August 12, 1966), 1719.

[48] "Civil Rights Lobbying," *ibid.,* 24 (August 5, 1966), 1713.

[49] New York *Times,* July 2, 1966, p. 24.

[50] "Senate Rejects Limit on Civil Rights Debate," *Congressional Quarterly Weekly Report,* 24 (September 16, 1966), 2141; "Controversy Over Public Housing: Pro or Con," 257.

lash." [51] The night before the cloture motion was rejected Senator Dirksen had informed the president that after the summer's racial violence in Illinois and in other parts of the country, "there would be no civil rights bill this year." [52] Senator Frank Lausche of Ohio declared on the day of the vote that "the Carmichaels and the McKissicks . . . have made it most difficult for every member of Congress to provide help where it is most needed." [53] At the same time, some liberals had lost enthusiasm for Title IV since it had been watered down so much.[54]

The senators voted once more on September 19, 1966, by 52–41 to reject a motion for cloture on the civil rights bill debate. This result ended all efforts for a bill in 1966, and it was the first time an administration's civil rights bill had been defeated since 1957.[55] Such black leaders as Whitney Young, Jr., and Dr. Martin Luther King, Jr., predicted a worsening of the racial crisis in the cities. Floyd McKissick, National Director of CORE, accused President Johnson of failing to exercise "strong and dynamic leadership." He also declared that the vote indicated "the climate of racism prevailing in the country at this time." Interestingly enough, Senator Dirksen claimed that in a meeting he had with the president, no great effort had been made by Johnson to cause the senator to vote for the bill.[56]

Apparently the president had not really pushed the bill, as McKissick and Dirksen charged. No doubt he was thinking about the midterm congressional elections and the growing white backlash. When compared to earlier civil rights bills, the one in 1966 with its "open" housing provision hit much closer to home for white Americans. As an article in *Time* magazine noted: "The sad, ever outrageous, but inescapable fact seems to be that the white is not yet acclimatized to the notion of having a Negro for a neighbor. So the bill last week became the first civil rights measure to be killed by Congress in nine years." [57]

[51] "The Issue Is Conduct," *Newsweek*, 68 (September 26, 1966), 32.
[52] *Ibid.*
[53] *Ibid.*
[54] Alexander M. Bickel, "Civil Rights' Dim Prospects," *New Republic*, 155 (September 17, 1966), 17.
[55] "Senate Kills Civil Rights Bill," *Congressional Quarterly Weekly Report*, 24 (September 23, 1966), 2199.
[56] *Ibid.*, 2220; "Civil Rights," *Time*, 88 (September 30, 1966), 21.
[57] "Civil Rights," 21; "Backlash Jitters," *New Republic*, 155 (October 22,

A growing white hostility toward blacks was indicated by the public opinion polls in 1966. A Gallup poll taken just before the November elections showed that 52 percent of the whites polled felt that the administration was pushing integration too fast. For this particular organization, it was the highest percentage on that question since 1962. About the same time, the Harris poll showed that some 75 percent of the whites polled thought that blacks were moving ahead too rapidly while in 1964 only 50 percent had felt that way.[58]

President Johnson once more requested new civil rights legislation in his State of the Union address in January, 1967. He repeated some of the same proposals he had made in 1966. Perhaps in part because of Republican gains in the midterm elections, Johnson modified them slightly. While he called for reform in the selection of juries, he did not specify whether he meant federal or state juries. He recommended a law protecting persons in the exercise of their civil rights and declared that "some solution" had to be found for "fair housing" problems. The president again recommended a strengthening of authority on the part of the Equal Employment Opportunity Commission (EEOC). He noted that while the House had passed a bill giving the EEOC the power to issue cease-and-desist orders and to accelerate coverage of unions and employers, the Senate had taken no action on the measure.[59]

In an effort to improve chances for the bill in the Senate, pro-civil rights forces attempted to modify the cloture rule. They wished to reduce the majority needed for cloture from two-thirds to three-fifths of those present and voting. A proposal came to a vote and received a 53–46 favorable majority, but that was 13 fewer votes than were needed to shut off a two-week-long debate that the southerners had conducted in opposition to the petition for modification of the rule. Thus the proponents of the rules change were not able to bring their petition up for a vote. Roy Wilkins referred to the failure of the vote

---

1966), 5–6. See also Lewis Chester, Godfrey Hodgson, and Bruce Page, *The Presidential Election of 1968* (New York: The Viking Press, 1969), 35–36, for a difference between black and white perceptions of the treatment of blacks in America.

[58] *Revolution in Civil Rights* (Washington, D.C.: Congressional Quarterly Inc., 1968), 73.

[59] "State of the Union Message, January 10, 1967," *Congressional Quarterly Weekly Report*, 25 (January 13, 1967), 45.

to cut off debate as a "kick in the teeth" to any civil rights legislation in 1967. He added, "I am not predicting riots, but this adds to the climate in which somebody could start something." [60]

Despite this setback, President Johnson delivered a civil rights message to Congress on February 15, 1967,[61] calling for a civil rights bill substantially the same as the one in 1966 except for minor revisions. He stated:

> I recommend the adoption of a national policy against discrimination in housing on account of race, color, religion or national origin. I propose the adoption of progressive steps to carry out this policy.
>
> I recommend the clarification and strengthening of existing federal criminal laws against interference with federal rights.
>
> I recommend requirements for the selection of juries in federal courts to guard against discrimination and insure that juries are properly representative of the community.
>
> I recommend legislation to eliminate all forms of discrimination in the selection of state juries.
>
> I recommend that the Civil Rights Act of 1964 be amended to authorize the Equal Employment Opportunity Commission to issue judicially enforceable cease-and-desist orders.
>
> I recommend the extension for an additional five years of the U.S. Commission on Civil Rights.
>
> I recommend a 90 percent increase in the appropriation for the Community Relations Service.[62]

After making these proposals the president proceeded to explain why legislation in each of those areas was needed. He concluded the speech by declaring:

> In our wars Americans, Negro and white, have fought side by side to defend freedom. Negro soldiers—like white soldiers—have won every medal for bravery our country bestows. The bullets of our enemies do not discriminate between Negro marines and white marines. They kill and maim whomever they strike.
>
> The American Negro has waited too long for first-class citizenship —for his right for equal justice. But he has accepted the full responsibilities of citizenship.
>
> The bullets at the battlefront do not discriminate—but the landlords at home do. The pack of the Negro soldier is as heavy as the white

---

[60] New York *Times*, January 25, 1967, p. 1.

[61] "Text of President Johnson's Civil Rights Message, February 15, 1967," *Congressional Quarterly Weekly Report*, 25 (February 17, 1967), 262–67.

[62] *Ibid.*, 264.

soldier's—but the burden his family at home bears is far heavier. In war, the Negro American has given this nation his best—but this nation has not given him equal justice.[63]

The housing section in the proposed bill was quite similar to Title IV in the 1966 measure, except that in the new bill the housing section would go into effect in three stages and gradually affect more housing units including single family dwellings by January 1, 1969.[64] However, in large part because of the housing section of the bill, its chance of passage was no better than in 1966. Senator Mansfield, majority leader in the Senate, compared 1967 with the previous year when he declared: "I would say, unfortunately, that the prospects would be the same." [65]

Just after the president introduced his omnibus civil rights bill, an editorial discussing its provisions appeared in the New York *Times*. It expressed the view that there was little likelihood of the bill becoming law. With regard to the sections on the protection of civil rights workers and blacks exercising their rights and on improvements in the judicial system, the article noted:

> The need for these improvements in Federal law enforcement and the judicial system in the South is reflected in the dismaying news that Byron de la Beckwith intends to run for Lieutenant Governor of Mississippi. His candidacy is proof of the open contempt in which the lives and opinions of Negroes are still held in parts of the South. Beckwith's sole claim to political preferment is that he has been twice tried though not convicted for the murder of Medgar Evers, the Mississippi leader of the National Association for the Advancement of Colored People.
> Tighter federal laws are imperative to make murder a crime, whatever the color of the victim's skin.[66]

If anything, there was more opposition to the bill than in 1966, as Representative Celler and Senator Hart introduced the bill in their respective houses. Since the omnibus bill seemed to be going nowhere, proponents of the bill decided to split it up into several measures with each section of the bill becoming a separate bill.[67] Heavy

---

[63] *Ibid.*, 267.

[64] New York *Times*, February 17, 1967, p. 23.

[65] "Fair Housing Again in Rights Bill," *U.S. News & World Report*, 62 (February 27, 1967), 69.

[66] New York *Times*, February 16, 1967, p. 38.

[67] "President Proposes New Civil Rights Legislation," *Congressional Quarterly Weekly Report*, 25 (February 17, 1967), 239.

opposition was anticipated not only in the Senate where the filibuster was still available, but also in the House as a consequence of its more conservative complexity resulting from the congressional elections of 1966. There were apparently several reasons for the decision to split the omnibus bill: there was a need for some movement, and the House was reluctant to take action on the omnibus bill after the debacle of 1966; there was the concern that the other sections of the bill had no chance as long as they were tied in with the "fair" housing title. At the same time, the strongest proponents of "fair" housing felt that its chances were doomed by its isolation. They believed that some legislators might vote for it even if they were not too enthusiastic, provided "fair" housing were part of a package.[68]

In spite of the division of the omnibus bill there was no rush in Congress to enact its various provisions into separate laws. Indeed, there was intense pressure in the House for the passage of an anti-riot bill which was introduced by Representative William Cramer of Florida as a result of continued riots in the cities.[69] A bill was considered in the House Judiciary Committee which combined civil rights protection with an effort to curb so-called outside agitators from inciting riots. However, Representative William M. Colmer of Mississippi, powerful chairman of the House Rules Committee, insisted on separate consideration of an anti-riot bill.[70]

The House Judiciary Committee yielded to Colmer's pressure and approved separate bills for riot control and civil rights protection. Colmer promised Representative Celler, chairman of the Judiciary Committee, that he would permit both bills to reach the floor, though he opposed the one providing for civil rights protection. Unquestionably in the House there appeared to be a greater demand for an anti-riot bill than for one providing protection for civil rights workers.

In spite of this situation, the administration let it be known that it opposed the anti-riot measure.[71] Moreover, Roy Wilkins of the NAACP stated at the annual NAACP convention in Boston that the anti-riot bill did not deal with the root of the problems blacks faced

[68] *Congressional Quarterly Almanac* (Washington, D.C.: Congressional Quarterly Inc., 1967) XXIII, 170.
[69] New York *Times*, March 18, 1967, p. 1.
[70] *Ibid.*, June 23, 1967, p. 1.
[71] *Ibid.*, June 28, 1967, p. 23.

in the cities. He charged that those congressmen opposed to the current civil rights legislation were "creating the atmosphere" for racial violence.[72]

In the meantime, on July 11 the House voted 282–89 to extend the life of the Commission on Civil Rights for five years. On the same day, the House Rules Committee also approved the anti-riot bill. At the presentation before the House Rules Committee Representative Cramer denounced Stokeley Carmichael as a "free lance insurrectionist." Representative Celler, apparently yielding to the growing backlash, stated that while he doubted the constitutionality of the bill, he did not wish to be placed in a position of opposing it. Representatives John Conyers, Jr., of Michigan, Herbert Tenzer of Nassau, and Don Edwards of California expressed the view that the bill violated both free speech and due process and, therefore, they opposed it.[73]

Tom Wicker, *New York Times* editorial writer, had the following to say about long-time civil rights advocate Celler's position on the anti-riot bill: "A Congress representing a predominantly white society that will not pass even a diluted open housing law or provide increased protection for civil rights workers, but which 'does not wish to be in a position of opposing' a demagogic anti-riot bill, is unlikely to persuade slum-dwelling, poorly educated, often ill-fed and ill-clad Negroes that they can get relief from the law before they can get it in the streets." [74]

In spite of the administration's opposition and that of many civil rights advocates, the House passed the anti-riot bill by a 347–70 vote. A similar bill had been passed by the House in the civil rights package. Representative Frank Thompson of New Jersey who voted against the bill, labeled it a "bill of attainder" aimed at Stokeley Carmichael.[75]

In the Senate the anti-riot bill faced considerable opposition. Senator Edward Kennedy promised that if the bill were to reach the Senate floor, he would attach some of the administration's civil rights proposals or a gun-control provision to it.[76]

[72] *Ibid.,* July 11, 1967, p. 15.
[73] *Ibid.,* July 12, 1967, p. 23.
[74] *Ibid.,* July 13, 1967, p. 36.
[75] *Ibid.,* July 20, 1967, p. 1; *Congressional Quarterly Almanac,* XXIII (1967), 771.
[76] New York *Times,* July 21, 1967, p. 35.

On August 16, 1967, the House voted 326–93 to approve a bill making it a crime to harm or intimidate persons exercising federally protected rights or policemen or firemen who attempted to quell a riot. Representative James Wright of Texas had succeeded in amending the bill to include policemen and firemen.[77] By that time, it had become apparent that the House would pass no other civil rights legislation in 1967.

By late in August the House-passed civil rights bill was sent to the Senate Judiciary Committee. Senator Eastland announced that he planned to kill it by adding the "open" housing provision to it. The Mississippi senator predicted that his action would halt further efforts to pass civil rights laws aimed at the South.[78]

As the months passed little action on civil rights occurred in the Senate. Finally, in October, 1967, the Senate Judiciary Committee approved the bill prolonging the life of the Civil Rights Commission. However, the committee tacked on a spending ceiling for the commission of $26 million.[79] A month later the Senate as a whole approved the bill dealing with the Civil Rights Commission. The bill then went back to the House, which refused to concur with the spending ceiling. However, the bill went to the conference committee, and the House members agreed to the Senate position. The committee's report was then adopted by both houses in essentially the same form as adopted by the Senate Judiciary Committee, with the spending ceiling.[80]

The bill extending the life of the Civil Rights Commission was signed into law on December 15. It was the only civil rights bill passed into law during 1967, although the Senate approved a federal jury reform bill on December 8.[81] Senator Mansfield announced, however, that the bill protecting persons engaged in civil rights activities would be the Senate's first order of business in 1968.[82]

Despite the rhetoric the administration had not pressured as much

[77] *Ibid.*, August 17, 1967, pp. 1, 24; *Congressional Quarterly Almanac*, XXIII (1967), 771.

[78] New York *Times*, August 26, 1967, p. 23.

[79] *Ibid.*, October 12, 1967, p. 50; *Congressional Quarterly Almanac*, XXIII (1967), 771.

[80] *Congressional Quarterly Almanac*, XXIII (1967), 777.

[81] *Ibid.*, XXIV (1968), 169.

[82] New York *Times*, December 16, 1967, p. 20.

for civil rights legislation in 1967 as it had in 1966. Being fully aware of the changed complexion of the House and the growing backlash, the president seemed to place a higher priority on support for other matters, especially the undeclared war in Vietnam. Even some of the traditional support of northern moderates and liberals warned: "The open bussing and equal employment bills affected the Northern homeowner and labor unionist, whose interests had not been touched by the civil rights movement. Northern members of Congress from both parties, many of whom had supported civil rights legislation previously, were keenly aware of the sensitive nature of those issues." [83] The coalition of northern Republicans and Democrats so crucial to the passage of the Civil Rights Act of 1964 and the Voting Rights Act of 1965 seemed to have faded away.

President Johnson returned to Congress to request more civil rights legislation in his annual message on January 17, 1968. In the course of his address the president declared: "I shall urge Congress to act on several other pending civil rights measures—fair jury trials, protection of Federal rights, enforcement of equal employment opportunity, and fair housing." [84]

There was considerable dismay among some of the black leaders that interest in civil rights was declining on the part of the president and Congress. Roy Wilkins and Floyd McKissick regretted that congressmen had applauded loudly when the president mentioned the need for anti-crime measures but none when he discussed the need for civil rights bills.[85] The chances for the enactment of any new civil rights bills appeared slight.

Perhaps in reaction to this situation, shortly thereafter, President Johnson sent a civil rights message to Congress in which he described the progress blacks had made; but he indicated that there was still much to be done in the areas of health, housing, education, and employment. He also mentioned some recent actions that had been taken by federal agencies in improving the status of blacks. At the same time, Johnson reiterated his request for additional civil rights

[83] *Congressional Quarterly Almanac*, XXIII (1967), 771.

[84] State of the Union Message, January 17, 1968, *Public Papers of the Presidents: Lyndon B. Johnson, 1968–69* (2 books; Washington, D.C.: U.S. Government Printing Office, 1970), I, 31; *Congressional Quarterly Weekly Report*, 26 (January 19, 1968), 99.

[85] New York *Times*, January 19, 1968, p. 19.

legislation and declared that action was urgently needed as follows:

> —To strengthen Federal criminal laws prohibiting violent interference with the right to exercise civil rights.
> —To give the Equal Employment Opportunity Commission the authority it needs to carry out its vital responsibilities.
> —To assure that Federal and state juries are seated without discrimination.
> —To make equal opportunity in housing a reality for all Americans.[86]

The administration and civil rights groups seemed to face a long uphill battle as there appeared to be little sentiment for civil rights in Congress. Nevertheless on February 26, 1968, the House passed a bill dealing with federal juries. It had already passed the Senate in the previous December, but the House version was somewhat different. On March 14, the senators accepted the House amendments and the bill was signed into law by the president on March 27. The bill provided that federal juries be selected at random "from a fair cross section of the community" without discrimination, and that each U.S. district court draw up a plan for jury selection meeting the standards of the bill. It also laid down guidelines for jury selection, established procedures for the degree of compliance with jury selection requirements, and raised fees for witnesses and jurors.[87]

At the time of his signing the federal jury bill into law the president declared:

> Too often the jury lists have tended to exclude citizens who were poor and who were not "in" or who may have lacked charisma or may have been members of a minority group.
>
> Now this discrimination—sometimes we call it "highhat"—was not always intentional. But sometimes it was intentional. And more often it was the result of a very haphazard selection system.
>
> So the bill I will sign shortly, takes a principle and makes it into a statute. From now on, all of our Federal jurors in this country will be, in the language of the law, "selected at random from a fair cross section of the community."
>
> This measure reinforces the precious legal rights of all citizens. And it does more than that alone. It advances the civil rights of those who

[86] Special Message to the Congress on Civil Rights, January 24, 1968, *Public Papers of the Presidents: Lyndon B. Johnson, 1968–69*, I, 58.

[87] *Congressional Quarterly Almanac*, XXIV, 169.

still reach for their full, and what we believe their proper, place in our society.[88]

Members of the Leadership Conference on Civil Rights continued to prefer that the president issue an executive order dealing with open housing. They had met with members of the administration on a number of occasions and urged that the president extend the coverage accorded by Kennedy's order in 1962. However, the president, as before, insisted on a law on the grounds that it would be more effective in the long run. The civil rights leaders were not happy with this approach; they felt that the president was evading the order so as to place the problem in the laps of the legislators, but they were unable to change Johnson's mind.[89]

Faced with the president's intransigence, Clarence Mitchell of the NAACP and other members of the Leadership Conference, decided to make the civil rights bill passed by the House in 1967 and still pending in the Senate, the vehicle for open housing legislation in 1968. The strategy for the measure was determined at a meeting on December 28, 1967, of Mitchell, Senator Hart of Michigan, Senator Mondale of Minnesota, and Senator Tydings of Maryland among others. They decided that Mondale and Senator Brooke of Massachusetts would cosponsor the housing amendment to the bill. Upon learning of this strategy, Attorney General Clark and Senator Mansfield of Montana were concerned that it might jeopardize the chances for any civil rights bill at all.

As debate on the civil rights bill began in the Senate on January 18, Senator Russell of Georgia, leader of the opposition to the measure, promised that there would be "extended" debate. When asked for his opinion about prospects for early passage of the bill by newsmen, Senator Mansfield said that they were "gloomy." [90]

On February 6 the liberals won a victory when the Senate rejected a southern substitute bill calling for the protection of civil rights but excluding state actions such as state elections or attendance in schools

---

[88] Remarks Upon Signing the Jury Selection and Service Act of 1968, March 27, 1968, *Public Papers of the Presidents: Lyndon B. Johnson, 1968–69,* I, 446.

[89] Wolk, *The Presidency and Black Civil Rights,* 57–59.

[90] New York *Times,* January 16, 1968, p. 23; *ibid.,* January 18, 1968, p. 1.

not receiving federal aid.[91] At the same time, Mondale and Brooke submitted an open housing amendment to the bill covering 91 percent of all housing. A filibuster by the southerners began at that point.

Senator Dirksen's role was crucial, just as it had been in earlier years with civil rights bills. A favorable cloture vote without his support was all but impossible. He had been against open housing in both 1966 and 1967, and it had failed. Things looked grim at first in 1968 as he took the same stance against open housing. On February 20 and 26, with Dirksen in the opposition, the first two cloture votes failed. Apparently President Johnson made no effort to change Dirksen's mind.[92] However, on the second vote, there was a 19–17 Republican majority vote in favor of cloture.

In the meantime, civil rights advocates were able to block a move by the Republican and Democratic leadership in the Senate to kill open housing by a 58–34 vote. Senator Mansfield, in sponsoring this proposal, had declared that it was unrealistic to hope for passage of the bill as long as it contained a housing provision.[93]

After the second attempt to achieve cloture had failed, Senator Dirksen seemed to have a change of heart. He began negotiations with Ramsey Clark and other civil rights advocates to modify the bill. They agreed to modify the coverage of the housing section of the bill. Dirksen then placed an amendment before the Senate which covered 80 percent of the nation's housing.[94] Why had he altered his strong stand against "open" housing? Tom Wicker of the *New York Times* speculated that the reasons were that his grip on Republican senators was slipping as was indicated in the second cloture vote, and that he faced possible strong opposition for reelection. His support for the bill might cause Mayor Daley and President Johnson not to support a strong Democratic opponent.[95]

When questioned by newsmen about what had happened, Dirksen claimed that "time and reality" had caused him to change his mind. It had been the "right thing to do." It was reported that Richard

91 *Ibid.*, February 7, 1968, p. 23.
92 MacNeil, *Dirksen*, 320.
93 New York *Times,* February 22, 1968, pp. 1, 26; MacNeil, *Dirksen*, 322.
94 MacNeil, *Dirksen*, 324.
95 New York *Times*, February 27, 1968, p. 42.

Nixon and Governor George Romney of Michigan were supporting Dirksen's changed attitude.[96]

In his memoirs, President Johnson gave much credit to Clarence Mitchell of the NAACP and his lobbying for changing the situation in the Senate. He also wrote that he had "never once discussed supporting Dirksen's 1968 Illinois election with him. No President could 'force' a strong local party; headed by as forceful a person as Mayor Richard Daley, to commit political hara-kiri—especially over a bill that most of his constituents did not want anyway." [97]

Whatever the real reason for Dirksen's change, the compromise covering 80 percent of housing was the approach supported by the administration and civil rights advocates. On May 1, 1968, however, a third attempt at cloture failed by a vote of 59–35. Clarence Mitchell and the administration at that point pulled out all the stops. A fourth attempt was made on March 4 to achieve cloture, and it succeeded by 65 to 32—the exact two-thirds majority needed. Republicans favored the motion 24–12, whereas Democrats approved it by a 41–20 margin. Among northern Democrats there was a 37–3 favorable vote, while among southern Democrats the vote was 17–4 against cloture. The vote of Senator Miller of Iowa was considered the crucial one putting the favorable vote over the top. He had switched after Senator Brooke had agreed to vote in favor of a weakening amendment which failed anyway.[98]

After the successful vote on cloture, approval of the bill with the section on housing was assured. On March 11, 1968, the senators, by a 71–20 vote, approved the bill which contained an "open" housing section. Republicans voted for it by a 29–3 margin, while Democrats did so by a vote of 42–17. Among northern Democrats the favorable vote was 39–0, while southern Democrats voted against the measure by a 17–3 margin.[99]

After the senators approved the bill, President Johnson declared that every American "can be proud today" in affirming "our nation's

[96] *Ibid.*, p. 35.
[97] Johnson, *The Vantage Point*, 177.
[98] Wolk, *The Presidency and Black Civil Rights*, 60–61.
[99] *Congressional Quarterly Almanac*, XXIV, 152.

commitment to human rights under law" [100] At the same time, he urged quick passage of the bill by the House.

At this point, Alexander Bickel of Yale Law School, made an evaluation of the new civil rights bill, particularly the housing section. He wrote that on the whole it would improve conditions somewhat for blacks and was a good bill. It provided largely for voluntary compliance, but private suits might be instituted by victims of discrimination through the attorney general, if there was a pattern or practice of resistance to any rights in the title and if such a denial raised an issue of general importance. He did write, however, that it would not "break up the ghettos, and would not do so even if its enforcement provisions were stronger." [101]

In the meantime, taking their cue from the president, and after consultation with the Leadership Conference on Civil Rights, labor, and the House Judiciary Committee, the House Democratic leaders, including Speaker John McCormack, urged their fellow House members to pass the bill without any change. However, on March 19 the bill ran into a temporary stumbling block in the House Rules Committee which voted 8 to 7 to delay the bill until April 9.[102] This step was probably taken to give the National Association of Real Estate Boards (NAREB), with their 85,000 members, time to mobilize pressure on the House from the local boards. In addition, there was the possibility that the bill would be delayed two weeks beyond April 9 since the Easter recess was at hand. That delay in turn might cause an adverse reaction to set in as a result of the scheduled poor people's march on Washington, D.C., which was being planned by Dr. Martin Luther King, Jr., and others.

Other pressure groups besides NAREB joined the battle against the bill. They were particularly opposed to "open" housing and included the Emergency Committee of One Million, the Liberty Lobby, and the Emergency Committee Against Forced Housing. Deeply disturbed by efforts at delay and fearful that the reaction to the poor people's campaign would endanger the bill, Clarence Mitchell of the NAACP and his lieutenants worked feverishly to push early passage

[100] New York *Times*, March 12, 1968, p. 1.
[101] Alexander M. Bickel, "The Belated Civil Rights Legislation of 1968," *New Republic*, 158 (March 30, 1968), 11–12.
[102] New York *Times*, March 20, 1968, p. 1.

of the bill. Knowing full well that some Republican support would be needed, Goodell of New York and Quie of Minnesota were recruited to organize GOP support for the bill. However, these efforts were hampered by Representative Gerald Ford of Michigan, House minority leader, who sought a conference committee with the Senate in order to obtain modifications of the housing section.[103]

While hearings were taking place in the House Judiciary Committee, on March 27 President Johnson publicly chided the House for "fiddling and piddling" and urged it to speed passage of the bill. He also declared that the time for excuses had ended and that the time for action had arrived.[104]

In the midst of the discussions in the House Dr. Martin Luther King, Jr., famed civil rights leader, was gunned down on April 4, 1968, in Memphis, Tennessee. On the same evening, President Johnson expressed to the nation his shock over this event.[105] The next day, while proclaiming a day of mourning for Dr. King, the president declared:

> The dream of Dr. Martin Luther King, Jr., has not died with him. Men who are white—men who are black—must and now will join together as never in the past to let all the forces of divisiveness know that America shall not be ruled by the bullet but only by the ballot of free and just men.
>
> In these years we have moved toward opening the way of hope and opportunity and justice in this country.
>
> We have rolled away some of the stones of inaction, of indifference, and of injustice.
>
> Our work is not yet done. But we have begun.
>
> We must move with urgency, with resolve, and new energy in the Congress, in the Courts, in the White House, the statehouses and the city halls of the Nation, wherever there is leadership—political leadership in the churches, in the homes, in the schools, in the institutions of higher learning—until we do overcome.[106]

Riots occurred in a number of American cities in the wake of Dr. King's murder. There also appeared to be increased activity in favor

[103] *Ibid.*, March 24, 1968, p. 24.

[104] *Ibid.*, March 28, 1968, p. 80.

[105] Statement of the President on the Assassination of Dr. Martin Luther King, Jr., April 4, 1968, *Public Papers of the Presidents: Lyndon B. Johnson, 1968–69*, I, 493.

[106] Address to the Nation Upon Proclaiming a Day of Mourning Following the Death of Dr. King, April 5, 1968, *ibid.*, 494.

of passage of the civil rights bill in the House. Moreover, John W. Gardner, former HEW secretary, joined with the Urban Coalition in urging passage of the bill.[107]

On April 9 the House Rules Committee rejected by an 8 to 7 vote an effort to send the bill to a House-Senate conference committee. A lone Republican, John Anderson of Illinois, had joined seven Democrats in this crucial vote. Following that action, the committee voted 9 to 6 to send the bill to the floor allowing one hour for debate.[108]

In an editorial the *New York Times* paid tribute to Dr. King and urged a favorable vote on the House floor. At the same time, in commenting on the one vote margin against sending the bill to conference, it insisted: "The narrowness of the vote demonstrates that, despite the murder of Dr. Martin Luther King and the ominous racial crisis developing in this nation, the Conservative Republicans and the Southern Democrats are dug in and refuse to move. These are truly the American Bourbons who have learned nothing and forgotten nothing." [109]

On April 10, 1968, the House voted 250–172 to adopt the Senate version of the bill without change. The Republicans helped to provide the margin of victory as they voted for the bill 100–84. The Democrats supported the measure by 150–88 with a breakdown of 137–13 among northern Democrats and 13–75 among southern Democrats.[110]

The new law which would go into effect fully in 1970 prohibited discrimination in the sale or rental of about 80 percent of all housing. Most housing built with federal assistance, such as public housing and urban renewal projects, was covered immediately on enactment of the bill.[111] Coverage was to be extended on January 1, 1969, to all multiple-unit dwellings except for owner-occupied dwellings with no more than four units. Also covered on that date were single-family houses, such as real estate developments, that were not owned by private individuals. Privately owned single-family houses sold or rented by real estate agents or brokers were covered as of January 1, 1970.

[107] New York *Times*, April 7, 1968, p. 56.
[108] *Ibid.*, p. 1.
[109] *Ibid.*, April 10, 1968, p. 46.
[110] *Congressional Quarterly Almanac*, XXIV, 152.
[111] Indeed, they were already covered.

Private owners selling or renting their house without the services of a real estate agent or broker were exempt. The prohibition against discrimination also applied to financing and brokerage services. The secretary of Housing and Urban Development was to administer this title.[112]

The bill also provided criminal penalties for injuring or interfering with a person who was exercising specific rights which included: to serve on a jury, to vote, to work, to participate in government or government-aided programs, to enjoy public accommodations, and to attend school or college. In addition, the measure provided similar protection to civil rights workers who urged or helped others to exercise the rights mentioned above.[113]

Moreover, there were anti-riot provisions which called for criminal penalties for traveling or using the facilities of interstate commerce, such as telephones, in order to take part in or incite a riot. Penalties were included for manufacturing or teaching the use of explosives or firearms for purposes of civil disorder.[114]

Finally, there was an Indian rights section which prohibited tribal governments from enforcing or making laws which violated certain constitutional rights. States were also prohibited from assuming criminal or civil jurisdiction over Indian areas without the consent of those Indian tribes affected.[115]

The next day, on April 11, the president signed the bill into law and declared:

> Now with this bill, the voice of justice speaks again.
>
> It proclaims that fair housing for all—all human beings who live in this country—is now a part of the American way of life.
>
> This afternoon, as we gather here in this historic room in the White House, I think we can all take some heart that democracy's work is being done. In the Civil Rights Act of 1968 America does move forward and the bell of freedom rings a little louder.[116]

---

[112] *Congressional Quarterly Almanac*, XXIV, 152. See also Edward Brooke, T. A. Smedley, Arthur Kinoy, and Sam J. Ervin, Jr., "Non-Discrimination in the Sale or Rental of Property: Comments on Jones v. Alfred H. Mayer Co. and Title VIII of the Civil Rights Act of 1968," *Vanderbilt Law Review*, 22 (April, 1969), 455–502.

[113] *Congressional Quarterly Almanac*, XXIV, 152.

[114] *Ibid.*

[115] *Ibid.*

[116] Remarks Upon Signing the Civil Rights Act, April 11, 1968, *Public Papers of the Presidents: Lyndon B. Johnson, 1968–69*, I, 510.

There was some dispute over why the bill passed the House as rapidly and easily as it did without any amendments. Some publications, such as the *New York Times* and the *Christian Century* attributed the passage to the assassination of Dr. King in large part.[117] However, Roy Wilkins in a letter addressed to the editor of the *New York Times*, denied that the death of Dr. King brought about the adoption of the bill by the House. Instead, Wilkins insisted, hard work, particularly on the part of Clarence Mitchell, had paid off. He wrote that Anderson's switch in the House Rules Committee had been rumored before Dr. King's death and supporters of the bill were claiming victory by April 2. If anything, the NAACP leader argued, the bill might have lost some votes in the wake of the riots following King's death.[118]

In any case,not everyone was persuaded that the bill would accomplish very much. On the one hand, Roy Innis of CORE declared, "This is a hoax on the black people"; on the other hand, Clarence Mitchell insisted, "Anyone making such a statement either has not read the bill or is just plain dishonest." [119] However, as one editorial noted:

> The measure does nothing directly—to conquer prejudice or poverty. Moreover, enforcement may prove forbiddingly difficult since a Negro who is refused housing because of his race must first appeal to the Department of Housing and Urban Development, then file suit in the courts. Yet the psychological effect of the act upon developers, homeowners and Negroes alike will open many doors. For the first time, by federal law, a Negro is as entitled as any white—or more accurately four-fifths as entitled—to buy or rent any house or apartment that he can afford.[120]

An editorial in another publication pointed out, "The fact that Washington could sigh with relief when such a minor bit of legislation stumbles through is an indication that the white power structure is still not prepared to do anything about the great injustices that perpetuate poverty." [121]

---

117 New York *Times,* August 4, 1968, IV, p. 14; *Christian Century,* 85 (April 24, 1968), 507.
118 New York *Times,* May 10, 1968, p. 46.
119 "Opening the Door," *Time,* 91 (April 19, 1968), 20.
120 *Ibid.*
121 "Racism Arrested?" *Christian Century,* 85 (April 24, 1968), 507.

A leading law journal contained an article pointing to some of the major weaknesses of the act. First of all, it disregarded zoning laws and building codes which were designed to retain *de facto* segregation. Second, HUD lacked enforcement authority. The only other action available was to bypass HUD and proceed directly to a federal district court.[122] However, "If the procedural and substantive difficulties do not vitiate Title VIII, it may eventually provide an escape valve for Negro frustration. Otherwise, it can best serve only as a temporary sedative. To at least a certain extent, however, exodus from the ghetto is now a practical possibility." [123]

The Civil Rights Act of 1968 had only been in existence about eight months when the Johnson administration came to an end. That act and the Voting Rights Act of 1965 were the two major civil rights bills that became law after 1964. Both measures had some significance, but both depended upon strong enforcement. Moreover, the acts accomplished little to relieve the poverty of most blacks.

[122] "The Federal Fair Housing Requirements: Title VIII of the 1968 Civil Rights Act," *Duke Law Journal* (August, 1969), 733–71.
[123] *Ibid.*, 771.

CHAPTER IV

Coordination of Federal Civil Rights Activities, Black Public Civilian Employment, and Blacks in the Armed Forces

John F. Kennedy had established a subcommittee on civil rights to coordinate federal civil rights activities. By the time Lyndon Johnson assumed the presidency the structure operated largely on paper and not in fact.[1] President Johnson did nothing about the situation for a time. On December 10, 1964, however, he announced that the new vice-president, Hubert Humphrey, would serve as the administration's coordinator on race equality.[2]

Soon after taking office as the vice-president, Humphrey sent a report to the president called "On the Coordination of Civil Rights Activities in the Federal Government." Humphrey noted that as a consequence of the numerous new programs created after the enactment of the Civil Rights Act of 1964, there was great need for coordination of them. The vice-president opposed the creation of a new structure that would require agencies to take action; instead he preferred an organization which would "offer leadership, support, guidance, advance planning, evaluation, and advice to foster and increase individual agency effectiveness, cooperation, and coordination."[3]

On February 5, 1965, the president issued Executive Order 11197. In it Johnson cited the need for coordination of all parts of the federal government involved in the elmination of discrimination and the promotion of equal opportunity. More specifically:[4]

Section 1 provided for the establishment of the president's Council on Equal Opportunity with the vice-president serving as chairman.

---

[1] See James C. Harvey, *Civil Rights During the Kennedy Administration,* 21. See also Wolk, *The Presidency and Black Civil Rights,* 177.

[2] New York *Times,* December 11, 1964, p. 1.

[3] Wolk, *The Presidency and Black Civil Rights,* 178.

[4] *Federal Register,* XXX (February 9, 1965), 1721–23.

Section 2 provided that the other members of the council were the attorney general, secretary of defense, secretary of agriculture, secretary of labor, secretary of commerce, secretary of HEW, chairman of the Civil Service Commission, administrator of the Housing and Home Finance Agency, the director of OEO, chairman of the United States Commission on Civil Rights, director of the Community Relations Service, chairman of the President's Committee on Equal Employment Opportunity, and other members the president might add from time to time.

Section 4 established the duties for the council as follows: (1) to recommend to the president policies and actions to promote the purpose of the Civil Rights Acts of 1957 and 1964 and other federal laws relative to the civil rights of all persons, without discrimination on the basis of race, creed, color, or national origin; (2) to advise the president of inadequacies in existing federal laws, policies, and programs relating to civil rights and make recommendations for their improvement; (3) to recommend to the president any changes needed in administrative structure and relationships; (4) to recommend to the president actions which would promote the coordination of federal activities with programs of state and local governments fostering civil rights and equal opportunity; (5) to assist federal agencies and departments to coordinate their programs and activities and to adopt uniform and consistent policies, procedures, and practices in dealing with civil rights and promoting equal opportunity; (6) to request reports and other information from federal agencies about their civil rights activities; (7) to consult with interested public and private interest groups and individuals.

Section 8 provided that each federal agency and department was to designate an official, of a mark no lower than deputy assistant secretary or its equivalent, to oversee and coordinate activities of each department or agency related to civil rights and equal opportunity, and serve as its liaison with the council.

Following the issuance of the executive order, the work of the President's Council on Equal Opportunity (PCEO) was undertaken by its own staff. Several meetings were held by the PCEO, and efforts were made to coordinate federal civil rights activity. At the second meeting William L. Taylor, staff director of the Commission on Civil Rights, gave a report to the group entitled "Enforcement of Federal

Civil Rights Policies in Alabama." The discussion centered on a plan for twelve federal agencies to institute a coordinated effort in which Alabama would have to rescind many of its racist policies or lose one billion dollars in federal revenue.[5]

Samuel Yette, special assistant on civil rights in OEO for a time during the Johnson administration, wrote that two events sealed the fate of PCEO. First of all, the council recommended federal intervention in behalf of Dr. King's Selma-to-Montgomery march on March 20, 1965. Secondly, there was the abortive attempt to cut off some federal funds to Chicago's de facto segregated school system. The alliance of George Wallace and Mayor Richard Daley, together with their supporters in Congress, against strenuous enforcement efforts helped to doom any meaningful coordinated effort in behalf of civil rights enforcement. Yette insisted that the challenge to Daley was the last straw.[6]

Apparently the relationship between the PCEO and the White House staff was never good and the president never liked the mechanism he had created by executive order.[7] In any case, whether it was of his volition or not, after a few months Vice-President Humphrey recommended to the president that the Justice Department be given the major responsibility for coodinating federal civil rights activities and called for the elimination of the council.[8] Most civil rights leaders were deeply disturbed by this change.

The president accepted Humphrey's recommendation and by executive order abolished the PCEO. He also shifted the Community Relations Service to the Justice Department (effective in 1966 after approval by Congress). Moreover, the order provided for the elimination of the President's Committee on Equal Employment Opportunity which made policies for the federal government and government contractors. Supervision of federal employment was placed under the Civil Service Commission, and the secretary of labor

[5] Samuel F. Yette, *The Choice: The Issue of Black Survival in America* (New York: Berkley Publishing Corporation, 1971), 62.

[6] *Ibid.*, 63–67.

[7] Wolk, *The Presidency and Black Civil Rights*, 185–89.

[8] See Executive Order 11246, September 24, 1965, *Federal Register*, XXX (September 30, 1965), 12319–12325. See also *Congressional Quarterly Almanac*, XXI, 566.

was given responsibility for assuring non-discrimination by government contractors. The clearing-house and data-gathering function of the Community Relations Service was shifted to the Civil Rights Commission.[9]

On the same day President Johnson issued another executive order which provided for the coordination by the attorney general of the enforcement of Title VI of the Civil Rights Act of 1964 (Title VI required desegregation of federally funded facilities and programs). The reason given was that the issues would be largely legal in the future and that the attorney general, being the nation's chief legal official, was the logical choice to direct the needed coordination. Executive Order 11197 of February 5, 1965, establishing the PCEO, was revoked in thirty days. Each federal agency and department was ordered to cooperate with the attorney general and to furnish information and reports as requested.[10]

Civil rights leaders had been caught unawares by the president's actions. Only a few days earlier, Johnson had taken a cruise on the *Honey Fitz* with some of them and, after listening to their complaints, had assured them that more rigorous civil rights enforcement would be undertaken.[11]

Why had the president decided to abolish the PCEO and the President's Committee on Equal Opportunity (established by President Kennedy in 1961) and diffuse authority among cabinet-level officials? Apparently there was considerable pressure from Congress, and Johnson succumbed in order to preserve his legislative program intact. Even the segregationists preferred the Equal Employment Opportunity Commission to process complaints since it had little power. Moreover, Congress had control over EEOC funds for staff and equipment.[12] Or had the president sought to diminish Humphrey's prestige and authority in the area of civil rights? Whatever the motive was, civil rights leaders feared that since the executive role would be lessened, enforcement efforts would be diluted also. Attorney Gen-

[9] Executive Order 11246, *Federal Register*, XXX, 12319–12325.
[10] Executive Order 11247, September 24, 1965, *ibid.*, 12327; *Weekly Compilation of Presidential Documents*, I (September 27, 1965), 310.
[11] Christopher Pyle and Richard Morgan, "Johnson's Civil Rights Shake-Up," *New Leader*, 48 (October 11, 1965), 3.
[12] *Ibid.*, 5.

eral Katzenbach had the reputation for favoring restraint in dealing with complaints of law violations.[13]

Allan Wolk, a political scientist, speculated that the Department of Justice was selected for this special role for four major reasons: (1) the department had the most expertise and experience in the field of civil rights enforcement; (2) Attorney General Katzenbach's philosophy was similar to the president's and Katzenbach was trusted by him; (3) the role of the department had traditionally been as the legal arm of the government; and (4) the department might serve as a front, appearing to liberal elements as "an affirmative control unit of coordination." [14]

The sudden death of PCEO was a hurried retreat from a brief co-ordinated attack on federally financed racism. But more than that, it signified a resurgence of the entrenched federal and local establishment, briefly threatened by a federally financed, federally directed move toward pacification, if not liberation. The bosses of the system would not be content with their mere victory of bolting the brief federal stand for civil rights; they would demand a reversal even of the basic pacification thrust. The federal establishment itself would have to be harnassed for a fast ride in the wrong direction.[15]

Two writers, Christopher Pyle and Richard Morgan, were deeply disturbed by the demise of the President's Committee on Equal Employment Opportunity. They insisted that neither the secretary of labor nor the chairman of the Civil Service Commission had the power, the prestige, and the available time to match that of the vice-president:[16] Furthermore, they argued that the president's committee, and not the much publicized Equal Employment Opportunity Commission, offered the best chance for an early reversal of current inability of Negroes to improve their employment prospects as rapidly as whites. This was the agency with the strongest legal powers, the largest force of trained investigators, and the most efficient techniques not only for fighting discrimination but for persuading corporations that employing Negroes and other minorities was good

13 See Ivor Kovarsky, "The Negro and Fair Employment," *Kentucky Law Journal*, 56 (Summer, 1967–68), 798. See also New York *Times*, October 17, 1965, p. 1.

14 Wolk, *The Presidency and Black Civil Rights*, 189.

15 Yette, *The Choice*, 67.

16 Pyle and Morgan, "Johnson's Civil Rights Shake-Up," 5.

business.[17] Pyle and Morgan wondered if the president had accepted the arguments of segregationists that enough had been done for blacks.[18]

After several months delay Attorney General Katzenbach issued "Guidelines for Enforcement of Title VI." Copies were sent to twenty-one government departments and agencies. Training programs were to be undertaken within forty-five or sixty days. In an accompanying letter Katzenbach wrote: "There should be no mistaking the clear intent and effect of the Guidelines—Title VI must and will be enforced. Assistance will be refused or terminated to non-complying recipients and applicants who are not amenable to other sanctions." [19] Despite the seemingly unequivocal langauge in the letter, however, the guidelines emphasized voluntary compliance before any resort to the termination or withholding of federal funds resulting from the failure of local or state agencies to meet the standards of the guidelines.[20]

Fears of those who anticipated a lessening of federal pressure for civil rights enforcement seemed to have been justified. Neither Katzenbach nor Ramsey Clark, his successor, believed that he had the power to order agencies and department heads to comply with the guidelines. Clark himself felt that the vice-president was better suited to do the job of coordination—provided he enjoyed the support of the president.[21]

No interdepartmental meetings concerned with civil rights were held until the first one was called by Attorney General Clark in July, 1967. After that time, Clark and his Title VI assistant, David Rose, held monthly meetings of special compliance assistants from a number of agencies and departments. Nevertheless, by Clark's own admission, interdepartmental coordination was at best "loose." The department's role was very limited.[22] The relationship between the Justice Department and the Civil Rights Commission was uneven

[17] *Ibid.*, 6.
[18] *Ibid.*
[19] *Congressional Quarterly Almanac*, XXI, 567.
[20] *Ibid.*
[21] Wolk, *The Presidency and Black Civil Rights*, 191–92.
[22] *Ibid.*, 195; "Comment: Title VI of the Civil Rights Act of 1964—Implementation and Impact," *George Washington Law Review*, 36 (May, 1968), 862.

during the Johnson administration, although better while Clark was in charge than with Robert Kennedy or Katzenbach.[23]

Professor Wolk summarized the overall effort of the Johnson administration to coordinate civil rights enforcement as follows:

> Lyndon Johnson's Council on Equal Opportunity was the first full-fledged official unit of coordination which had specific powers and responsibilities as stated in an executive order. It, however, was created reluctantly by a President who always had reservations as to its need. Its short existence was an indication that the administration preferred decentralized civil rights implementation, with White House control vested in the trusted Justice Department. This was further reflected in the delegation of Title VI coordination responsibilities to Attorney General Nicholas Katzenbach, who did not view his new duties as calling for czar-like action. Katzenbach, rather, saw the Justice Department as a moderating force which kept civil rights enforcement advancing at a steady and even speed. Thus, the Attorney General, as coordinator, did not engage in the pushing type of operation that was desired by civil rights groups, but rather assumed a more passive coordination role, one in which he used his power to keep the various departments working in tandem, and in which he tried to prevent political embarrassment of the President.[24]

Not much changed when Clark assumed the reins as attorney general.

APPOINTMENT OF BLACKS
TO IMPORTANT FEDERAL GOVERNMENTAL POSITIONS

Among blacks who were appointed to important posts in the federal government were the following: Robert Weaver, secretary of Housing and Urban Development; Andrew Brimmer, board of governors of the Federal Reserve System; Hobart Taylor, Jr., board of directors of the Export-Import Bank; Thurgood Marshall, solicitor general and Associate Justice of the Supreme Court; Samuel Nabrit, Atomic Energy Commission; Clifford Alexander, chairman of the Equal Employment Opportunity Commission; Walter Washington, mayor of Washington, D.C.; Emmet J. Rice, United States alternate director of the World Bank; Patricia Harris, ambassador to Luxemburg; Roger Wilkins, director of the Community Relations Service; Carl Rowan, director of the United States Information Agency (USIA);

---

[23] Wolk, *The Presidency and Black Civil Rights,* 196.
[24] *Ibid.,* 205.

James Nabrit, Jr., ambassador to the United Nations; Hugh Johnson, military aide to the president; Lisle C. Carter, assistant secretary for Individual and Family Services, HEW; Theodore M. Berry, assistant director of OEO; Wiley Branton, special assistant to the attorney general; Ruby Martin, director of the Office of Civil Rights, HEW; Samuel Johnson, commissioner, EEOC; Howard B. Woods, deputy director, USIA; Merle Cook, ambassador to Gambia; Clinton E. Knox, ambassador to Dahomey; Franklin H. Williams, ambassador to Ghana; Marjorie Lawson, member of the United States delegation to the United Nations; and Samuel F. Yette, special assistant on civil rights, OEO. Some of them held more than one position during the Johnson administration.

Lyndon Johnson stated in his memoirs that he appointed these blacks to major posts "for their competence, wisdom, and courage, not for the color of their skin. But I also deeply believed that with these appointments Negro mothers could look at their children and hope with good reason that someday their sons and daughters might reach the highest offices their government could offer." [25]

His former secretary of HUD, Robert Weaver, praised Johnson for bringing more blacks into the federal government than any earlier president. He also held that Johnson exposed some of them to important areas of power which could be transferred to the private economy. [26]

In spite of these surface gains, one writer, Benjamin Muse, pointed out that they meant little to the black masses whose income was half that of whites and the gap seemed to be increasing. [27] A black writer, Samuel Yette, wrote: "While the black appointees were highly visible, they were, for the most part, powerless. And their powerless visibility in and around the bureaucratic councils added an aura of legitimacy to illegitimate acts, providing a smokescreen for dirty dealing." [28]

Still another leading black spokesman, Chuck Stone, referred to

[25] Johnson, *The Vantage Point*, 179.
[26] Robert C. Weaver, "Eleanor and LBJ and Black America," *Crisis*, 79 (June–July, 1972), 191–92. See also "Negroes Move Up in Government," *U.S. News & World Report*, 63 (July 3, 1967), 57–58.
[27] Benjamin Muse, "Climax of a Revolution," *New South*, 23 (Summer, 1968), 6.
[28] Yette, *The Choice*, 16.

the Johnson policy as that of the "revolving door." He wrote:

> Historically a "revolving door negro" could be a militant or he could be one who was forthright and uncompromising in his fight for equality. More often than not, however, he was usually the safest the congressional traffic could bear without provoking a united opposition to the appointment. In the Johnson appointments, the "revolving door negro" has either been an "Uncle Tom" or one who could be counted upon not to cause any serious emotional dislocation of the body politic. Still, a Southerner by temperament and in his relations with negroes, President Johnson has gravitated toward those negroes who did not make him feel personally uncomfortable and who could assure him that everything he was doing in the area of race relations was right, good, and proper. Thus, one of Johnson's favorite negroes, to whom he often turned for advice, was the moderate-conservative executive secretary of the NAACP, Roy Wilkins.[29]

Stone also insisted:

> High level negro appointments are still rare, and because they are, they must be categorized as symbolic appointments. Symbolic appointments do not control power. Usually they are more honorific than substantial and are extremely impressive to black people. The appointment of a negro does not guarantee any improvements in the economic, educational or political conditions of the black masses, however. Not a single additional negro receives an increase in his wages because one negro is appointed to the Supreme Court.[30]

Stone noted that the appointments had been carried out with P. T. Barnum fanfare and had given the impression that Johnson, who had fought vigorously against civil rights as a member of Congress, "has done more for the cause of civil rights" than any previous president in American history.[31] He called the whole thing a charade. A detailed examination of various agencies and departments, starting with the executive office of the president, where there was 1 black out of 125 staff members, showed that blacks were largely excluded from policy-making and responsible positions in the federal government.[32]

In comparing Kennedy and Johnson in the area of black appoint-

[29] Chuck Stone, "Measuring Black Political Power" in Edward Greer (ed.), *Black Liberation Politics: A Reader* (Boston: Allyn and Bacon, Inc., 1971), 272.

[30] *Ibid.*, 258.

[31] *Ibid.*

[32] *Ibid.*, 266–70.

ments, Stone judged Kennedy to have been superior in that he had appointed fewer "revolving door" blacks than did Johnson. While Kennedy was determined to have appointed a number of competent black administrators, Johnson often did not appoint another black in his post when one was moved to a different position.[33]

BLACKS AND PUBLIC EMPLOYMENT
(Largely Federal)

In general, public employment of blacks increased during the Johnson administration, and they fared better in obtaining employment in the public (federal) sector than in the private sector.[34] In addition, they held a higher percentage of management positions. Nevertheless, blacks were likely to be found in those offices having a black clinetele or in new programs or new governmental agencies. As one political scientist noted:

> Negro representation is relatively high in welfare, housing, and urban affairs agencies and in those units of the State Department dealing with African affairs. A significant exception to the principle of Negro clientele-Negro employment opportunities seldom occurs in the Department of Agriculture. The political impotence of the Negro clients(southern rural Negroes) has limited the opportunities for Negro employees. . . .
>
> Even in recent years, some offices in the Department of Agriculture have not permitted Negro employees to serve white farmers, have isolated Negroes in separate offices and at segregated meetings, and have provided Negro staff members with less in-service training than that provided whites. Where equal opportunity is provided in the Agriculture Department, it is likely to be in newer programs dealing with food inspection and consumer services.[35]

The Department of Labor reported that between June, 1961, and June, 1964, the civilian work force of the federal government had increased by 3.3 percent, and the number of blacks increased in the

---

[33] *Ibid.*, 258.

[34] See Timothy Jenkins, "Study of Federal Efforts to End Job Bias: A History, a Status Report, and a Prognosis," *Howard Law Journal*, 13 (Winter, 1967), 261.

[35] Ira Sharkansky, *Public Administration: Policy-Making in Government Agencies* (Chicago: Markham Publishing Co., 1972), 153–54. See also U.S. Commission on Civil Rights, *Equal Opportunity in Farm Programs. An Appraisal of the Services Rendered by Agencies of the Department of Agriculture* (Washington, D.C.: U.S. Government Printing Office, 1965), 105–11.

same period by 5.9 percent. The 5.9 percent increase represented 16,911 more black employees raising the total number of blacks engaged in civilian employment with the federal government to 299,527 or 13.2 percent. While blacks were distributed among the government's major pay positions, they constituted a larger proportion of the work force under the Postal Field Service and the Wage Board than under the Classification Act. Furthermore, blacks were largely employed in the lower-paying positions.[36]

Statistically, the situation as of June, 1964, was as shown in Table 2.[37]

These figures show that about 60 percent of the blacks employed under the Classification Act were found in the four lower grades. However, only 30 percent of the other employees held the four lowest

Table 2

Pay System and Grade or Salary Group	Number	Blacks Employed by the Federal Government as Percent of all Employees
Classification Act		
(or similar pay plan)	102,697	9.3
GS–1 to GS–4	63,911	19.0
GS–5 to GS–8	28,304	9.1
GS–9 to GS–11	8,145	3.1
GS–12 to GS–18	2,337	1.1
Wage Board	102,918	19.3
less than $4,500	33,486	47.2
$4,500–6,499	57,481	22.1
$6,500–7,999	10,697	6.9
$8,500 or more	624	1.5
Postal Field Services	90,078	15.5
PFS–1 to PFS–4	83,078	16.8
PFS–5 to PFS–8	6,165	9.1
PFS–9 to PFS–11	223	1.7
PFS–12 to PFS–20	40	1.1

[36] "Employment of Negroes in the Federal Government," *Monthly Labor Review*, 88 (October, 1965), 1222.

[37] *Ibid.*, 1223; U.S. Civil Service Commission, *Study of Minority Group Employment in the Federal Government* (Washington, D.C.: U.S. Government Printing Office, 1967), 5.

grades. Almost an equal proportion of blacks and others were employed in the GS-5 through GS-8 range. However, in jobs classified GS-9 and above, only about 10 percent were employed in that category. The Wage Board situation was similar, Approximately one-third of the black workers earned less than $4,500 per year, compared with one out of twelve of other employees at that lowest scale. While only 11.3 percent of the blacks held positions paying $6,500 or more, 43.9 percent of all other Wage Board Workers were so employed. With regard to the Postal Field Service, 92.9 percent of the blacks were PFS-1 to 4, while 84.1 percent of the others were so employed. In the range of PFS-5 to 8, blacks constituted 6.8 percent, while 12.6 percent of other races were so employed; and 0.2 percent of blacks and 2.6 percent of others served in PFS-9 to 11 categories. Finally, 0.5 percent of blacks were employed in the PFS-12 to 20 categories, whereas 0.7 percent of the others were so employed.[38]

By Executive Order 11246 which President Johnson issued in 1965 the responsibility for widening equal employment opportunities within the federal government was transferred from the President's Committee on Equal Employment Opportunity to the Civil Service Commission. The commission almost immediately undertook efforts to recruit and train personnel and to police various efforts at equal employment opportunity within the federal government. A number of governmental agencies took independent action in that direction too. In 1966 the commission established a new program called MUST (Maximum Utilization of Skills and Training) to assist other federal agencies to recruit and train workers who did not or could not enter the civil service through regular testing procedures. The commission in 1966 for the first time made intensive efforts to recruit personnel at black colleges. Finally, it made attempts to revise entrance examinations in order to eliminate "cultural bias." [39]

Change was slow to come in spite of these efforts at reform. An interesting study was published in 1967 by the Civil Service Commission. The study compared black employment in the federal govern-

[38] "Employment of Negroes in the Federal Government," 1223–24.

[39] "Government Hiring More Negroes—But in Low Paid Jobs," *Congressional Quarterly Weekly Report*, (February 14, 1969), 263; Anthony M. Rachel, Jr., "EEO: We Must Not Settle for Less," *Civil Service Journal*, 7 (July–September, 1966), 1–5.

ment in various regions in 1965 with those so employed in 1967. This breakdown by region was as follows:[40]

Table 3

Atlanta Region (Alabama, Fla., Ga., Miss., N.C., S.C., Tennessee, and the Virgin Islands)

November, 1967			June, 1965		
Total Employment	Negro Number	%	Total Employment	Negro Number	%
317,187	41,620	13.1	277,110	31,805	11.5

Boston Region (Conn., Maine, Mass., N.H., R.I., and Vt.)

1967			1965		
Total Employment	Negro Number	%	Total Employment	Negro Number	%
119,367	4,485	3.8	108,071	3,830	3.5

Chicago Region (Ill., Indiana, Ky., Michigan, Ohio, and Wisconsin)

1967			1965		
Total Employment	Negro Number	%	Total Employment	Negro Number	%
351,177	74,410	21.2	313,501	61,141	14.8

Dallas Region (Ark., Okla., and Texas)

1967			1965		
Total Employment	Negro Number	%	Total Employment	Negro Number	%
241,722	22,823	9.4	202,180	17,359	8.6

Denver Region (Arizona, Colo., N.M., Utah, and Wyoming)

1967			1965		
Total Employment	Negro Number	%	Total Employment	Negro Number	%
135,408	4,322	3.2	117,247	3,836	3.3

[40] U.S. Civil Service Commission, *Study of Minority Group Employment with the Federal Government*, 47–56.

New York Region (N.J. and N.Y.)

1967			1965		
Total Employment	Negro Number	%	Total Employment	Negro Number	%
239,986	43,325	18.0	227,932	34,452	15.1

Philadelphia Region (Del., Md., Penn., Va., and W. Va.)

1967			1965		
Total Employment	Negro Number	%	Total Employment	Negro Number	%
288,739	59,739	20.5	258,451	46,451	18.0

St. Louis Region (Iowa, Kansas, Minn., Mo., Neb., N.D., and S.D.)

1967			1965		
Total Employment	Negro Number	%	Total Employment	Negro Number	%
157,330	14,513	9.2	140,517	11,248	8.0

San Francisco Region (California and Nevada)

1967			1965		
Total Employment	Negro Number	%	Total Employment	Negro Number	%
319,260	46,256	14.5	255,684	32,176	12.6

Seattle Region (Alaska, Idaho, Montana, Oregon, and Washington)

1967			1965		
Total Employment	Negro Number	%	Total Employment	Negro Number	%
108,542	3,705	3.4	90,263	2,236	2.5

A comparison of black employment among states was also revealing for 1967:[41]

Table 4

FEDERAL EMPLOYMENT BY STATES AND WASHINGTON, D.C.

State	Total Federal Employment (1967)	Negro Federal Employees (1967)		State's Negro Percentage (1960)
		Number	Percentage	
Ala.	55,138	5,626	10.2	30.0
Alaska	13,946	567	4.1	3.0
Ariz.	24,894	640	2.6	3.3
Ark.	14,789	1,490	10.1	21.8
Calif.	311,484	45,917	14.7	5.6
Colo.	40,977	2,731	6.7	2.3
Conn.	17,878	1,340	7.5	4.2
Del.	4,057	579	14.3	13.6
D.C.	187,669	57,314	30.5	53.9
Fla.	64,749	5,247	8.1	17.8
Ga.	74,616	12,879	17.3	28.5
Idaho	7,273	38	0.5	0.2
Ill.	108,717	32,825	30.2	10.3
Ind.	39,836	5,803	14.6	5.8
Iowa	16,321	378	2.3	0.9
Kansas	20,536	1,445	7.0	4.2
Ky.	34,993	3,384	9.7	7.1
La.	29,319	5,460	18.6	31.9
Maine	8,040	40	0.5	0.3
Md.	114,602	23,684	20.7	16.7
Mass.	62,782	2,615	4.2	2.2
Mich.	49,725	11,424	23.0	9.2
Minn.	22,508	670	2.4	0.7
Miss.	18,506	2,222	12.3	42.0
Mo.	63,719	11,225	17.6	9.0
Mont.	9,828	46	0.5	0.2
Neb.	14,051	694	4.9	2.1
Nev.	7,776	339	4.4	4.7
N.H.	12,837	65	0.5	0.3

[41] "Government Hiring More Negroes—But in Low Paid Jobs," 264.

State	Total Federal Employment (1967)	Negro Federal Employees (1967)		State's Negro Percentage (1960)
		Number	Percentage	
N.J.	65,887	9,091	13.8	8.5
N.M.	24,653	407	1.7	1.8
N.Y.	173,989	34,144	19.6	8.4
N.C.	34,538	5,125	14.8	24.5
N.D.	6,821	54	0.8	0.1
Ohio	95,406	19,802	20.8	8.1
Okla.	53,964	3,491	6.5	6.6
Ore.	22,458	464	2.1	1.0
Pa.	138,863	26,086	18.8	7.5
R.I.	14,869	413	2.8	2.1
S.C.	29,073	4,655	16.0	34.8
S.D.	8,374	47	0.6	0.2
Tenn.	40,860	5,801	14.2	16.5
Tex.	143,650	12,382	8.6	12.4
Utah	40,494	503	1.3	0.5
Vt.	3,141	12	0.4	0.1
Va.	122,951	25,996	21.1	20 6
Wash.	55,037	2,590	4.7	1.7
W. Va.	11,682	510	4.4	4.8
Wis.	22,500	1,172	5.2	1.9
Wyo.	4,790	41	0.9	0.7

As Samuel Krislov noted:

The discrepancy between central headquarters and the regions in the employment of Negroes is striking. Negroes in 1965 constituted nearly one of four employees in the Washington metropolitan area, but only about one in eight throughout the federal service. One in five Negro employees is employed in Washington, while only about one in eight or nine of all employees is so located. The difference in distribution by classification is similar. Thus nearly 1,100 Negroes are employed at GS–12 to 18 levels in Washington out of 2,800 in the total federal service; i.e., nearly 40 percent are in the metropolitan area. Similarly 27 percent of all Negroes at GS–9 to 11 levels are so employed. (This picture is slightly modified, however, by the relatively greater number of Negroes in wage board positions in the District of Columbia than elsewhere and by a somewhat less concentrated situation in the postal services.) As one moves away from the core in the periphery of the federal service one finds sharp variation based on local custom, with the obvious result that the Negro is sadly disadvantaged in the Deep South. Alabama and its roughly 30 percent Negro population has 60,000 federal employees of whom only about 11 percent are Negro. Mississippi with almost a 40 percent Negro population has 16,000 federal employees of whom only about 9 percent are Negro—this, however, represents a dramatic 450 percent increase over the situation in 1964, when the first regional census began to be published.[42]

The Civil Rights Commission also furnished a comparison between composite figures for all agencies in 1967 with those of 1966. These figures are shown in Table 5.

As one political scientist pointed out, although more blacks were being employed than ever before, and in total numbers slightly above their percentage of the total population, that did not tell the whole story. Blacks still largely occupied the lowest positions with very few at the GS-12 through GS-18 levels (or their equivalents outside of the Classification Act). The federal government still did not serve as a model for the rest of society to follow.[43] Black women had added difficulties. A large proportion of the Wage Board and similar positions were held by black males which helped to boost total black employment figures with the federal government. Black women, however, competed largely for the lower clerical positions in the government.[44]

Furthermore, there was the feeling among blacks occupying middle range positions that theirs were make-work positions. Krislov wrote:

> Negroes all too often found that their newly created jobs have no real duties. Often the accoutrements of the office are obviously beyond the level of work demanded. The suspicion that he is there to perform the function of Art Buchwald's Negro Ph.D. with an engineering background who speaks ten languages to sit by the door to convince everyone of the egalitarian principle of the business office in which he is employed—haunts every Negro bureaucrat.[45]

In 1968 the Post Office Department increased its efforts to recruit

[42] Samuel Krislov, *The Negro in Federal Employment: The Quest for Opportunity* (Minneapolis: University of Minnesota Press, 1967), 104.

[43] Krislov, *The Negro in Federal Employment*, 101.; "Government Hiring More Negroes—But in Low Paid Jobs," 262; William Ryan, "Uncle Sam's Betrayal," *The Progressive*, 32 (May, 1968), 28.

[44] Krislov, *The Negro in Federal Employment*, 97.

[45] *Ibid.*, 100.

Table 5

NEGRO EMPLOYMENT [46] November, 1967, and June, 1966

Pay Category	1967			1966**		
	Employment	Negro Number	%	Employment	Negro Number	%
Total all Pay Plans	2,621,939	390,842	14.9	2,303,906	320,136	13.9
Total General Schedules or Similar	1,270,051	133,626	10.5	1,126,985	109,658	9.7
GS–1 thru GS–4	369,968	75,846	20.5	352,514	65,548	18.6
GS–5 thru 8	349,020	40,494	11.6	309,754	31,205	10.1
GS–9 thru 11	296,560	12,631	4.3	254,635	9,642	3.8
GS–12 thru 18	254,503	4,655	1.8	210,082	3,263	1.6
Total Wage Board	596,647	121,829	20.4	537,681	110,596	20.4
Up thru $4,499	45,023	24,464	54.3	78,587	33,886	43.1
$4,500 thru $6,499	235,082	65,227	27.7	233,096	58,943	25.3
$6,500 thru $7,999	233,218	28,879	12.4	172,490	16,223	9.4
$8,000 and over	83,214	3,259	3.9	53,508	1,538	2.9
Postal Field Services	696,346	132,011	18.9	594,220	94,449	15.9
PFS 1 thru 4*	601,160	123,632	20.6	507,602	87,686	17.3
PFS 5 thru 8	77,746	7,805	10.0	69,225	6,410	9.3
PFS 9 thru 11	14,985	467	3.1	13,514	296	2.2
PFS 12 thru 20	4,455	107	2.4	3,879	57	1.5
Total Other Plans	56,895	3,376	5.9	45,020	5,439	12.1
Up thru $4,499	6,523	1,252	19.2	11,927	3,997	33.5
$4,500 thru $6,499	10,970	1,073	9.8	9,843	899	9.1
$6,500 thru $7,999	7,107	359	5.1	4,176	146	3.5
8,000 and over	32,295	692	2.1	19,074	397	2.1

* Includes 4th-class postmasters and rural carriers.   ** Of 2,511,052 employees, 207,146 (8.2%) are unidentified.
[46] U.S. Civil Service Commission, *Study of Minority Group Employment in the Federal Government*, 3.

and train blacks and other minority groups. During the same year an institute for postmasters and supervisors was held which contained minority-group problems in its curriculum. Moreover, the department established five job opportunity programs for minority groups throughout the country.[47]

The next study made of black employment in the federal government appeared in 1969. Although the investigation necessarily included the early months of the Nixon administration, for the most part the figures reflected developments under Johnson who ended his tenure in January, 1969. About two years had elapsed since the study made in 1967. (See Table 6)

Despite the Johnson administration's commitment to equality of opportunity and despite the fact that a higher percentage of blacks had been hired than they constituted of the total population, the black employees were still largely employed at the lowest paid and most menial positions. Furthermore, as formerly, more blacks proportionally were under the wage system and the postal service system.[48]

Another area of public employment was that at the state and local level. The United States Commission on Civil Rights made a study which was published in 1969. The investigation covered the cities of San Francisco-Oakland, Philadelphia, Detroit, Atlanta, Houston, Memphis, and Baton Rouge. As was the case elsewhere in society blacks largely held the least-skilled and lowest-paid jobs. Indeed, the positions held by blacks tended to be so-called "Negro jobs," largely those of common laborer and general service workers. In two of the cities, Memphis and Houston, such jobs were exempted from civil service coverage and job security.[49]

When blacks held white collar jobs they were largely in areas having large black clienteles—health and welfare services.[50] Bad as the situation was, except for Baton Rouge, of the cities studied, black employment in the public sector was significantly higher than in

[47] "Government Hiring More Negroes—But in Low Paid Jobs," 263.
[48] See Garth L. Mangum and Lewell M. Glenn, *Employing the Disadvantaged in the Federal Civil Service* (Washington, D.C.: University of Michigan, Wayne State University and National Manpower Policy Task Force, 1969).
[49] U.S. Commission on Civil Rights, *For All the People: A Report on Equal Opportunity in State and Local Government Employment* (Washington, D.C.: U.S. Government Printing Office, 1969), 1.
[50] *Ibid.*, 2.

Table 6

MINORITY GROUP STUDY
Full-Time Employment in All Agencies
As of November 30, 1969 [51]

Pay System	Total Full-Time Employees	Negro Number	%
Total All Pay Systems	2,601,639	389,251	15.0
Total General Schedules or Similar	1,289,114	137,919	10.7
GS–1 thru 4	312,047	67,252	21.6
GS–5 thru 8	367,410	47,838	13.0
GS–9 thru 11	321,140	16,318	5.1
GS–12 thru 13	213,260	5,370	2.5
GS–14 thru 15	69,937	1,078	1.5
GS–16 thru 18	5,317	63	1.2
Total Wage Systems	554,443	109,356	19.7
Up thru $5,499	48,012	21,705	45.2
$5,500 thru $6,999	149,327	47,683	31.9
$7,000 thru $7,999	140,355	21,896	15.6
$8,000 thru $8,999	113,357	11,755	10.4
$9,000 thru $9,999	50,863	4,150	8.2
$10,000 thru $13,999	48,675	2,033	4.2
$14,000 thru $17,999	3,035	117	3.9
$18,000 and over	819	17	2.1
Total Postal Field Service	700,304	136,322	19.5
PFS 1 thru 5*	595,654	124,173	20.8
PFS 6 thru 9	84,311	11,343	13.5
PFS 10 thru 12	15,359	623	4.1
PFS 13 thru 16	4,509	170	3.8
PFS 17 thru 19	439	11	2.5
PFS 20 thru 21	39	2	5.1
Total Other Pay Systems	57,778	5,654	9.8
Up thru $6,499	11,792	2,782	23.6
$6,500 thru $9,999	18,488	2,053	11.1
$10,000 thru $13,999	11,809	496	4.2
$14,000 thru $17,999	6,063	141	2.3
$18,000 thru $25,999	5,935	132	2.2
$26,000 and over	3,691	50	1.4

[51] U.S. Civil Service Commission, *Preliminary Report of Minority Group Employment, 1969* (Washington, D.C.: U.S. Government Printing Office, 1969), 23.

the private sector. In addition, more than half of the blacks were employed by central city governments.[52]

The Commission concluded its report as follows:

> The basic finding of this report is that State and local governments have failed to fulfill their obligations to assure equal job opportunity. In many localities, minority group members are denied equal access to responsible government jobs at the state and local levels and often are excluded from employment except in the most menial capacities. In many areas of government, minority group members are excluded almost entirely from decision-making positions, and, even in those instances where they hold jobs carrying higher status, these jobs tend to involve work only with the problems of minority groups and tend to permit contact largely with other minority group members.[53]
>
> Not only do State and local governments consciously and overtly discriminate in hiring and promoting minority group members, but they do not foster private programs to deal with discriminatory treatment on the job. Too many public officials feel that their responsibility toward equal employment opportunity is satisfied merely by avoiding specific acts of discrimination. Rarely do State and local governments perceive the need for affirmative programs to recruit and upgrade minority group members for jobs in which they are inadequately represented. When recruiting programs do exist, minority group applicants are frequently subjected to a variety of screening and selection devices which bear little if any relation to the needs of the job, but which place them at a disadvantage in their effort to secure government employment. There have been few efforts by State and local governments to eliminate such unequal selection devices.[54]

Unquestionably blacks had been hired in greater numbers to work for federal bureaucracy during the Johnson administration. Certainly when compared with private employment, the federal government more accurately reflected the notion of the equal opportunity employer. However, relatively few blacks occupied higher positions and played a major role where policies were made. Black employment at the state and local level even more accurately than in the case of the federal government, reflected the prevailing discrimination in private employment.

52 *Ibid.*, 5. See also Sharkansky, *Public Administration*, 155.
53 U.S. Commission on Civil Rights, *For All the People*, 131.
54 *Ibid.*, 131–32.

BLACKS AND THE ARMED FORCES

The Kennedy administration had continued the efforts of Truman and Eisenhower to desegregate the armed forces. Nevertheless, despite the fact that some limited progress had been made in eliminating discrimination on the bases, there was still too high a percentage of blacks to be found in the lower ranks at both the officer and enlisted levels. The situation for black servicemen was especially difficult off base. The first report issued by the President's Committee on Equal Opportunity in the Armed Forces in 1963 pointed the direction for some significant reforms.[55]

Even before Johnson took office, on July 26, 1963, Secretary of Defense McNamara had issued a directive designed to curtail racial discrimination in communities located near bases. However, on January 27, 1964, a spokesman from the same department acknowledged to the press that little had been done to implement the program. At the time of the issuance of the directive in 1963, Representative Carl Vinson of Georgia, chairman of the House Armed Services Committee, had demanded that Congress make it a court-martial offense for military officers to carry out the off-base sanctions proposed by McNamara. When asked if the pressure from Vinson had caused a delay in the program, the spokesman denied that it had done so. Instead, he claimed that "unexpected delays in preparing the regulations and manuals were solely responsible for the delay" beyond September 1, 1963, when the directive was supposed to have gone into effect. In the meantime, complaints by blacks of discrimination by private businesses were mounting.[56]

The so-called Gesell Committee on the President's Committee on Equal Opportunity in the Armed Forces completed the final part of its investigation in November, 1964. It found one segment of the armed forces that had not been fully integrated—the National Guard. Most of the ten southern states—Mississippi, Florida, Alabama, Arkansas, Georgia, Louisiana, North Carolina, South Carolina, Tennessee, and Virginia (all of which had had no blacks in their National Guard units as of June, 1962)—had eliminated formal and technical

---

[55] See Harvey, *Civil Rights During the Kennedy Administration*, 32–35.
[56] New York *Times*, January 28, 1964, p. 22.

racial restrictions and had provided for token integration.[57] Major General Winston P. Wilson, head of the National Guard Bureau, admitted that only tokenism prevailed in some of the states, but he hailed the progress that had been made as a "milestone in the history of the National Guard." [58] The Gesell Committee was not impressed by General Wilson's appraisal and insisted that was not enough. It pointed out that over 90 percent of the guard's financial support came from the federal government. Since the Defense Department was on the record with a policy of equal opportunity and integration, all federal support should be withdrawn from any state refusing to integrate its National Guard units as provided in the Civil Rights Act of 1964.[59]

The last two states to abandon formal racial discrimination in their National Guard units were Alabama and Mississippi, with Mississippi doing so on December 1, 1964.[60] On December 29, 1964, General Wilson announced that all racial barriers had been eliminated in the National Guard, that token integration had been achieved in all units, and that "a steady growth was expected." [61]

In January, 1965, President Johnson sent a message to Secretary of Defense McNamara insisting that all discrimination in the National Guard had to be ended.[62] McNamara then sent a directive to all states and the National Guard Bureau detailing the actions that were to be taken, including the possibility that funds might be withdrawn from any state persisting in its denial of equal opportunity in the guard. Despite this warning, integration of the guard proceeded very slowly.[63] By March 31, 1965, there were only 380 blacks in the National Guards of eleven southern states.[64]

[57] John P. Davis (ed.), *The American Negro Reference Book* (Englewood Cliffs, N.J.: Prentice-Hall, 1966), 660.

[58] *Ibid.*

[59] Milton R. Konvitz, *Expanding Liberties: Freedom's Gains in Postwar America* (New York: The Viking Press, 1966), 262; Richard M. Dalfiume, *Desegregation of the United States Armed Forces* (Columbia, Mo.: University of Missouri Press, 1969), 222.

[60] Konvitz, *Expanding Liberties*, 262.

[61] *Ibid.*; Richard Stillman III, *Integration of the Negro in the U.S. Armed Forces* (New York: Frederick A. Praeger, 1968), 115.

[62] Ruth Morgan, *The President and Civil Rights: Policy-Making by Executive Order* (New York: St. Martin's Press, 1970), 26.

[63] Dalfiume, *Desegregation of the U.S. Armed Forces*, 223.

[64] Konvitz, *Expanding Liberties*, 262.

In comparing 1964 and 1965 figures for the National Guard it was noteworthy that as of February 1, 1964, only 5,780 of 442,410 Air and Army National Guardsmen in the entire country—1.5 percent of the total—were black. Only twenty states had black officers in their guards. Of 122,670 men in the Air National Guard and Army National Guard units in the eleven southern states in 1965, 539 were nonwhite or .004 percent of the total. That 539 figure represented an increase of 169 over the 1964 total.[65]

Statistics for the southern states, 1964–65, are shown in Table 7:

Table 7

CHANGE IN THE NUMBER OF NEGROES SERVING
IN THE NATIONAL GUARD (ARMY/AIR GUARD)[66]

State	1964 Army	Air	1965 Army	Air	% of Negroes in State Pop.	Total No. of Men in Guard (1964)
Ala.	0	2	5	1	30 0	16,800
Ark.	3	1	7	1	22.3	8,845
Fla.	21	2	44	2	21.8	—
Ga.	2	2	1	2	31.1	—
La.	3	2	1	2	30.9	—
Miss.	1	1	24	6	42 0	—
N.C.	80	1	106	1	24.9	—
S.C.	1	5	5	5	34.5	—
Tenn.	94	6	118	13	18.3	—
Tex.	146	2	178	5	14.15	—
Va.	5	0	8	4	20.9	—
Totals	358	24	497	42		122,670

In December, 1964, the Defense Department decided to place all members of the Army Reserve in the National Guard "in a pool of fillers," and to abolish Army Reserve units. The Senate Appropriations Committee, however, killed the merger effort in September, 1965. The Southern Governors' Conference and Senator John Stennis of Mississippi, chairman of the Senate Preparedness Subcommittee, probably played a key role in the defeat of the plan which would

[65] Stillman, *Integration of the Negro in the U.S. Armed Forces*, 104.
[66] *Ibid.*

also have led to a larger amount of integration. The reason given for the attempt at merger, according to a Pentagon spokesman, was "to improve war plans and to increase readiness of top priority divisions and brigades." [67] The opposition to the plan was too great, however, and the Pentagon had to drop it.

Although statistics for each state for the latter part of the Johnson administration were lacking, it was well known that the number of blacks entering the National Guard did not improve very much, not even in non-southern states. In addition to the failure of the National Guard to try to recruit blacks in most instances, it was also doubtless true that blacks showed little interest even when some effort was made. Moreover, although the authority was there in Title VI of the Civil Rights Act of 1964, federal funds were never cut off from any state for its failure to recruit more blacks into the National Guard.[68]

After the National Guard participated in the quelling of the riots during the summer of 1967, the spotlight turned on the guard. The President's Commission on Civil Disorders in 1968 lamented that blacks constituted but 1.15 percent of the Army National Guard and 0.6 percent of the Air National Guard in the entire country. The commission recommended to the president that he should take steps immediately to correct the situation.[69]

These low figures caused Senator Margaret Chase Smith of Maine to criticize McNamara, who had told the Senate Preparedness Subcommittee in March, 1965: "There are no segregated state guards today." Senator Smith declared that the secretary's claim "would be ludicrous if it weren't so tragically dishonest." McNamara bristled when replying that it had been "true then" and was "true today." The secretary insisted that he had caused some states to drop their exclusionary policies and added defensively: "That was a great stride but it does not mean that Negro representation in the Guard is adequate." [70]

Meanwhile, the various services made organizational efforts to set

[67] Konvitz, *Expanding Liberties*, 263.

[68] Richard Stillman III, "Negroes in the Armed Forces," *Phylon*, 30 (Summer, 1969), 155.

[69] Dalfiume, *Desegregation of the U.S. Armed Forces*, 223; "National Guard and Negroes," *America*, 117 (September 2, 1967), 213.

[70] Ulysses Lee, "The Draft and the Negro," *Current History*, 55 (July, 1968), 47. See also "National Guard and Negroes," 213.

their own houses in order. The army established an Equal Rights Branch in the Office of the Deputy Chief on Personnel and on July 2, 1964, issued guidelines for military commanders to follow which were called "Equal Opportunity and Treatment of Military Personnel." The navy took a different tact by creating an *ad hoc* committee in the Bureau of Personnel to deal with problems of blacks. It also issued guidelines to naval commanders called "Equal Opportunity and the Treatment of Military Personnel." On April 19, 1963, the air force had created an "Air Force Committee on Equal Opportunity," and on August 19, 1964, it issued regulations to commanders entitled "Equal Opportunity and the Treatment of Military Personnel." [71]

On July 10, 1964, Secretary of Defense McNamara sent a memorandum to the military service secretaries. He wrote:

> The Civil Rights Act of 1964 is an immensely important historic expression of this nation's commitment to freedom and justice. It has special meaning to our Armed Forces all of whom have already given a personal commitment to defend freedom and justice, and some of whom have not always been accorded full freedom and full justice in this country.
>
> The President has made it very clear that he expects each Department to move with dispatch within its area of concern in developing programs and policies which will give full effect to the Civil Rights Act.
>
> In the Department of Defense this means, primarily, the vigorous, determined, sensitive commitment by military commanders to a program of fostering and securing equal treatment for every serviceman, and we cannot afford to lose an opportunity to gain a goal so simple, so just, so compelling.
>
> I want to make it clear that it is and will be a continuing responsibility for all commanders to foster equal treatment for every serviceman, and to support him in the lawful assertion of the rights guaranteed to him by the Constitution and the Civil Rights Act of 1964.
>
> The Department was created to defend the freedom of the United States. The denial of rights of members of the Armed Forces is harmful to the very purpose in which we are engaged, for discrimination against our people saps the military effectiveness we strive so much to maintain. This last reason alone compels an affirmative commitment by all members of the Department of Defense to the cause of equal treatment and equality.[72]

[71] Stillman, *Integration of the Negro in the U.S. Armed Forces*, 117.
[72] Davis, *The American Negro Reference Book*, 660.

In the meantime, the changes in the number of blacks in the armed services between 1962 and 1964 were as follows:[73]

Service	1962	1964
Army	11.1%	12.3%
Air Force	7.8%	8.6%
Navy	4.7%	5.1%
Marine Corps	7.0%	9.0%
Total	8.2%	9.0%

Though lower than the black proportion of the nation's population, one analyst wrote:

> It is virtually certain that among those eligible, a higher proportion of Negroes than whites enter the armed forces. That is, a much larger number of Negroes do not meet the entrance standards required by the military forces. . . . Because of the relatively low number of Negroes obtaining student or occupational deferments, it is the Army drawing upon the draft that is the only military service where the percentage of Negroes approximates the national proportion. Thus, despite the high number of Negroes who fail to meet induction standards, army statistics for 1960–65 show Negroes constituted about 15 percent of those drafted.[74]

It was all too obvious that blacks held few of the higher ranks in the armed services. Table 8 illustrated the story.

For all four services blacks reenlisted at about twice the rate of whites. Approximately one half of the blacks reenlisted for a second hitch after serving the first one.[75]

In 1965 the military forces were 9 percent black and the percentage was expected to increase. At that time, the first term reenlistment rate for whites was 17 percent; whereas for blacks it was 45.1 percent.[76] Furthermore, one writer pointed out:

> Given their educational background and previous level of skills,

[73] Charles C. Moskos, "Racial Integration in the Armed Forces," *American Journal of Sociology*, 72 (September, 1966), 136. See also Davis, *The American Negro Reference Book*, 656, for slightly different figures, but the conclusions to be drawn from them are the same.

[74] Moskos, "Racial Integration in the Armed Forces," 136.

[75] *Ibid.* See also "Negroes in the Army," *Trans-Action*, 4 (December, 1966), 5.

[76] Morris Janowitz, "American Democracy and Military Service," *Trans-Action*, 4 (March, 1967), 7.

Negroes have tended to concentrate in the combat arms of the Army where the opportunities for advancement are greatest for rapid advancement into non-commissioned officer positions. In some units such as the airborne the percentage of Negroes is near 40. Overall participation of Negroes in Vietnam for the last part of 1965 showed the Army had the highest proportion with 15.8 percent, and the Navy 5.1 percent. From 1961 to 1965 Negro fatalities were 237 out of 1,620 or 14.6 percent.[77]

In 1966 another writer reported that 18.3 percent of the army combat dead were blacks in the more than four years of fighting in

Table 8

NEGROES AS PERCENTAGE OF TOTAL PERSONNEL
IN EACH GRADE FOR EACH SERVICE, 1964 [78]

Grade	Army	Air Force	Navy	Marine Corps
Officers*				
General/Admirals	—	0.2	—	—
Colonels/Captains	0.2	0.2	—	—
Lt. Cols./Commanders	1.1	0.5	.06	—
Majors/Lt. Commanders	3.6	0.8	0.3	0.3
Capt./Lieutenants	5.4	2.0	0.5	0.4
1st Lts./Lts. j.g.	3.8	1.8	0.2	0.4
2nd Lts./ensigns	2.7	2.5	0.7	0.3
Total Officers	3.4	1.5	0.3	0.4
Enlisted*				
E–9 (sgt. maj.)	3.5	1.2	1.5	0.8
E–8 (master sgt.)	6.1	2.2	1.9	1.2
E–7 (sgt. 1st class)	8.5	3.2	2.9	2.3
E–6 (staff sgt.)	13.9	5.3	4.7	5.0
E–5 (sgt.)	17.4	10.8	6.6	11.2
E–4 (corp.)	14.2	12.7	5.9	10.4
E–3 (pvt. 1st class)	13.6	9.7	6.6	7.8
E–2 (private)	13.1	11.7	5.7	9.5
E–1 (recruit)	6.8	14.4	7.1	9.1
Total Enlisted Men	13.4	10.0	5.8	8.7

* Equivalent pay grades in Air Force and Navy.

[77] *Ibid.*
[78] *Ibid.*, 137.

Vietnam. This was 5 percent higher than their total proportion in the army and 7 percent higher than their proportion of the total American population. He also wrote that blacks made up 18 percent of the combat units in Vietnam and 14 percent of the service units there. Moreover, blacks constituted 13.4 percent of the enlisted men in the army and 3.5 percent of the officers.[79]

In addition, there was a strong feeling among black soldiers that they were often discriminated against, particularly in the lower grades, in terms of punishment and promotions. In spite of the Gesell Committee's recommendations several years earlier, there were no effective procedures to deal with complaints, nor was there a periodic review of NCO promotions to determine if equal opportunities policies were being implemented. Furthermore, blacks still had to face offbase discrimination.[80]

Late in 1966, *Time* magazine reported that the Vietnam war was the first to be fought by the Americans on a truly integrated basis. While blacks made up 11 percent of the population, they constituted 23 percent of the combat troops. There were still few black officers, less than one half of 1 percent in the navy and marine corps. There were not many blacks in the service academies, but the number was growing.[81]

In 1967 the Defense Department took action to open more housing located near military bases to black servicemen. It prohibited all servicemen stationed at certain bases from renting apartments or spaces in trailer courts that engaged in discrimination against blacks and were located within a certain radius of the bases. The directive applied to several bases in the Washington, D.C.-Baltimore area, and the department indicated that it was considering a similar move at stations in California, Illinois, and Florida. Under the then-existing rules, the department listed only apartments and trailer courts open

[79] Gene Grove, "The Army and the Negro," *New York Times Magazine*, July 24, 1966, p. 5. See also Julian Bond, *A Time to Speak, A Time to Act: The Movement in Politics* (New York: Simon and Schuster, 1972), 20, for an explanation as to why so many blacks have been involved in the fighting in Vietnam.

[80] Grove, "The Army and the Negro," 49–50.

[81] "Armed Forces: The Integrated Society," *Time*, 88 (December 23, 1966), 22.

to all servicemen, but the regulations did not prohibit servicemen from renting in segregated trailer courts or apartments.[82]

The National Advisory Commission on Selective Service headed by Burke Marshall, former head of the Civil Rights Division in the Justice Department, reported that in the spring of 1967 blacks constituted 11 percent of the total enlisted strength in Vietnam, 14.5 percent of the army, and 22.4 percent of all army troops killed in action. In the spring of 1968 it was reported that blacks made up nearly 20 percent of the combat forces, about 25 percent of the front-line noncommissioned officers, about 2 percent of the commissioned officers, and some 14 percent of those killed in action.[83] At the same time, while 30.2 percent of the qualified blacks were drafted, some 18.8 percent of the qualified whites were drafted. As late as mid-1966, 1.3 percent of all draft board members were black; by mid-1968 there were about 600 black members altogether, with some 316 added in 1967.[84]

On July 26, 1968, the twentieth anniversary of Truman's desegregation order, Secretary of Defense Clark Clifford sent a memorandum to President Johnson describing the progress that had been made in integrating the armed services over a twenty-year span. It read as follows:

> Twenty years ago the Army had 1,306 Negro officers, with only one a colonel. Now there are 5,637, of whom 27 are colonels, and one has been nominated for brigadier general.
> The Navy in 1948 had only 4 Negro officers, now it has 330.
> The Marine Corps, which had one Negro officer in 1948, now has 180.
> In 1948 the Air Force had 310 Negro officers, with a colonel. Today it has 2,417 with 19 colonels, and a lieutenant general.
> There were 14 Negroes at the service academies in 1948. Today, there are 116, of whom 47 entered as plebes earlier this month.
> Enlisted grades—Negroes made up 10.7% of all Army enlisted men in 1948 but only 5.7% of the top enlisted grade. In 1968 the overall

---

[82] *Congressional Quarterly Almanac*, XXIII, 803; Morgan, *The President and Civil Rights*, 26.

[83] Lee, "The Draft and the Negro," 33. See also New York *Times*, November 23, 1967, p. 33, for somewhat different figures in November, 1967.

[84] Lee, "The Draft and the Negro," 47.

percentage is 12.1%, but now Negroes make up 13.9% of the grade which corresponds to 1948's top grade.

By 1967 it was apparent that while many forms of shameful off-base treatment of Negro servicemen had been eliminated or substantially ameliorated, housing discrimination in some communities nearby military installations continued to have a corrosive and damaging impact on black Americans wearing this country's uniform. As a consequence, military effectiveness was impaired.

A year ago commanders were told to seek out landlords and urge them to rent to all servicemen without regard to color, pointing out that if they refused to deal with all servicemen fairly, then no servicemen would be authorized to deal with them.

Only 30% of all landlords nationwide were on our nondiscriminating list a year ago. Now 84% are. This has meant a gain of nearly 630.000 rental units open to all servicemen in all parts of our nation.

We are determined to push forward with our campaign to achieve 100% housing justice for all our servicemen. We have stated that no other goal is acceptable. I announced in June that beginning in August the sanctions which we have imposed in certain areas on certain discriminatory landlords will be extended throughout the country wherever we have military bases.[85]

In spite of the improvements for blacks in the armed services there was still much to be done by the end of the Johnson administration. There were still too few blacks officers and noncoms, especially in the higher grades. As one authority noted also:

Negroes are concentrated in the infantry, the Navy's food services, medical corps and dental jobs, and with the quartermasters. Fewer are in the growing skills of electronics, communications and mechanical repair. For example, 16.4 percent of the infantry, 11.8 percent of the medical and dental corpsmen, and 16.9 percent of service and supply workers are Negroes, but only 5.5 percent of the electronic equipment repairmen, 6.7 percent of communications and intelligence experts, and 0.3 percent of craftsmen are nonwhite.[86]

The same authority noted that the worst situation was outside the post gate. There was still discrimination in the schools, churches, and housing, particularly near bases located in parts of the South.[87]

[85] Memorandum for the President from Secretary of Defense Clark M. Clifford on the 20th Anniversary of the Desegration Order, July 26, 1968, *Weekly Compilation of Presidential Documents*, 4 (July, 29, 1968), 1154–55.

[86] Stillman, "Negroes in the Armed Forces," 145.

[87] *Ibid.*, 150–51.

Moreover, 18.3 percent of the army combat deaths in Vietnam were black.[88]

Another writer about the armed forces, Richard Dalfiume, took cognizance of some paradoxes in the situation. He wrote:

> The conclusion that the United States armed forces is the most integrated institution in American society is inescapable. This fact together with the Vietnam war and the black nationalism current among today's Negro radicals, however, poses a number of ironies. The Vietnam conflict is constantly labeled "the most integrated war in history," a fact that must result in a feeling of well done by the Negro radicals of yesterday whose slogan was "the fight for the right to fight." But the black radicals of today charge that the war and the military are too integrated, that Negroes are doing more than their share of dying. Negro soldiers, Stokeley Carmichael, of the Student Nonviolent Coordinating Committee and Floyd McKissick of the Congress of Racial Equality proclaim they are "black mercenaries" of a white government fighting against their colored brothers in Vietnam. They call upon the young Negro to resist the draft.[89]
>
> Certainly part of this indictment is a reflection of the general radical and liberal opposition to United States involvement in Vietnam. But the black radicals of today charge that the military is too integrated has some basis in fact. Comprising 11 percent of the population, Negroes are only 9.5 percent of all the armed forces. In Vietnam, however, black soldiers are 14.5 percent of the combat units and 22.4 percent of all troops killed in Vietnam. The Negro radical of today also finds cause for complaint when he examines the draft statistics! Negroes make up approximately 13.4 percent of the draftees inducted. This is especially galling to the radical because, as of May, 1967, only 1.3 percent of all draft board members were Negroes, and there was not a single black member on the draft boards of Alabama, Arkansas, Louisiana, and Mississippi.[90]

In evaluating the overall accomplishments of the Johnson administration in terms of civil rights coordination, appointment of blacks to significant positions in the federal government, black employment with the federal bureaucracy, and blacks in the armed service, one must make some positive and some negative statements. As far as coordination of civil rights activities is concerned, the Johnson administration seemed to have set up the strongest mechanism in 1965,

[88] *Ibid.*, 157.
[89] Dalfiume, *Desegregation of the U.S. Armed Forces*, 223–24.
[90] *Ibid.*, 224.

but it was abandoned within a few months. After that, efforts to co-ordinate were at best uneven and too much dependent upon voluntarism. Quite a number of blacks were appointed to important posts in the federal government, but all too often they were of the "revolving door" type and had little or no real power. More blacks were hired to work in the bureaucracy than ever before, but they still held very few of the higher positions; there was still too much tokenism above the lower levels. Strides were made in desegregating the armed forces, but here too, blacks tended to be top heavy in the lower ranks and to be too heavily involved in the combat units for their numbers. Furthermore, black servicemen still faced much prejudice off base.

CHAPTER V

Housing
and Private Employment

HOUSING

The federal government had been heavily involved in housing since the depression years of the 1930s. However, it was not until the Kennedy administration that the federal government began to recognize that it had any responsibility to bring about equal opportunity in this area. The chief role of the federal government in the 1930s had been to facilitate credit and the relief of depressed economic conditions. The federal government did establish a low-rent public-housing program in 1937 in order to provide housing for low-income families. Again, however, the main purpose was economic. Following the depression, the emphasis changed to that of meeting the housing needs of American families. In 1949 a national goal was enunciated of providing a decent home and living environment for every American family.

Unfortunately, when the federal government did become involved in housing it accepted and even magnified the discriminatory attitudes and practices of private industry, e.g., lenders, brokers, and real estate boards.[1] For instance, FHA not only condoned discriminatory practices but actively encouraged them. The Federal Home Loan Bank and the Home Owners' Loan Corporation overtly espoused racial exclusionary policies in residences.[2]

With regard to public housing, the federal government adopted a policy based on equitable participation of minorities, not only as tenants, but also in terms of management and construction. Nevertheless, most of the public-housing projects produced during the first twenty-five years were either all white or all black. Down to 1962 when President Kennedy issued the housing order, the racial compo-

[1] See George W. Grier, "The Negro Ghettos and Federal Housing Policy, *Law and Contemporary Problems*, 32 (Summer, 1967), 550–60, for a survey of the federal government's role in maintaining and even expanding segregation in housing.

[2] See U.S. Commission on Civil Rights, *Federal Civil Rights Enforcement Effort* (Washington, D.C.: U.S. Government Printing Office, 1970), 426.

sition of the tenants in public-housing units was a matter determined by local public-housing authorities. Even in the case of urban renewal, the federal government subsidized private developers who practiced discrimination.

Kennedy's order in 1962 covered FHA- and VA-insured housing, but most housing units—those financed by conventional loans from mortage lending institutions whose deposits or accounts were regulated and insured by agencies of the federal government—were excluded from the order. Moreover, the chief thrust of the order had related almost entirely to housing provided through federal-aid agreements after November 20, 1962. Another section of the order had merely provided "good offices" to deal with federal-aid agreements made before the date of the order. That part of the order proved to be singularly ineffective.

Title VI of the Civil Rights Act of 1964 covered all federally assisted housing except where the assistance provided was solely in the contracts of insurance of guaranty (FHA and VA—already covered in 1962). Title VI was applied to all urban renewal, housing rehabilitation, code enforcement grants, low-rent public housing, and relocation grants.

The Civil Rights Act of 1968 called for coverage in three phases. The first phase, down to December 31, 1968, merely included what had been done in Kennedy's executive order. The second phase, lasting from January 1, 1969, to December 31, 1969, extended coverage to private, non-federally assisted housing, except single-family housing and buildings of no more than four housing units, including one occupied by the owner. Private clubs and religious institutions were not covered. The third phase went into effect on January 1, 1970. It limited the exemption of single-family dwellings to such housing sold or rented without the use of a real estate broker.[3] Some 80 percent of the nation's housing would be covered after the third phase had been entered.

While coverage was weak in the executive order of 1962 and Title VI of the Civil Rights Act of 1964, the sanctions were fairly substantial if enforced. However, the coverage of the Civil Rights Act of 1968 was its strong point; its sanctions were weak—largely be-

[3] *Ibid.*, 433.

cause of time-consuming litigation. Either the individual discriminated against or the Department of Justice could undertake a suit in
the case of "pattern or practice of discrimination." HUD, which had
the major responsibility for enforcement and administration of the
law, had only the "informal" methods of conference, conciliation,
and persuasion as its weapons.[4]

Two months after the passage of the Civil Rights Act of 1968 the
United States Supreme Court made a very significant decision dealing with housing. In *Jones* v. *Alfred H. Mayer, et al.* (392 U.S. 409,
1968) the Court held that a provision of the Civil Rights Act of 1866
had been meant to apply to private as well as public discrimination in
the sale or rental of housing. This decision made all housing open
without regard to race. The said law was held to have been in har-
mony with the Thirteenth Amendment to the Constitution. Under the
enabling clause of that amendment Congress had been allotted the
power to pass all laws necessary and proper for the abolishment of all
badges and incidents of slavery in the nation.

Furthermore, the Court declared:

> Just as the Black Codes, enacted after the Civil War to restrict the
> free exercise of those rights, were substitutes for the same system, so
> the exclusion of Negroes from white communities became a substitute
> for the Black Codes, and when racial discrimination herds men into
> ghettos and makes their ability to buy property turn on the color of
> their skin then it too is a relic of slavery.
>
> Negro citizens, North and South, who saw in the Thirteenth Amend-
> ment a promise of freedom to "go and come at pleasure" and "to buy
> and sell when they please" would be left "with a mere paper guarantee"
> if Congress were powerless to assure that a dollar in the hands of a
> Negro will purchase the same thing as the dollar in the hands of a white
> man. At the very least, the freedom that Congress is empowered to se-
> cure under the Thirteenth Amendment includes the freedom to buy
> whatever a white man can buy, the right to live wherever a white man
> can live. If the Congress cannot say that being a free man means at
> least this much, then the Thirteenth Amendment made a promise the
> Nation cannot keep.

One legal writer hailed the court for acting in its greatest tradition.
The decision served as a "frank recognition of the overwhelming
problems confronted by the nation's black citizens." The court had

[4] *Ibid.*, 434–35.

publicly acknowledged that the structure of slavery had never been fully uprooted and that black citizens were still oppressed by the remaining existence of the badges of the supposedly outlawed system.[5]

Housing integration, probably more than integration of schools, had long brought fear into the minds of many whites in American society. The romantic image of a boy marrying the girl next door caused many whites to fear miscegenation if blacks lived where whites did. What many whites did not recognize, however, was that blacks found themselves beautiful and for the most part preferred to marry among themselves. The whole fear of miscegenation, of course, was tied in with the racist idea that whites were superior to blacks.

Ironically, particularly since discrimination had restricted the amount of housing available to blacks in the ghettos, they frequently obtained less for their money in housing than whites. In turn, since the average black's income was less than that of his white counterpart anyway, blacks often had to live in substandard housing.

One authority on the subject, Donald King, wrote:

> Discrimination has the effect of creating over-crowded conditions and makes families, solely because of their race, victims of an increasingly undesirable environment. It is one factor contributing to the perpetuation of slums and blighted areas. It creates poor health and living conditions, which in turn undermine the ability of the individual to contribute to society and to enjoy the blessings of liberty.[6]

The black man had a very difficult time obtaining credit for housing. In the first place, his generally low income served as a tremendous handicap. However, even if a black borrower had good credit, he often found the lender unwilling to finance his purchase of a home in a predominantly white neighborhood. The lender rationalized this decision on the incorrect assumption that if a black owned it, property values would ipso facto decrease. Therefore the lender would want to "protect" the investments he had already made. Furthermore, it was considered a matter of "good" public relations. No mat-

---

[5] Arthur Kinoy, "Jones v. Mayer Co.: An Historic Step Forward," *Vanderbilt Law Review*, 22 (April, 1969), 476–77.

[6] Donald B. King, "Housing: The Right of Occupancy Without Discrimination," in Donald B. King and Charles W. Quick (eds.), *Legal Aspects of the Civil Rights Movement*, (Detroit: Wayne State University Press, 1965), 145.

ter how the lender might rationalize, however, residential segregation was the result.[7]

The role of the broker was also crucial in the housing field. He almost always steered the nonwhite buyer away from the all-white neighborhoods. The techniques for doing so were often dictated by the local real estate boards. Real estate boards, through their ability to expel members and to mobilize business sentiments against those who did not conform, could generally control the action of members who might not otherwise go along with discriminatory policies. Realtors were also reluctant to contravene neighborhood norms, unless a neighborhood had already begun a racial transition.[8] In a transitional situation, of course, all restraints were dropped, realtors often resorted to "blockbusting" techniques in order to pressure fleeing whites to sell at a low price and then turn around and sell to in-moving blacks at a much higher price.

Karl Tauber, a sociologist from the University of Wisconsin, wrote in 1965 that there was little hope of ending the de facto segregation of Negroes in the nation's major cities. He argued that this was the case because segregation was not the result of poverty, lack of education, or other factors that could be remedied by government programs, national policy, or the courts. Instead, Tauber insisted that segregation resulted from "unchanging and apparently unchangeable human prejudice." He concluded that basically discrimination was the major cause of residential segregation and that there was no basis for "anticipating major changes in the segregated character of American cities until patterns of housing discrimination can be altered." [9]

Whitney Young, Jr., executive director of the National Urban League, had this to say about the problem:

> The ghetto poses problems in the civic and political as well as the economic area. It can mean degeneration of government, and power in the hands of second-rate persons, demagogues and extremists. In

[7] Linton C. Freeman and Morris H. Sunshine, *Patterns of Residential Segregation* (Cambridge, Mass.: Schenkman Publishing Co., 1970), 43.

[8] *Ibid.*, 43–44.

[9] New York *Times*, August 8, 1965, p. 58. See also Henry Clark, "Desegregated Housing: Still Worth Waiting For," *Social Action*, 33 (May, 1967), 8–14, who holds out hopes for integrated housing in the long run.

the past, it was believed by many people, including many Negroes, that education provided the entree to American society. This has been shown to be inaccurate. Ralph Bunche cannot move into Cicero, Illinois, though Al Capone could and did.[10]

Young pointed out that at the heart of the problem was the recent rise of a large group of whites to middle-class status, but who lacked the educational and cultural background generally associated with the middle class. It was a very insecure group, and "most vulnerable to believing in easy solutions to complex problems." He charged that they were among the most bigoted and most militant in opposing equal opportunity for blacks and were the pawns of right-wing groups in society. Young stated that societal indifference was also a problem, and those who were indifferent outnumbered the active haters. Young concluded:

> Any approach to the problem must be based on the dual recognition that Negroes will not return to Africa and that white society will not collapse. We are dealing largely with attitudes. Whiteness means status. The whiter the neighborhood the better. Such attitudes must be changed by giving the people "the facts of life." There is nothing creative in a child's growing up in a homogeneous neighborhood. It compounds mediocrity, while heterogeneity provides security. You don't shut others out, you fence yourself in.[11]

For a considerable time after World War II FHA and VA had been heavily involved in providing homes for whites who sought to flee from the central city to the suburbs. Often the federal government itself had required the exclusion of blacks as a condition for its guarantee of loans.[12] Kennedy's executive order had not been effective in reversing the continued segregation of housing. Each major operating agency, in effect, had been allowed to police itself under the general guidance of the president's committee. The FHA apparently feared that vigorous enforcement would cause builders and lenders to shift to conventional loans. Undoubtedly, too, many FHA

[10] National Committee Against Discrimination in Housing, April 13–14, 1967, *Model Cities and Metropolitan Desegregation* (New York: National Committee Against Discrimination in Housing, 1967), Conference Report No. 8, p. 25.

[11] *Ibid.*

[12] See George and Eunice Grier, *Equality and Beyond: Housing and the Goals of the Great Society* (Chicago: Quadrangle Books, 1966).

personnel subscribed to the tenet of the real estate people that property values declined when neighborhoods became racially mixed.[13]

The "stroke of the pen" had also done little for public housing. Integration was a vain hope in many cities. Public-housing projects in the South were normally either black or white, rarely both. On December 31, 1965, Tampa, Florida, reported that it had ten housing projects: five all black and five all white. Savannah, Georgia, had nine projects: six black and three white. As late as June of 1968 there were six projects in Jacksonville, Florida; two were all white and four were all nonwhite. Segregation was also widespread in the North. On December 31, 1965, the Raymond Rosen Apartments in Philadelphia contained 1,122 dwelling units; all of the tenants were black. In St. Louis, Missouri, as of December 31, 1964, 83.3 percent of the occupants of public housing were black; the whites were concentrated in five projects, with a bare majority in one of them. Thus, public housing in St. Louis meant low income blacks, and if a neighborhood accepted public housing it also had to accept blacks. The most extensive case, perhaps, was in Chicago. The Robert Taylor Homes had some 28,000 units, and at the end of 1965 black families occupied every one of them. There were other projects in Chicago that were all white. In general, the public in this country supported public housing for blacks and the poor across the board if they remained geographically isolated.[14] Of course, blacks were more likely to be poor than whites.

Late in 1968 Mark Killingsworth charged that although the Johnson administration had obtained fair housing laws and had quadrupled the number of public housing units available, federal funds were still being used to finance what was the largest block of segregated housing in the nation. He pointed out that HUD "continued to approve the construction of public housing on sites and in areas which reinforce and perpetuate segregated living patterns." As late as 1968 the Kerner Commission had charged: "To date, housing programs serving low-income groups have been concentrated in the

[13] Morton J. Schussheim, *Toward New Housing Policy* (New York: Committee for Economic Development, 1969), 46–47.

[14] Lawrence M. Freidman, *Government and Slum Housing: A Century of Frustration* (Chicago: Rand McNally & Co., 1968), 124–26; U.S. Commission on Civil Rights, *Federal Civil Rights Enforcement Effort*, 43–44.

ghettos." Killingsworth said that many whites, otherwise eligible, were avoiding public housing because it was so terrible. The problem was one of a stingy Congress and stingy resources.[15]

Nathan Wright, Jr., writing in 1967, had perhaps the best solution to the black people's housing problems. He noted that most blacks were renters. He felt that furnishing them with public rental housing was not conducive to the revitalization of city life for blacks. Instead, he urged that blacks be furnished with housing on the basis of ownership which would give them pride in its upkeep and maintenance. He even predicted that such low-cost housing would be less costly to taxpayers than would the rental type.[16]

In 1967, the National Committee Against Discrimination in Housing (NCADH) charged that funds of the federal government were still being used to build racial ghettos, and that the federal government was primarily responsible for their continued existence. More specifically, it had notified the White House of this problem in 1966 and nothing had changed. HUD continued to approve loans and grants to municipalities where equality of opportunity in housing had been denied by law to racial or ethnic minorities.[17] The organization urged that Title VI sanctions be implemented to alleviate that condition. The NCADH pointed out that the metropolitan and regional bodies receiving federal funds from a variety of programs were not required to develop comprehensive plans for eliminating community-wide segregation. It recommended that they be required to do so in the future.[18]

The sin of the federal government was held by the NCADH to be blandness and a lack of will. Its policies appeared murky since:

> On the one hand, the Government is officially committed to fighting

[15] Mark Killingsworth, "Desegregating Public Housing," *The New Leader*, 51 (October 7, 1968), 13–14; Charles O. Jones, *An Introduction to the Study of Public Policy* (Belmont, Calif.; Wadsworth Publishing Co., Inc., 1970), 41. See also Report of the National Advisory Commission, *The Kerner Report* (New York: Bantam Books, 1968).

[16] Nathan Wright, Jr., *Black Power and Urban Unrest* (New York: Hawthorn Books, Inc., 1967), 93–94.

[17] Robert Weaver, Secretary of Housing and Urban Development, was a former president of the National Committee Against Discrimination in Housing.

[18] Edward Rutledge and Jack E. Wood, Jr., "Government and the Ghettos," *Social Action*, 33 (May, 1967), 16–18.

segregation on all relevant fronts; on the other, it seems temperamentally committed to doing business as usual—which, given our current social climate, means more segregation. It hires many intergroup relations specialists—HUD had forty-seven—but deprives them of the power and prestige to achieve meaningful integration. Similarly, it cranks out hundreds of inter-office memoranda on how best to promote open occupancy, but it fails to develop follow-up procedures tough enough to persuade bureaucrats to take these missives seriously. The federal files are bulging with such memoranda—and our racial ghettos are expanding almost as quickly.[19]

As if to confirm the charges made by the National Committee Against Discrimination in Housing, the United States Commission on Civil Rights in its 1970 report noted that the denial of equal opportunity remained an acute and persistent problem. In 1959, before the federal government had adopted fair housing laws and policies, it was estimated that less than 2 percent of the new homes provided by FHA mortgage loans had been available to minority groups. The situation had not changed much by 1967, although five years had passed since Kennedy had issued his "stroke of the pen." In 1967, FHA made a national survey of subdivisions built after the 1962 order and found that of the more than 400,000 units surveyed, only 3.3 percent were reported as sold to blacks. In some areas, the situation was worse than in others. In the St. Louis area, for example, it was reported that 56 units or 0.85 percent of the total had been sold to blacks.[20]

The FHA took some minor steps against discrimination between November, 1962, and November, 1968. It received 195 complaints alleging discrimination by builders or landlords who had been recipients of federal funds. Eighty-six of the offenders were found guilty and given relatively light sentences—eighteen of the eighty-six were banned from HUD programs; however, twelve of the eighteen were later reinstated. The greatest black successes were forty-five instances in which the complainant actually acquired the rental unit or home.[21] The VA lagged behind the FHA in such policies, as in the case of racially restrictive covenants and one- and two-family homes. One

19 *Ibid.*, 18–19.
20 U.S. Commission on Civil Rights, *Federal Civil Rights Enforcement Effort*, 42–43.
21 *Ibid.*, 487.

exception occurred in the fall of 1968 when the VA took steps to determine the extent of participation by minority groups in the loan guaranty program. The FHA did not follow suit.

Nevertheless, some minor administrative changes were made within HUD to lessen discrimination in housing. In 1967 the FHA initiated a free counseling service in fifteen cities for low-income and minority persons who sought advice about housing. That action complemented FHA's efforts to liberalize mortgage insurance payments in inner city neighborhoods. Moreover, HUD tightened its rules on site selection for low-rent public housing and in the re-use of urban renewal locations and the provision of aid for commuity facilities. The purpose of such changes was to prevent the excessive concentration of minority group families and, at the same time, to widen housing choices for them outside the ghettos. Apparently HUD had intended to implement the Civil Rights Act of 1968 rather vigorously. It requested nine million dollars to do so, but received only two million dollars for the first year.[22]

Nevertheless, HUD continued to come under attack in 1968 for its failure to push non-discrimination in housing. One study charged:

> The Department of Housing and Urban Development has been exceedingly cautious and painfully slow in implementing Title VI objectives. To date, HUD has directed its energies toward improving the quality and expanding the quantity of available housing, sacrificing civil rights goals where necessary to meet this end. The recurrent tension in HUD programs over the order of priority of various policy objectives has relegated civil rights and Title VI to a secondary status in every major HUD program. While HUD administrators feel that they are making contributions to the solution of the housing problem by increasing the housing supply, they are doing so in open contradiction of Congress, which was to provide not maximum housing units, but maximum desegregated housing.[23]

On other fronts in 1961 the Federal Home Loan Bank Board had issued a policy statement against discrimination but had undertaken no enforcement actions. The banking agencies, e.g., the FDIC, the Federal Savings and Loan Insurance Corporation, and the Board of Governors of the Federal Reserve System, had taken no action at all.

22 Schussheim, *Toward New Housing Policy*, 47–48.

23 "Comment: Title VI and the 1964 Civil Rights Act-Implementation and Impact," *George Washington Law Review*, 36 (May, 1968), 1006.

Data were not even collected upon which a non-discriminatory policy might have been based.[24]

In 1968, since section 805 of the Civil Rights Act of that year barred discrimination in mortgage lending, the United States Commission on Civil Rights sent notices to the FHLBB, the FDIC, the Board of Governors of the Federal Reserve System, and the FSLIC that as of January 1, 1969, discrimination was prohibited and they should notify mortgage lenders and builders and developers that the policy of nondiscrimination was to be required.[25]

In July 1968, the FHLBB followed up the notice from the Commission on Civil Rights by sending a letter to all member savings and loan associations describing the requirements of section 805 and calling attention to the sanctions that could be imposed for violation of the prohibition against discrimination in mortgage lending. The three financial agencies did not follow suit until 1969. Nothing was done to require lending institutions to impose non-discrimination standards on developers and builders, however.[26]

Meanwhile, President Johnson tried to alleviate housing conditions for blacks in a different way. He had set up a committee in 1965 to study slum conditions and to make recommendations for solving them. The group made recommendations, and based on them the president proposed legislation to Congress. The result was the Model Cities Act of 1966. The president noted that the new approach was:

based on the proposition that a slum is not merely decaying brick and mortar but also a breeding ground of human failure and despair, where hope is as alien as sunlight and green grass. Along with new buildings to replace the crumbling hovels where slum dwellers wore out their deprived existences, we needed to offer those slum dwellers a genuine opportunity to change their lives—programs to train them for jobs, the means of giving their children a better chance to finish school, a method for putting medical clinics and legal services within their reach. The proposal was an approach to the rebuilding of neighborhoods in a total way, bringing to bear on a blighted community all the programs that could help in that task.[27]

24 U.S. Commission on Civil Rights, *Federal Civil Rights Enforcement Effort*, 515.
25 *Ibid.*, 517.
26 *Ibid.*
27 Johnson, *The Vantage Point*, 330.

On another front the president appointed the President's Committee on Urban Housing in 1967 to study the overall housing needs of the country for the coming decade. The group recognized that there were two interrelated needs—one for the population in general and one for low-income families of whom many were black. Of those with low income who would need housing, 70 percent would be white and 30 percent nonwhite. However, while one out of four nonwhite families would require assistance in obtaining the needed housing, only one out of twelve white families would require such help.[28]

The president's committee also urged enforcement of civil rights laws and constructive and affirmative actions by society to deal with discrimination. Finally, the committee recommended that 26 million housing units were needed by 1978, six million of those to be built for low-income families.[29] Based on the study and recommendations made by this committee, he proposed and Congress passed the Housing and Urban Development Act of 1968. It established a blueprint for the number of units recommended by the committee.

The need for housing was demonstrated in a statistical analysis made by the Urban Institute comparing the amount of substandard housing whites and nonwhites had in 1960 and 1968.[30]

Housing		1960	1968	Annual Imputed Rate of Change, 1960–1968
% Substandard				
Housing	W	13%	6%	−9.2%
	NW*	44%	24%	−7.3%

* 92% were black.

The above figures showed that the gap between whites and non-

---

[28] *Ibid.*, 331; The President's Committee on Urban Housing, *A Decent Home* (Washington, D.C.: U.S. Government Printing Office, 1968), 8.

[29] Johnson, *The Vantage Point*, 331; The President's Committee on Urban Housing, *A Decent Home*, 3.

[30] Michael J. Flax, *Blacks and Whites: An Experiment in Racial Indicators* (Washington, D.C.: The Urban Institute, 1971), 20. See also *The Kerner Report*, 467–474.

whites had been 31 percent in 1960, while in 1968 it was 18 percent. However, the rate of improvement for nonwhites was less than that for whites.[31]

Of course, the central cities in the country were becoming increasingly black in the 1960s. In the urban poverty areas, two writers noted, four out of five of all housing units were occupied by nonwhites; three out of four substandard units were located in the central cities; nine out of ten of the substandard units were occupied by nonwhites in the central cities; five out of six of the overcrowded units occupied by nonwhites had been built before 1940, and approximately a third were one hundred years or older. Race, therefore, appeared to continue to be a factor in bad housing.[32]

PRIVATE EMPLOYMENT
(Includes Government Contract Employees)

Just as in every area of American life, blacks were discriminated against when trying to locate jobs. Undoubtedly this area of discrimination made life the most difficult for blacks in their efforts to survive in a hostile society. Racism in obtaining jobs meant inevitably high unemployment rates, as well as low-paying and low-status jobs for most black Americans.

As one management expert wrote on this matter of blacks having the lowest-paid and lowest-status jobs:

> Nonwhites in many parts of the country have been taught that there are "white" jobs and "colored" jobs, and because of the racial practices of some state employment services that have helped to institutionalize this pattern, they expected to be treated with indifference by any state employment service as well as by private employment agencies. Much of the same feeling is shared by hardcore unemployed workers who inquire about openings or arrive for a job interview in private industry. Thus they look lightly upon advertisements and sports radio announcements that attempt to attract them to interviews.
>
> Many of the disadvantaged have experienced indifference and condescending treatment at the hands of middle-class interviewers—who might indeed be black. Many unemployed men and women prefer to

[31] Flax, *Blacks and Whites*, 21.
[32] William L. Henderson and Larry C. Lidebur, *Economic Disparity: Problems and Strategies for Black Americans* (New York: The Free Press, 1970), 8.

remain in the slums than suffer indignities from insensitive and discriminating people.[33]

Unfortunately, this side of the problem was often misunderstood, especially in much of the white community.

The fact that blacks appeared to be "locked" into low-paying and low-status jobs affected not only their standard of living but their attitude toward life. While there were more white poor than black poor in America, in proportion to their percentage of the population, blacks were much more likely to be poor than whites. Jobs, of necessity, were far more important to the black masses than integration.[34]

In the meantime, whites in the North were flocking to the suburbs, and the central cities were becoming increasingly black with the continuous influx from the South. The same phenomena was happening in the southern metropolitan areas at a slower pace. Along with the population shifts, there was an exodus of industries to the suburbs. This situation meant that from the standpoint of suburban location alone, regardless of other considerations, whites would hold most of the better jobs. Lack of personal transportation and the cost of finding some other means presented overriding problems for many blacks. In addition, blacks had little information and little opportunity to learn about jobs located far from the ghetto.

There was considerable concern, among those who cared about black employment, that the riots in the 1960s might accelerate the flight of industries to the outlying parts of the metropolitan areas.[35] Furthermore, employers located outside the ghettos discriminated against blacks by not bringing blacks into the all-white areas in the suburbs for fear of retaliation by white customers. Finally, since the industries were located where there were few if any blacks, there were few pressures not to discriminate.[36]

[33] William D. Drenan (ed.), *The Fourth Strike: Hiring and Training the Disadvantaged* (New York: American Management Association, Inc., 1970), 14–15.

[34] See C. Eric Lincoln, *Sounds of the Struggle: Persons and Perspectives in Civil Rights* (New York: William Morrow & Co., 1967), 142.

[35] Joseph D. Mooney, "Housing Segregation, Negro Employment and Metropolitan Decentralization: An Alternative Perspective," *Quarterly Journal of Economics*, 83 (May, 1969), 299–300.

[36] John F. Kain, "Housing Segregation, Negro Employment, and Metropolitan Decentralization," *Quarterly Journal of Economics*, 82 (May, 1968), 179–80.

A meaningful method of comparing the nonwhite and white employment situation was to examine the income and degree of poverty between the two groups from 1960 to 1968. One study showed the following.[37]

Income and Poverty		1960	1968	Imputed Rate of Annual Change, 1960–1968
Median family income	W	$6,857	$8,937	+ 3.4%
(in 1968 dollars)	NW	$3,794	$5,590	+ 4.9%
% Persons below	W	18%	10%	− 7.1%
poverty level	B	55%	35%	− 5.5%
% Families with				
incomes greater	W	39%	58%	+ 4.8%
than $8,000	NW	15%	32%	+10.0%
(in 1968 dollars)				

An analysis showed that the size of the white/nonwhite gap was $3,060 in 1960 and $3,347 in 1968. While the ratio of improvement for nonwhites was greater than that of whites between 1960 and 1968, the size of the gap between the two groups was increasing for whites over nonwhites. The data on employment is shown on page 106.[38]

On analysis and evaluation, the size of the unemployment gap in 1960 for white and nonwhites was 5.3 percent, the 1968 spread was 3.5 percent. The size of the white/nonwhite gap in unemployment was decreasing in the 1960–1968 period; however, the rate of nonwhite improvement was less than that for whites. The size of the white/nonwhite gap for unemployed teenagers was 15.1 percent in 1960, and it had decreased to 14 percent by 1968. The size of the gap was decreasing, but the nonwhite rate of improvement was less

[37] Flax, *Blacks and Whites*, 22; Alan B. Bachelder, "Decline in the Relative Income of Negro Men," *Quarterly Journal of Economics*, 78 (November, 1964), 525–48; Rashi Fein, "Relative Income of Negro Men: Some Recent Data," *Quarterly Journal of Economics*, 80 (May, 1966), 336; David Rasmussen, "A Note on the Relative Income of Nonwhite Men 1948–1968," *Quarterly Journal of Economics*, 84 (February, 1970), 168–72; Andrew Brimmer, "Employment Patterns and the Dilemma of Desegregation," *Integrated Education*, 5 (October–November, 1965), pp. 17–23.

[38] Flax, *Blacks and Whites*, 22–23.

Employment		1960	1968	Imputed Annual Rate of Change
% Unemployed	W	4.9%	3.2%	−5.2%
	NW	10.2%	6.7%	−5.1%
% Teenagers	W	19.1%	11.0%	−6.7%
Unemployed	NW	34.2%	25.0%	−3.9%
% in Clerical	W	15.8%	17.5%	+1.3%
Occupations	NW	7.3%	12.1%	+6.6%
% in Professional	W	12.1%	14.2%	+2.0%
and Technical	NW	4.8%	7.8%	+6.2%
Occupations				

than that for whites. The white/nonwhite gap in clerical positions was 8.5 percent in 1960; it was 5.4 percent in 1968. The spread was decreasing and the rate of nonwhite improvement was greater than for whites. The gap in professional and technical occupations between whites and nonwhites was 7.3 percent in 1960; in 1968 it was 6.4 percent. The size of the gap was decreasing, and the nonwhite rate of improvement was greater than that for whites.[39] Generally speaking, too, nonwhites earned less than whites in all occupations.

In 1969 the Department of Labor published the unemployment rates for persons sixteen years of age and older between 1948 and 1968.[40] (See Tables 9-12)

The "last hired and the first fired" all too frequently characterized the situation of blacks in the labor market. The black employment rate in the 1960s was lower than it had been in 1930. Moreover, unemployment for nonwhite males had been half again higher than for whites between 1948 and 1954; however, from 1955 into the 1960s nonwhite unemployment was more than twice as high as for whites. While things were somewhat better in the 1960s for middle class

[39] *Ibid.*, 23.
[40] See U.S. Department of Labor, *Statistics on Manpower: A Supplement to the Manpower Report to the President* (Washington, D.C.: U.S. Government Printing Office, 1969), 15.

Table 9
UNEMPLOYMENT RATE OF PERSONS SIXTEEN YEARS AND OLDER BY COLOR, SEX AND AGE: ANNUAL AVERAGES, 1948–68

White Male	Totals, 16 Years and Over	16 and 17	18 and 19	20 to 24	25 to 34	35 to 44	45 to 54	55 to 64	65 and Over	14 and 15
1948	3.4	10.2	9.4	6.4	2.6	2.1	2.4	3.0	3.3	5.9
1949	5.6	13.4	14.2	9.8	4.9	3.9	4.0	5.3	5.0	5.1
1950	4.7	13.4	11.7	7.7	3.9	3.2	3.7	4.7	4.6	5.8
1951	2.6	9.5	6.7	3.6	2.0	1.8	2.2	2.7	3.4	4.7
1952	2.5	10.9	7.0	4.3	1.9	1.7	2.0	2.3	2.9	5.5
1953	2.5	8.9	7.1	4.5	2.0	1.8	2.0	2.7	2.3	4.6
1954	4.8	14.0	13.0	9.8	4.2	3.6	3.8	4.3	4.2	4.9
1955	3.7	12.2	10.4	7.0	2.7	2.6	2.9	3.9	3.8	5.1
1956	3.4	11.2	9.7	6.1	2.8	2.2	2.8	3.1	3.4	6.1
1957	3.6	11.9	11.2	7.1	2.7	2.5	3.0	3.4	3.2	6.8
1958	6.1	14.9	16.5	11.7	5.6	4.4	4.8	5.2	5.0	7.9
1959	4.6	15.0	13.0	7.5	3.8	3.2	3.7	4.2	4.5	7.2
1960	4.8	14.6	13.5	8.3	4.1	3.3	3.6	4.1	4.0	8.1
1961	5.7	16.5	15.1	10.0	4.9	4.0	4.4	5.3	5.2	8.0
1962	4.6	15.1	12.7	8.0	3.8	3.1	3.5	4.1	4.1	7.6
1963	4.7	17.8	14.2	7.8	3.9	2.9	3.3	4.0	4.1	7.9
1964	4.1	16.1	13.4	7.4	3.0	2.5	2.9	3.5	3.6	7.7
1965	3.6	14.7	11.4	5.9	2.6	2.3	2.3	3.1	3.4	7.1
1966	2.8	12.5	8.9	4.1	2.1	1.7	1.7	2.5	3.0	7.6
1967	2.7	12.7	9.0	4.2	1.9	1.6	1.8	2.2	2.7	8.9
1968	2.6	12.3	8.2	4.6	1.7	1.4	1.5	1.7	2.8	8.3

Table 10
UNEMPLOYMENT RATE OF PERSONS SIXTEEN YEARS AND OLDER BY COLOR, SEX AND AGE: ANNUAL AVERAGES, 1948–68

White Female	Totals, 16 Years and Over	16 and 17	18 and 19	20 to 24	25 to 34	35 to 44	45 to 54	55 to 64	65 and Over	14 and 15
1948	3.8	9.7	6.8	4.2	3.8	2.9	3.1	3.2	2.4	7.6
1949	5.7	13.6	10.7	6.7	5.8	4.5	4.0	4.3	4.1	7.5
1950	5.3	13.8	9.4	6.1	5.2	4.0	4.3	4.3	3.1	8.0
1951	4.2	9.6	6.5	3.9	4.1	3.5	3.6	4.0	3.3	7.1
1952	3.3	9.3	6.2	3.8	3.2	2.8	2.4	2.5	2.3	7.6
1953	3.1	8.3	6.0	4.1	3.1	2.3	2.3	2.5	1.4	4.0
1954	5.6	12.0	9.4	6.4	5.7	4.9	4.4	4.5	2.8	6.8
1955	4.3	11.6	7.7	5.1	4.3	3.8	3.4	3.6	2.2	7.1
1956	4.2	12.1	8.3	5.1	4.0	3.5	3.3	3.5	2.3	7.8
1957	4.3	11.9	7.9	5.1	4.7	3.7	3.0	3.0	3.5	6.8
1958	6.2	15.6	11.0	7.4	6.6	5.6	4.9	4.3	3.5	5.8
1959	5.3	13.3	11.1	6.7	5.0	4.7	4.0	4.0	3.4	5.2
1960	5.3	14.5	11.5	7.2	5.7	4.2	4.0	3.3	2.8	6.3
1961	6.5	17.0	13.6	8.4	6.6	5.6	4.8	4.3	3.7	5.6
1962	5.5	15.6	11.3	7.7	5.4	4.5	3.7	3.5	4.0	5.6
1963	5.8	18.1	13.2	7.4	5.8	4.6	3.9	3.5	3.0	5.9
1964	5.5	17.1	13.2	7.1	5.2	4.5	3.6	3.5	3.4	4.1
1965	5.0	15.0	13.4	6.3	4.8	4.1	3.0	2.7	2.7	4.4
1966	4.3	14.5	10.7	5.3	3.7	3.3	2.7	2.2	2.7	4.4
1967	4.6	12.9	10.6	6.0	4.7	3.7	2.9	2.3	2.6	5.2
1968	4.3	13.9	11.0	5.9	3.9	3.1	2.3	2.1	2.7	5.4

Table 11
UNEMPLOYMENT RATE OF PERSONS SIXTEEN YEARS AND OLDER BY COLOR, SEX AND AGE: ANNUAL AVERAGES, 1948–68

Nonwhite Male	Totals, 16 Years and Over	16 and 17	18 and 19	20 to 24	25 to 34	35 to 44	45 to 54	55 to 64	65 and Over	14 and 15
1948	5.8	9.4	10.5	11.7	4.7	5.2	3.7	3.5	4.6	3.2
1949	9.6	15.8	17.1	15.8	8.5	8.1	7.9	7.0	6.2	6.1
1950	9.4	12.1	17.7	12.6	10.0	7.9	7.4	8.0	7.0	10.8
1951	4.9	8.7	9.6	6.7	5.5	3.4	3.6	4.1	4.7	4.9
1952	5.2	8.0	10.0	7.9	5.5	4.4	4.2	3.7	4.7	5.5
1953	4.8	8.3	8.1	8.1	4.3	3.6	5.1	3.6	3.1	5.1
1954	10.3	13.4	14.7	16.9	10.1	9.0	9.3	7.5	7.5	5.1
1955	8.8	14.8	12.9	12.4	8.6	8.2	6.4	9.0	7.1	12.7
1956	7.9	15.7	14.9	12.0	7.6	6.6	5.4	8.1	4.9	13.0
1957	8.3	16.3	20.0	12.7	8.5	6.4	6.2	5.5	5.9	14.1
1958	13.8	27.1	26.7	19.5	14.7	11.4	10.3	10.1	9.0	13.0
1959	11.5	22.3	27.2	16.3	12.3	8.9	7.9	8.7	8.4	12.7
1960	10.7	22.7	25.1	13.1	10.7	8.2	8.5	9.5	6.3	13.3
1961	12.8	31.0	23.9	15.3	12.9	10.7	10.2	10.5	9.4	14.3
1962	10.9	21.9	21.8	14.6	10.5	8.6	8.3	9.6	11.9	15.2
1963	10.5	27.0	27.4	15.5	9.5	8.0	7.1	7.4	10.1	16.9
1964	8.9	25.9	23.1	12.6	7.7	6.2	5.9	8.1	8.3	19.1
1965	7.4	27.1	20.2	9.3	6.2	5.1	5.1	5.4	5.2	20.3
1966	6.3	22.5	20.5	7.9	4.9	4.2	4.1	4.4	4.9	20.0
1967	6.0	28.9	20.1	8.0	4.4	3.1	3.4	4.1	5.1	24.1
1968	5.6	26.6	19.0	8.3	3.8	2.9	2.5	3.6	4.0	26.0

Table 12

UNEMPLOYMENT RATE OF PERSONS SIXTEEN YEARS AND OLDER BY COLOR, SEX AND AGE: ANNUAL AVERAGES, 1948–68

Nonwhite Female	Totals, 16 Years and Over	16 and 17	18 and 19	20 to 24	25 to 34	35 to 44	45 to 54	55 to 64	65 and Over	14 and 15
1948	6.1	11.8	14.6	10.2	7.3	4.0	2.9	3.0	1.6	(1)
1949	7.9	20.3	15.9	12.5	8.5	6.2	4.0	5.6	1.6	(1)
1950	8.4	17.6	14.1	13.0	9.1	6.6	5.9	4.8	5.7	(1)
1951	6.1	13.0	15.1	8.8	7.1	5.6	2.8	3.4	1.6	(1)
1952	5.7	6.3	16.8	10.7	6.2	4.0	3.5	2.4	1.5	(1)
1953	4.1	10.3	9.9	5.5	4.9	3.5	2.1	2.1	1.6	(1)
1954	9.3	19.1	21.6	13.2	10.9	7.3	5.9	4.9	5.1	(1)
1955	8.4	15.4	21.4	13.0	10.2	5.5	5.2	5.5	3.3	(1)
1956	8.9	22.0	23.4	14.8	9.1	6.8	5.6	5.3	2.8	(1)
1957	7.3	18.3	21.3	12.2	8.1	4.7	4.2	4.0	4.3	(1)
1958	10.8	25.4	30.0	18.9	11.1	9.2	4.9	6.2	5.6	(1)
1959	9.4	25.8	29.9	14.9	9.7	7.6	6.1	5.0	2.3	(1)
1960	9.4	25.7	24.5	15.3	9.1	8.6	5.7	4.3	4.1	(1)
1961	11.8	31.1	28.2	19.5	11.1	10.7	7.4	6.3	6.5	(1)
1962	11.0	27.8	31.2	18.2	11.5	8.9	7.1	3.6	3.7	(1)
1963	11.2	40.1	31.9	18.7	11.7	8.2	6.1	4.8	3.6	(1)
1964	10.6	36.5	29.2	18.3	11.2	7.8	6.1	3.8	2.2	(1)
1965	9.2	37.8	27.8	13.7	8.4	7.6	4.4	3.9	3.1	(1)
1966	8.6	34.8	29.2	12.6	8.4	5.0	5.0	3.3	4.0	(1)
1967	9.1	32.0	28.3	13.8	8.7	6.2	4.4	3.4	3.4	(1)
1968	8.3	33.7	26.2	12.3	8.4	5.0	3.2	2.8	2.4	(1)

(1) Rate not shown where base was less than 50,000.

young blacks, they were worse for the young black masses.[41] In addition, when seeking a job for the first time, nonwhites took much longer to find work. In every industry unemployment was higher for nonwhites than for whites having less than eight years of schooling. Furthermore, blacks were not employed at occupational levels comparing with white occupational levels.[42]

Moreover, as Nathan Wright, Jr., wrote in reflecting a black viewpoint:

> It is commonplace that Negroes of great potential are excluded from middle-management and other higher level positions simply on the basis of color. Middle class-oriented Negroes and those trained to high levels of high competence are being summoned to see their plight as being one with that of the Negro poor. They see as the first necessity not training, but immediate opportunity at every level for substantial numbers of competent Negroes, coupled with massive new training opportunities for others after them. The basic empasis of industry and government upon means of overcoming lack of training among the Negro community has come increasingly to be seen as a perhaps unconscious dodge to delay giving immediate and significant opportunity to Negroes who are more than adequately prepared for jobs for which they could apply.
>
> A common joke in the Negro community is that business people are looking for every black super Ph.D. they can find to replace white high school dropouts and others with not much more advanced skill or training. That practice is, obviously, overdrawn but the truth is evident that black people are largely dealt into the current free enterprise system only after the economic needs of non-black people are first substantially fulfilled.[43]

[41] Arthur Ross and Herbert Hill (eds.), *Employment, Race and Poverty* (New York: Harcourt, Brace & World, Inc., 1967), 21–23; Ray Marshall, "The Job Problems of Negroes," in Herbert R. Northrup and Richard L. Rowan, *The Negro and Employment Opportunity: Problems and Practices* (Ann Arbor: The University of Michigan Press, 1965), 5–6; Adrian Sinfield, *The Long-Term Unemployed* (Paris: Organization for Economic Co-operation and Development, 1968), 34; Richard C. Wilcox, "Who Are the Unemployed?," in Joseph J. Becker (ed.), *In Aid of the Unemployed* (Baltimore: The John Hopkins University Press, 1965), 330.

[42] Arthur Pearl, "Education, Employment, and Civil Rights for Youth," in William Kvoraceus, John S. Gibson, and Thomas J. Curtin, *Poverty, Education and Race Relations* (Boston: Allyn and Bacon, 1968), 49. See also Claire C. Lodge, "The Negro Job Situation: Has It Improved?," *Monthly Labor Review*, 82 (January, 1969), 20–28.

[43] Wright, *Black Power and Urban Unrest*, 92. See also Timothy Lionel Jenkins, "A Study of the Federal Effort to End Job Bias: A History, A Status

The Department of Labor published statistics for 1966 concerning whites and nonwhites and their rates of joblessness.

Table 13

WHITE AND NONWHITE UNEMPLOYMENT

Percentage of Persons with work who had specified numbers of weeks and spells of unemployment by color and occupation, 1966.[44]

	5 Weeks or More	15 Weeks or More	27 Weeks or More	2 Spells or More	3 Spells or More
	WHITE				
Total	5.7	2.4	0.8	3.5	1.9
Professional and Technical Workers	2.1	.7	.3	.9	.5
Farmers and Farm Managers	——*	——	——	——	——
Managers, Officials and Proprietors	1.8	.6	.2	.7	.4
Clerical Workers	4.3	1.7	.6	2.1	.9
Sales Workers	4.4	2.1	.9	2.4	1.1
Craftsmen and Foremen	7.8	2.8	.6	5.9	3.7
Operatives	9.2	3.9	1.2	5.7	3.0
Private Household Workers	5.6	2.4	.9	4.3	2.4
Service Workers, exc. private households	6.4	3.0	1.3	3.6	1.9
Farm Laborers and Foremen	6.7	2.9	1.8	4.9	3.3
Nonfarm Laborers	13.9	6.7	2.2	9.6	6.3

Report, and a Prognosis," *Howard Law Journal*, 13 (Winter, 1967), 261; and Lincoln, *Sounds of the Struggle*, 185.

[44] See U.S. Department of Labor, *Manpower Report of the President including a Report on Manpower Requirements, Resources, Utilization and Training 1968* (Washington, D.C.: U.S. Government Printing Office, 1968). See also Henderson and Lidebur, *Economic Disparity*, 6–7, for commentaries about the 1968 report.

Table 14

	5 Weeks or More	15 Weeks or More	27 Weeks or More	2 Spells or More	3 Spells or More
	NONWHITE				
Total	11.7	6.3	2.3	7.8	4.7
Professional and Technical Workers	——	——	——	——	——
Farmers and Farm Managers	——	——	——	——	——
Managers, Officials and Proprietors	——	——	——	——	——
Clerical Workers	7.4	4.8	1.8	4.4	1.7
Sales Workers	——	——	——	——	——
Craftsmen and Foremen	14.5	9.2	3.0	9.5	7.0
Operatives	14.4	6.6	2.5	8.3	4.8
Private Household Workers	7.7	4.5	2.2	6.0	3.9
Service Workers, exc. private households	12.2	6.8	2.5	7.4	4.3
Farm Laborers and Foremen	13.0	6.8	2.6	12.6	8.1
Nonfarm Laborers	19.4	10.3	3.3	14.6	9.2

* Percentage not shown where base was less than 100,000.

The president's manpower report in 1969 summarized developments between 1961–1968. In the report it was noted that overall unemployment among blacks was the lowest since 1953; however, their rate was still twice that of whites and their incomes lagged far behind. Blacks were still under-represented in many of the higher-skilled jobs, and they continued to suffer from job discrimination, poor education, and poor living conditions. During the 1961–1968 period black employment rose by 1.3 million or 20 percent; white employment increased by 15 percent during that time. Among males, black employment rose by 14 percent, while that of white males increased by 8 percent. Among females, the increase was greater for

Over a longer period, 1930–1966, the ratio of male nonwhite to white unemployment rates were shown.

Table 15
WHITE AND NONWHITE MALE UNEMPLOYMENT
Ratio of Nonwhite to White Male Unemployment Ratio By Age[45]

Year	Total 16 Years and Over	14– 15	16– 17	18– 19	20– 24	25– 34	35– 44	45– 54	55– 64	65+
1930	82	——	53	——	86	115	105	91	80	65
1939	114	——	——	79	93	138	135	153	131	——
1948–50	171	119	100	128	168	204	230	188	142	138
1951–53	177	105	86	133	183	259	215	208	148	145
1954–56	216	191	117	128	180	271	283	222	217	171
1957–59	213	182	158	181	184	293	264	212	193	183
1960–62	212	181	164	171	163	266	235	204	204	237
1963–66	209	219	169	188	181	243	250	220	211	201

black females than males; however, that condition was offset by a corresponding increase in white female employment. Thus there was no relative improvement for black women.[46]

Among black teenagers there was an increase of employment of 42 percent between 1961 and 1968. However, since their numbers increased at an even faster rate, their level of joblessness had increased too. In 1967 unemployment among black teenagers was two and a half times that for white teenagers; the ratio had been less than two to one in 1960. If there had not been a number of special federal programs, such as the Neighborhood Youth Corps, the situation might have been even worse for black teenagers.[47]

There was an increase in the number of blacks employed full-time between 1961 and 1968. In 1961, 78 percent of the total, or 4.5 mil-

[45] Alan L. Sorkin, "Education, Migration and Negro Employment," *Social Forces*, 47 (March, 1969), 266.
[46] U.S. Department of Labor, *Manpower Report of the President, Including a Report on Manpower Requirements, Resources, Utilization and Training, 1969* (Washington, D.C.: U.S. Government Printing Office, 1969), 39.
[47] *Ibid.*; and *ibid., 1968*, 60.

lion, blacks worked full-time. By 1968, however, there were 6 million employed or, 83 percent of the total black work force. Among whites, there was no substantial change during that same period.[48]

Between 1961 and 1968 there was a sharp decrease in the number of blacks employed part-time in northern industries. Moreover, the number of blacks employed on short work weeks dropped from 680,000 to 410,000 during this period. In percentage terms this decrease was greater than that for whites; however, the gap between them had not narrowed. Black gains in goods-producing industries and white-collar positions were factors in this movement into full-time positions. During the same period there was a decline in number of blacks engaged in private household work.[49]

Occupational upgrading for blacks occurred between 1961 and 1968. There was an increase of 320,000 blacks in professional and technical positions; 430,000 more in clerical jobs; 220,000 more in craftsman and foreman positions; and 520,000 more in operative jobs. At the same time, there was a decline in lower paid and less secure positions. By 1968 there were some two million blacks in white-collar positions, a rise from 16 percent to 24 percent by 1968 in terms of total black employment. However, blacks represented only 8 percent of the total white-collar employment in 1968; in 1964 the figure had been 4 percent.[50]

In blue-collar occupations black employment gains in 1961–1968 occurred among the relatively high-wage craftsmen and operative categories. The number of black craftsmen increased by more than 50 percent, with the most rapid gains among mechanics, repairmen, metal workers, and construction workers. Blacks had started from a very small base, however. Most of the black's employment gains in blue-collar ranks occurred in operative occupations, which had traditionally employed large numbers of blacks. However, in spite of the blue-collar and white-collar gains, 3.6 million blacks, or 44 percent of all those employed, worked on farms, in service, or as unskilled laborers in 1968. The percentage of whites in these categories was 18 perecent.[51]

The manpower report made special reference to the Kerner Com-

48 *Ibid., 1969*, 39–40.   49 *Ibid.*, 40.
50 *Ibid.*   51 *Ibid.*, 40–41.

mission's study of urban conditions for blacks, particularly that part dealing with the high level of unemployment and the tendency of blacks to hold low-paid and unskilled jobs. If an upgrading occurred in order that their occupational distribution became equal to that of the male labor force as a whole, there would be a 30 percent increase in income among black males. It was estimated that reducing black unemployment to the same level of whites would add less than 10 percent to black income even if the pay scale were the same as for whites. In riot-torn cities, of those blacks surveyed who said they would join in a possible future riot, 43 percent claimed that they had been denied a job because of discrimination and 60 percent believed that blacks were discriminated against in hiring practices. However, among those who did not sympathize with rioting, 21 percent felt that they had not gained positions as a result of discrimination, and only 31 percent thought blacks were discriminated against in hiring practices.[52]

A writer labeled the effort to deal with job discrimination against blacks a failure. He wrote that part of the problem concerned short-comings in legislation and executive orders, as well as failures of those who had the duty to enforce them. However:

> In a larger sense the failure of performance has depended on the limited conception with which the entire nation has approached the task of this second reconstruction in this area, or in a real sense the first real construction, of wage earning opportunity for Negroes. Here-to-fore, it has been assumed that the problem is one which is the result of the discrete evil acts of a few or of less than a majority of bigoted men. Therefore, it seemed reasonable to expect that by righting individual wrongs it would best be possible to undo the whole social evil. Whatever might be cited to support that conception it would still seem to leave unaddressed those myriads of reinforcing business and industrial practices which have, with racial indifference, reinforced the disastrous cycle of economic deterioration which encircles the nonwhite community. These factors have to do not only with the veneration of past practices in the form of seniority but also with the trends in locating new industry within or beyond the suburbs, the ever increasing fashion to require skills beyond those needed for immediate performance, and the constant automation of unskilled and semi-skilled functions out of existence. The national response needed to deal with these developments as they especially affect the nonwhite worker would seem to be

[52] *Ibid.*, 195–96. See also *The Kerner Report.*

in the direction of a new definition of discrimination in terms more relevant than mere race, terms that have to do with arbitrary seniority practices, educational levels, remoteness from job markets, and limited skill capacity, etc.—for which handicaps, it would then be necessary to fashion new legal remedies such as enforced quota hirings, the compulsory establishment of training programs, and the governmental and private requirement for the creation of new jobs each year.[53]

Executive Order 11246 and OFCC

Executive Order 11246, issued by President Johnson on September 24, 1965, placed in the hands of the secretary of labor the responsibility for supervising and coordinating non-discriminatory employment activities of contracting agencies using federal funds. Federal contractors were required to take affirmative action to ensure that applicants were employed and treated during employment without regard to race, color, or national origin.[54] About one third of the national labor force was employed by government contractors and 100,000 facilities were affected by the order. Most of the major industrial employers in the nation were government contractors. On October 5, 1965, the Office of Federal Contract Compliance was established on paper in the office of the secretary of labor. It was not ongoing until 1966.

An equal opportunity clause was required of all contracts and subcontracts, except those under $10,000, those outside the United States, and contracts with state and local governments. Moreover, the director of OFCC could exempt any agency from the nondiscriminatory clause, if he found that "special circumstances in the national interest" required it. In addition, labor unions were not directly covered although they were affected by it. Oddly enough, employers were not required to assure that unions did not discriminate. Although the order did not compel unions to assume any equal opportunity obligation, the secretary of labor was to use his best efforts, e.g., "voluntarism," to encourage unions to cooperate.

Pyle and Morgan voiced fears that this new set up would work less

[53] Jenkins, "A Study of the Federal Effort to End Job Bias: A History, A Status Report, and a Prognosis," 328–29.

[54] See Richard P. Nathan, *Jobs and Civil Rights* (Washington, D.C.: U.S. Government Printing Office, 1969), 86. See also Frederick D. Anderson, "Civil Rights and Fair Employment," *Business Lawyer,* 22 (January, 1967), 513–31.

effectively than the PCEEO could.[55] In evaluating the role of the OFCC in effectuating the order during the Johnson administration, the United States Commission on Civil Rights insisted that the OFCC had failed to carry out its mission and thus confirmed the fears of Pyle and Morgan. The commission gave the following reasons for the failure of the OFCC:

1. Its staff as well as that of the contracting agencies was too small. In 1967 the OFCC had a full-time staff of 28 in Washington, while the contracting agencies employed 228 full-time contract compliance specialists and 40 others, on a part-time basis.[56]

2. OFCC failed to exercise effectively its own role as leader or co-ordinator. It did not even issue regulations for the contracting agencies for two and a half years. During that period there was no explicit definition of what "affirmative" meant in the non-discriminatory clause. This vacuum in turn gave rise to vague and ineffectual standards on the part of the contracting agencies. Moreover, the OFCC did not undertake aggressive action to require that they comply with the order.[57]

3. The reporting system used in evaluating employment practices of government contractors was inadequate. The data were often out of date and were not systematically gathered.[58]

4. The OFCC failed to impose sanctions on noncomplying contractors. Civil rights groups attributed this failure to political considerations, particularly with regard to the construction industry. The first notices of debarment from future contracts were not sent out to any contractors until May 24, 1968. Those affected by the order were: Bethlehem Steel Corporation, Timken Roller Bearing Company, Allen-Bradley, B & P Motor Express, and Pullman Inc. Another company, Hennis Freight Lines, Inc., was debarred in August, 1968, but the company requested a hearing and none was held. No cancellation or termination of contracts occurred at all. Only two contractors had been sued or recommended for suit. The administra-

[55] Pyle and Morgan, "Johnson's Civil Rights Shake-Up," 5–6.

[56] U.S. Commission on Civil Rights, *Federal Civil Rights Enforcement Effort*, 101–102; Nathan, *Jobs and Civil Rights*, 156.

[57] U.S. Commission on Civil Rights, *Federal Civil Rights Enforcement Effort*, 159–61.

[58] *Ibid.*, 161–62.

tive authority to suspend government contractors while hearings were pending had never been used; indeed, only one hearing had been held by a contracting agency since the beginning of the compliance program. Perhaps one of the most striking instances of an agency's priorities was that of the Department of Defense. While the department often canceled defense contracts when there were shortcomings in the quality of production, it never canceled a contract because a firm engaged in unfair hiring practices.[59]

The Civil Rights Commission made an investigation in the San Francisco Bay area in May, 1967. During its hearings the commission delved into the affairs of a large federally funded construction project, the Bay Area Rapid Transit system (BART). It was anticipated that BART would receive eighty million dollars in federal funds and employ a peak of eight thousand workers. The commission found that there were no blacks among the ironworkers, plumbers, and electricians employed on the project.[60]

In April–May, 1968, the Civil Rights Commission held a five-day hearing in Montgomery, Alabama, in order to investigate the economic security of blacks in a predominantly rural sixteen-county area in Alabama. The commission found that blacks had been largely excluded from new industrial jobs; that government contractors in the area had done little to improve conditions for blacks there; and that contractors had instead contributed significantly to patterns of segregation and oppression.[61]

The American Can Company located in Choctaw County, Alabama, had General Services Administration contracts for 1.7 million dollars. The company employed 1,550 persons; only 108 (7 percent) were black and only "several" held skilled positions. Yet, the company drew its employees from an area about 57 percent black in population. The company had a segregated company town at Bellamy, Alabama. Eight of the 123 black-occupied houses had running water and inside toilet facilities; all white-occupied houses had both.

The Alabama Power Company was also a government contractor.

[59] *Ibid.*, 162–65; Nathan, *Jobs and Civil Rights*, 141.

[60] U.S. Commission on Civil Rights, *Federal Civil Rights Enforcement Effort*, 135.

[61] The Alabama findings discussed in the following paragraph are all recorded in *ibid.*, 136–38.

It earned some 2.5 million dollars from a contract with the General Services Administration. The company had 5,394 employees of whom 472 were black, and about three fourths of the blacks held unskilled positions. The company maintained segregated facilities at locations in Birmingham.

The Dan River Mills in Greenville, Alabama, produced uniforms for the armed forces. It had two hundred employees of whom three were black—a watchman, warehouseman, and janitor-truck driver. The restroom facilities at the plant were inside for whites and outside for blacks.

The Allied Paper Company in Jackson, Alabama, was a large GSA contractor. The company officials told the commission that they believed their company was in compliance with federal equal employment requirements. The personnel manager reported that there were about 445 employees of whom 47 were black. None of the blacks held supervisory or clerical positions.

The OFCC finally did issue guidelines in May, 1968. It covered those contractors receiving an excess of $10,000 in federal funds. Employers having over fifty employees had to maintain records showing efforts made to hire blacks.[62]

In the light of these and other episodes, Congressman William Ryan wrote that Executive Order 11246 had been the most far-reaching and least-utilized tool available to the federal government to deal with discrimination in employment:

> If the government took this order seriously, it could open new, formerly denied opportunities to millions of minority Americans. Yet the history of Executive Order 11246 is an inexcusable story of bureaucratic betrayal. Since that order was issued in September, 1965, not one contract has been canceled for non-compliance. Nor has any contract ever been canceled under any earlier orders, dating back to 1941.[63]

Ryan charged that the labor unions were not desegregating. He insisted, however, that "if Executive Order 11246 were implemented, unions would have to choose between admitting minorities as mem-

---

[62] *Ibid.*, 156; Ivor Kovarsky and William Albrecht, *Black Employment, The Impact of Religion, Economic Theory, Politics, and Law* (Ames, Iowa: The Iowa State University Press, 1970), 62–63.

[63] Ryan, "Uncle Sam's Betrayal," 25.

bers and apprentices or losing work on government contracts." [64]

In a report prepared for the Civil Rights Commission, Richard Nathan concluded:

> There is widespread skepticism as to the seriousness of the government's commitment to the Executive Order 11246. The principal problems are not the kind that can be corrected by new procedures, agency reorganizations, or clearer guidelines to compliance agencies. The key is political. Our conclusion is that more determined application of sanctions under Executive Order 11246 is *imperative* if this program is to be effective and respected as such.
>
> This is not to deny that some Federal agencies are pressing hard and getting results. For instance, the OFCC's selected cities campaign for Federal and federally assisted construction has been effective in a number of areas. But the overall implementation of the contract compliance order has been decidedly cautious. [65]

Just prior to the end of the Johnson administration, Herbert Hill, national labor director of the NAACP, gave testimony on December 5, 1968, before the *ad hoc* House of Representatives committee holding hearings on federal contract compliance. He complained that although many government contractors had been found guilty of following discriminatory employment practices, not one government contract had ever been terminated as a result. Hill stated: "The history of the failure of federal contract compliance provides a classic example of the administrative nullification of civil rights laws and executive orders. [66]

Hill argued that blacks had benefited very little from what might have been the most effective weapon to end institutional racism in the nation's major industrial and other business enterprises. Indeed, he insisted:

> The consequences of the failure of federal officials to enforce the anti-discrimination provision in government contracts are far reaching and have broad social implications. Throughout the nation high public officials are calling upon Negroes to observe law and order but the

[64] *Ibid.*, 28.

[65] Nathan, *Jobs and Civil Rights*, 143.

[66] Herbert Hill, *Testimony of Herbert Hill, National Labor Director, National Association for the Advancement of Colored People Before the Ad Hoc Committee Hearings on Federal Contract Compliance, House of Representatives* (Washington, D.C.: U.S. Government Printing Office, December 5, 1968), 1.

irony is not lost upon the Negro citizen of Newark, Detroit, Buffalo, Watts, Cleveland and many other cities where the rates of unemployment and under-employment in the Black ghetto areas have reached crisis proportions. They have noted that they are the same public officials who refuse to enforce the law in protecting the rights of Negroes against discrimination in employment, especially where job discrimination is directly subsidized by federal funds. . . . The failure of the United States Government to enforce civil rights laws and executive orders is directly contributing to the racial crises in the urban centers of our country.[67]

In the face of this utter failure of OFCC and the contracting agencies to enforce the executive order, Hill made the following recommendations:

1. That the OFCC be removed from the Department of Labor to the Justice Department since the Department of Labor was too much the captive of institutions resisting changes in discriminatory practices.

2. That contract compliance agencies regard violations of the executive order as a fundamental breach of contract and that sanctions be rapidly applied.

3. That pre-award contract compliance become a reality.

4. That the executive order be modified so that it would cover labor unions more directly.

5. As a matter of policy, contract compliance agencies should regard a finding of "reasonable cause" by the Equal Employment Opportunity Commission as adequate grounds for contract liability. Most assuredly, if a contract were found to violate Title VII of the Civil Rights Act of 1964 and the Justice Department began a lawsuit after a contractor had failed to comply, the contract ought to be revoked.

6. That the OFCC issue new specifications redefining the meaning of "affirmative action" which contractors were expected to follow.[68]

Title VII and Employment

Title VII of the Civil Rights Act of 1964, in attempting to deal with discriminating in private employment, "made it illegal to hire or discharge any individual, or otherwise to discriminate against any individual with respect to his compensation, terms, conditions, or privileges of employment, because of such individual's race, color, religion, sex, or national origin." [69] Coverage under the title was at

[67] *Ibid.*, 2.
[68] *Ibid.*, 31–33.
[69] Nathan, *Jobs and Civil Rights*, 13.

one and the same time broader and narrower than that of any other state employment practices law or federal labor statute. Unlike the Fair Labor Standards Act no employee was exempted because he was employed in a bonafide administrative, professional, or executive capacity or in any of the many industrial exceptions provided in section 13 of the Fair Labor Standards Act. Moreover, no employee was excluded, as under most state laws, because he was engaged in domestic service or agriculture. However, even when Title VII went fully into effect, it covered only the work force of employers having twenty-five or more employees. Illinois was the only state having a law with such a high cut-off number. However, Alaska law covered employers with one or more persons, while a California statute covered employers with five or more workers.[70]

Title VII went into effect gradually. From July 2, 1965 (when it went into effect), to July 1, 1966, it covered employers of one hundred or more persons; from July 2, 1966, to July 1, 1967, it covered employers of seventy-five or more persons; from July 2, 1967, to July 1, 1968, employers of fifty or more workers; from July 2, 1968, on it covered employers of twenty-five or more persons. One expert expressed the following opinion:

> Congress apparently believed that some limitation on the size of the employer was necessary if enforcement procedures were not to be overwhelmed with complaints. This writer would conjecture that a very significant proportion of the discrimination this Title wishes to prevent occurs in small organizations where both the personal preferences of the employer and the prevailing community influences are likely to have greater impact. Thus employees who may be the most in need of the protections provided in Title VII may be precisely those who have the fewest protections under the Title.[71]

Title VII provided for the creation of the Equal Employment Opportunity Commission for its enforcement. The jurisdiction of the EEOC extended beyond employers, labor unions, and employment

---

[70] Maurice C. Benewitz, "Coverage Under Title VII of the Civil Rights Act," *Labor Law Journal*, 17 (May, 1966), 285. See also Ray Marshall, "Prospects for Equal Employment: Conflicting Portents," *Labor Law Journal*, 88 (June, 1965), 650–53.

[71] Benewitz, "Coverage Under Title VII of the Civil Rights Act," 291. See also Richard Berg, "Title VII: A Three Years View," *Notre Dame Lawyer*, 44 (February, 1969), 311–44, for a somewhat more realistic view.

services. No public employees at any level of government were covered by it, however. In spite of its broad jurisdiction, EEOC had little means at its disposal to enforce Title VII. It might try to eliminate discrimination through persuasion, conference, or conciliation, but it had no means of its own to deal with those who might persist in violating the law.

Of the procedures available to EEOC to eliminate discrimination, the most significant was the one for the handling of a discrimination complaint. Whenever an individual or a member of the EEOC charged that a violation of the law had taken place, the EEOC was to make an investigation. If the EEOC determined that there was reasonable cause that the charge was true, then it was to use the methods of persuasion, conference, or conciliation to resolve the problem. If the act of discrimination occurred in a state having machinery to deal with employment discrimination, then the EEOC had to defer action for sixty days to give the state a chance to settle it. If the EEOC could not resolve the problem, then the complainant could institute a civil suit in federal court. However, if a pattern or practice of discrimination were revealed, then EEOC might recommend that the Justice Department file suit against the perpetrator of the discrimination.[72]

Title VII also empowered the EEOC to use certain affirmative action methods in an effort to reduce discrimination in employment. They included: offering technical assistance to those covered by the title; conducting promotional and educational activities such as hearings and collecting employment data; publication of studies dealing with the job bias; and cooperation of the EEOC with state and local fair employment commissions.[73]

Very early, one legal expert, Michael Sovern, called attention to the weaknesses in Title VII. He wrote:

> Title VII's enforcement machinery has no precise precedent anywhere in the history of fair employment practices legislation. Predecessors can be found, however, for each of its major elements. The Commission with the power to conciliate but not to compel has been tried and regularly found wanting. Letting the complainant sue was one of

[72] U.S. Commission on Civil Rights, *Federal Civil Rights Enforcement Effort*, 267–68; Fleming, "The Federal Executive and Civil Rights," 934–35.
[73] Frances Reisman Cousens, *Public Civil Rights Agencies and Fair Employment: Promise vs. Performance* (New York: Frederick A. Praeger, Publishers, 1969), 12.

the original modes of anti-discrimination law enforcement (criminal prosecution was the other) and it has never worked.

Effective enforcement machinery is indispensable to an effective equal employment opportunity law. The experience of state and local agencies shows that impotence will frequently be met by intransigence, that conciliation works best when compulsion is waiting in the wings.

Whether this model will become reality may well depend on the Attorney General. If he believes vigorous enforcement desirable, if he interprets Title VII to permit him to sue and intervene frequently, and if the courts sustain his interpretation, respondents can be expected to conciliate in droves. But if any of these conditions is not met, the employment title of the Civil Rights Act of 1964 could prove a serious disappointment.[74]

Sovern's comments about Title VII were to prove all too meaningful during the rest of the Johnson administration. Richard Berg, earlier an adviser to Hubert Humphrey during the Senate debates over the Civil Rights Act of 1964, and later deputy general counsel to the EEOC, felt that civil rights forces had suffered a defeat with Title VII. This conclusion was based on two reasons: (1) Congress had rejected hearings and cease-and-desist orders and left enforcement up to the courts; and (2) a series of amendments designed to lessen the fears of conservatives on the scope of the law had been agreed to by the Democratic leaders as a part of the process which stopped the filibuster and secured passage of the measure.[75] Still another writer noted that since the EEOC would have the prestige, power, and financial resources of the national government, "it was regarded by civil rights practitioners as having the potential to make a significant difference in equality of employment opportunity. However, the EEOC was destined to become yet another source of frustration for disadvantaged minorities for some of the reasons that rendered the state and local agencies relatively ineffective and also, for reasons that are unique to the federal establishment."[76]

The same writer, Cousens, insisted that the federal government

[74] Michael I. Sovern, *Legal Restraints in Racial Discrimination in Employment* (New York: Twentieth Century Fund, 1966), 79–80. See also Joseph Parker Witherspoon, *Administrative Implementation of Civil Rights* (Austin: The University of Texas Press, 1968), 13–15.

[75] Alfred W. Blumrosen, *Black Employment and the Law* (New Brunswick, N.J.: Rutgers University Press, 1971), 57.

[76] Cousens, *Public Civil Rights Agencies and Employment*, 12.

had become a huge bureaucracy and could not be physically close to the local communities. Furthermore, she pointed out:

> Programs frequently are placed under the direction of political appointees, who may be entitled to the patronage but lack the commitment and/or competence needed to achieve the desired objective. Staff members are often selected by the same procedures and display the same weaknesses. Those who have both the commitment and the competence may be prevented from working at maximum effectiveness for various reasons and therefore either resign in frustration or become resigned to the bureaucratic posture and cease trying to be effective. These problems may be present in other types of agencies but are particularly restrictive in civil rights programs. There have been numerous instances of a President's urging Congress to enact legislation and then emasculating the law's power by his appointment. One wonders if this is motivated by the dual political advantage of winning favor with proponents by enacting the law while reassuring opponents that the status quo will not be seriously threatened.[77]

Moreover, Cousens argued that the EEOC program had been undermined from the start by including sex discrimination since it diverted attention from the more serious allegations of the racial, ethnic, and religious form. The EEOC was inundated by complaints of sex discrimination. In addition, the president had crippled the EEOC by waiting a full eleven months before appointing the members of the commission. They were compelled to find a staff and be ready to enforce the act in one month. The EEOC was to be plagued throughout the rest of the Johnson administration with a small staff and inadequate funds.[78]

The first chairman of the EEOC, Franklin D. Roosevelt, Jr., was an unfortunate choice. Cousens insisted that his selection was an example of emasculation of a law by appointment. Most persons active in the field of civil rights felt that he was a poor choice and were concerned that he had no record of championing civil rights causes. This was regarded as especially tragic since the EEOC was just starting.[79] A former attorney for the EEOC had this to say about Roosevelt: "When he paid attention to the commission, he was the best chairman of the four men who have held the job. He was knowledgeable,

[77] *Ibid.*, 12–13.
[78] *Ibid.*, 13; Blumrosen, *Black Employment and the Law*, 55; U.S. Commission on Civil Rights, *Federal Civil Rights Enforcement Effort*, 271.
[79] Cousens, *Civil Rights Agencies and Fair Employment*, 13.

sophisticated and had good judgment. But he was forever chasing the will-o'-the-wisp of political office." [80]

An example of what happened to enthusiasts who joined the commission was that of Aileen Hernandez, a black female Democrat from California. She was aggressive and most concerned that the EEOC achieve its social objectives. But she became disenchanted and frustrated by the obstacles in attaining her goal and by the neglect of the commission by President Johnson. Therefore, she resigned in the middle of her term.[81]

After Blumrosen joined the EEOC as an attorney he found that the President's Committee on Equal Employment Opportunity (PCEEO) had collected much data about the racial and ethnic composition of the work force of most of the contractors doing business with the government. There were lists of employers with a low percentage of black employees or none in white- and blue-collar jobs. However, the PCEEO had no program to deal with this situation. As Blumrosen looked through the list his sense of indignation grew. He noted:

> Many of the industrial giants of the nation, many of them members of the much-vaunted Plans for Progress, were either on the zero list or low utilization lists. The abdication of decency and social responsibility, the implication of discriminatory practices of these blue chip organizations, and the shabby failure of even minimum enforcement of the executive order tumbled through my mind. The sense of outrage thus struck high in the establishment. Lyndon Johnson, while Vice-President, had been in charge of the PCEEO. A strengthened PCEEO had been one of the early acts of the Kennedy administration. I learned later that Johnson himself had chosen a soft rather than tough enforcement policy by backing Hobart Taylor, the Executive Vice-Chairman over the more aggressive John Field.[82]

The EEOC published its first annual report in 1966 on job patterns for minorities and women in private industry. It was a survey of forty-three thousand employers with twenty-six million employees. The general conclusion of the EEOC was that "Discrimination in employment is widespread and takes many forms in almost every area, occupational group, and industry; and it has a crushing impact. In short, it is a profound condition, national in scope, and it consti-

[80] Blumrosen, *Black Employment and the Law*, 55.
[81] *Ibid.*, 56. [82] *Ibid.*, 76.

tutes a continuing violation of the American ideal of fair play in the private enterprise system." [83]

The specific findings of EEOC were as follows: [84]

1. With few exceptions, minority group workers were found largely in lower-paying occupations and were under-represented in higher-paying ones.

2. Women were under-represented in the highest-paying occupations; and Negro, Spanish-surnamed, and American Indian women were heavily concentrated in the low-paying service worker and laborer class.

3. The lower educational level of some minority groups was a factor in their lower occupational status, but that accounted for only about one third of the difference between Negro men and majority group men. Conclusion: two thirds had to be attributed to discrimination.

4. A study of forty-one industries—in which educational level was taken as a variable—indicated that relatively few industries offered real equal opportunity throughout the occupational range.

5. Negro and Spanish-surnamed men and women were clustered in the low-paying industries and were under-represented in the highest-paying industries.

6. Only one out of every seven Negroes had a white-collar job; the ratio was three out of every seven for the population as a whole.

7. For Negro males discrimination was greatest in the skilled trades; for Negro women it was greatest in the clerical category.

8. One seventh of all workers were classified as skilled craftsmen; only one fourteenth of all Negroes were so classified.

9. Four fifths of Negroes were employed in semi-skilled and unskilled blue collar jobs; for the population as a whole it was around two fifths.

10. While 28 percent of the Negro women were employed in white-collar jobs, only 7 percent of the Negro men were so em-

[83] *Ibid.*, 103; Equal Employment Opportunity Commission, Equal Employment Report No. 1, *Job Patterns for Minorities and Women in Private Industry, 1966* (3 pts.; Washington, D.C.: U.S. Government Printing Office, 1968), pt. 1, 1.
[84] See Blumrosen, *Black Employment and the Law*, 107; Equal Employment Opportunity Commission, *Patterns for Minorities and Women in Private Industry*, pt. 1, 3–4.

ployed. For the population as a whole: 57 percent of women workers and 37 percent of men workers held white-collar positions.

Some nine thousand complaints about job discrimination were lodged during the first year—about two thirds from blacks.[85] Job discrimination among black males was strongest in those industries which: had a high proportion of black employees; had black and white employees with high average educational levels; had a high proportion of well-paid positions; had a large part of their operations in the South. Another way to look at it was that if a large number of blacks succeeded in getting jobs in industry, relatively few could expect promotions; if large numbers of blacks in an industry had high educational attainments, the bias against them would be stronger; if an industry had many well-paid jobs, a relatively higher proportion would be restricted to majority group employment; and there was generally lower employment status for blacks in the South. A table was provided which showed the employment situation in 1966.[86] See Tables 16 and 17.

In March, 1966, what seemed like a major breakthrough occurred with the Newport News Agreement. The federal government negotiated with the Newport News Shipbuilding and Dry Dock Company to change the pattern of discrimination against black workers. While negotiating, the federal government brought in the EEOC, the Departments of Labor, Justice, Defense, and the Navy to deal with the situation. A written agreement resulted with the initial stage of it taking about one year to go into effect. As a result, over three thousand of the five thousand black workers in the yard were promoted, and some one hundred became or were designated to become supervisors. The EEOC estimated that the agreement brought about one million dollars more into the black community in the Newport News area.[87]

This agreement came under heavy attack from conservatives, es-

[85] Remarks at the Swearing in of Stephen Shulman as Chairman, Equal Employment Opportunity Commission, September 21, 1966, *Public Papers of the Presidents: Lyndon B. Johnson, 1966* (2 books; Washington, D.C.: U.S. Government Printing Office, 1967), II, 1052.

[86] Blumrosen, *Black Employment and the Law*, 107–109. See Equal Employment Opportunity Commission, *Job Patterns for Minorities and Women in Private Industry*, pt. 2.

[87] Blumrosen, *Black Employment and the Law*, 328.

Table 16

PERCENTAGE OF DISTRIBUTION OF ANGLO AND MINORITY GROUP
Employment in the U.S. by Occupation and Sex, 1966.

Occupation	Negro	MALE Oriental	Am Ind.	SSA*	Anglo
Managers, Officials, Proprietors	.97	6.95	6.49	2.54	12.01
Professional Workers	.85	21.50	3.38	2.38	9.03
Technical Workers	1.19	7.84	3.23	2.33	4.83
Sales Workers	1.25	4.80	4.74	3.00	7.35
Clerical Workers	2.70	8.31	3.89	5.14	7.13
Craftsmen	7.90	13.60	19.32	13.92	20.44
Operatives	37.22	14.01	29.94	32.08	25.49
Laborers	29.82	10.91	22.27	26.38	8.37
Service Workers	18.10	12.08	6.73	12.23	5.35
Total No. Employed	1,449,810	84,787	37,857	445,128	15,519,583
% of all Males Employed	8.17	.48	.21	2.51	88.62

* Spanish-surnamed Americans.

Table 17

Occupation	FEMALE				
	Negro	Oriental	Am. Ind.	SSAA*	Anglo
Managers, Officials, Proprietors	.68	1.86	2.19	.80	2.64
Professional Workers	1.55	9.48	2.28	1.10	3.30
Technical Workers	4.55	8.75	3.32	2.53	4.35
Sales Workers	3.95	5.92	12.50	6.92	9.25
Clerical Workers	17.52	41.05	21.67	24.05	40.77
Craftsmen	2.53	2.28	5.13	4.81	2.80
Operatives	24.93	11.39	24.18	29.81	21.67
Laborers	14.14	7.04	11.18	17.61	6.39
Service Workers	30.25	12.23	16.92	12.39	9.10
Total No. Employed	639,677	45,177	17,136	198,551	7,155,656
% of all Females Employed	7.91	.56	.21	2.46	88.86

* Spanish-surnamed Americans.

pecially Senator Fannin of Arizona. Unfortunately, no repeat performance of this kind of governmental coordination occurred down to the end of the Johnson administration. That was tragic as it was a more effective means than with just one agency or with several working at cross purposes. Nevertheless, the United States Commission on Civil Rights charged in 1970 that the Newport News Agreement had never been fully honored, that none of the federal agencies had done anything, and it was still a pending matter.[88] Apparently little progress was made after the first stage had been reached.

In the meantime, the EEOC issued a second report for 1967. Black men and women had increased only slightly their share of private employment in the nation. Black males constituted 8.7 percent of the male work force, while black women had 8.6 percent of all female employment. Black women had less than 1 percent of the upper-level white-collar positions (officials and managers), while 2.4 percent of all women held such posts; 11.2 percent of all men, but only 1.1 percent of black males were officials or managers. Minority men, particularly blacks, were disproportionately overrepresented in laborer, operative, and service jobs and underrepresented in skilled craft occupations. Only 8.4 percent of black males were craftsmen, yet 19.3 percent of all males were craftsmen; 82.7 percent of all black males were in operative, service, or laborer jobs. Minority women tended to hold the lowest-paying jobs. While a little over one third of all women held these positions, 67.1 percent of black women did so. While the earning power of the black male had been 77.4 percent of that of Anglo males in 1966, it was 77.7 percent in 1967. The earning power of black women had been 84.7 percent of Anglo women in 1966; the percentage was 85.8 in 1967.[89]

In the industries survey, total employment was 28,292,395; and black employment was 2,445,775 (8.6 percent). Total white-collar employment was 12,769,334; blacks totaled 383,355 (0.3 percent)

---

[88] See U.S. Commission on Civil Rights, *Federal Civil Rights Enforcement Effort*, 388–89.

[89] Equal Employment Opportunity Commission, Equal Employment Opportunity Report No. 2, *Jobs for Minorities and Women in Private Industry, 1967* (2 pts., Washington, D.C.: U.S. Government Printing Office, n.d.), pt. 1, pp. xxxv–xxxviii.

in this category. There was a total of 13,737,862 blue-collar workers, of whom 1,575,319 (11.5 percent) were black. Finally, there were 485,101 (27.3 percent) black service workers, out of a total of 1,785,187.[90]

In its second annual report the EEOC noted that discrimination was a nationwide problem with some of it overt and much of it more subtle and sweeping. Employers or unions often required recommendations for each new candidates from a current union member or employee while the present work force was all white. Also verbal aptitude tests were often required of jobs requiring few verbal skills which worked a hardship on minority groups.

The greatest number of complaints came from the South, with the mid-Atlantic area second, Great Lakes region third, and the West Coast last. During the first year of the existence of EEOC, 53.1 percent—3,234 out of a total of 6,133 complaints—were based on racial discrimination. During the second year, 4,786 (56.2 percent) out of 8,512 complaints were based on racial discrimination.[91]

During fiscal 1966 EEOC had begun to utilize EEO-1 data on employment patterns in an effort to promote equal job opportunity. These data concerning employment patterns in the North and South Carolina textile industry were the focal point of EEOC's forum in Charlotte, North Carolina, in 1967 and would ultimately be used to evaluate the follow-up activity carried on in that industry by EEOC and cooperating governmental agencies in order to improve minority job participation. The EEOC pointed out that the textile industry was important in the South even though it might not be a growth industry, because it could serve as medium of transition from an agricultural to an industrial economy.[92]

The data revealed that for the 406 textile mills in 73 counties in North and South Carolina, only 8.4 percent of all textile employees and 3.4 percent of all female textile workers were black. However, nonwhites made up 22.3 percent of the population in North Carolina and 30.5 percent in South Carolina. Moreover, 99 percent of the

90 *Ibid.*, xlv.

91 See Equal Employment Opportunity Commission, *Second Annual Report, June, 1967* (Washington, D.C.: U.S. Government Printing Office, 1968), 6.

92 *Ibid.*, 21–22.

black employees were either blue-collar or service employees, and blacks held only 2.3 percent of the craftsman, foreman, and similar jobs. For the 406 establishments the following figures showed total and black employment in the white-collar and skilled categories.[93]

	Total	Negro
Officials and Managers	10,211	11
Professionals	2,338	3
Technicians	2,104	13
Sales Workers	526	0
Office and Clerical	11,784	149
Craftsmen	29,845	690

After the forum was held at Charlotte the EEOC brought together federal and legal agencies with representatives of the textile industry in a follow-up program to open new job opportunities for minorities. By the end of July, 1967, ten South Carolina textile mills had voluntarily, with EEOC assistance, provided 246 new jobs (41 percent of the employees) for blacks with total annual wages expected to be in excess of $750,000.[94]

The Atlanta regional office of EEOC visited one hundred Carolina facilities in 1967 calling on personnel managers and officers to review their hiring, promotion, and job classification procedures. The EEOC officials pointed out some of the subtle forms of discrimination in the lower supervisory levels. The second annual report stated:

> In one city, the president of a textile firm organized a meeting between seven of his plant managers and commission representatives to discuss screening methods for applicants and existing testing procedures to determine if they were job-related and validated or simply a matter of custom. As a result of the one day conference, plant managers agreed to discard the tests and to develop new ones with greater relevance to job openings.[95]

In some instances, EEOC representatives were able to bring company representatives in contact with local minority group organizations in order to improve techniques of recruiting. A manager and personnel manager at one plant agreed that the firm had an "unfavorable" image with minority groups. EEOC technical assistance

[93] *Ibid.*, 22.   [94] *Ibid.*, 23.   [95] *Ibid.*

officers conducted a county-wide recruitment drive resulting in thirty-five black applicants in two weeks; twenty-seven were hired.[96]

In August, 1967, EEOC made public the industry-by-industry statistics for Atlanta, Cleveland, Chicago, Kansas City, Los Angeles, San Francisco, New Orleans, New York City, and Washington, D.C. The major industry lagging in minority employment in all areas was wholesaling. It was closely followed by banking, air travel, printing and publishing and communications. Even where blacks fared well percentage-wise, they largely held the lowest-paid jobs. EEOC chairman Clifford Alexander threatened an increase in lawsuits if action were not taken to correct the situation. As before, though discrimination was widespread, the southern cities were the worst. For example, the following figures on black employment explained the situation:[97]

Atlanta
Negro Share of population 23%
Negro Share of employment 15%

Top 6 industries
Retailing 12.9%
Communications 3.2%
Wholesaling 9.5%
Transport equipment 13.2%
Food products 24.8%
Rail transport 20%

Cleveland
Negro share of population 13%
Negro share of employment 11.2%

Top 6 industries
Transport equipment 12.4%
Primary metals 18.7%
Non-electrical machinery 5.9%
Fabricated metal products 9.8%
Electrical machinery 7.1%
Medical services 31.8%

Chicago
Negro share of population 14%
Negro share of employment 13.5%

Top 6
electrical machinery 13%
retailing 16.9%
non-electrical machinery 7.8%
wholesaling 7.5%
food products 22.1%
fabricated metal products 12.9%

Kansas City
Negro share of population 11%
Negro share of employment 8.9%

Top 6
transport equipment 7.5%
electrical machinery 6.1%
retailing 5.7%
food products 12.9%
wholesaling 3.7%
medical services 26.4%

[96] *Ibid.*, 24.
[97] "Opening the Record on Jobs for Negroes," *Business Week*, August 12, 1967, 128, 130.

Los Angeles	*New York City*
Negro share of population 7.6%	Negro share of population 11.5%
Negro share of employment 6.9%	Negro share of employment 10%
Top 6	Top 6
electrical machinery 5.1%	retailing 12%
transport equipment 6.8%	communications 10.2%
wholesaling 3.4%	banking 6.5%
retailing 7.5%	wholesaling 4.4%
medical services 13.6%	medical services 28.8%
business services 12.6%	insurance carriers 5.6%

The EEOC held special hearings on discrimination in white-collar employment in New York City in January, 1968. The city was considered to be of special importance as it had the largest concentration of white-collar employees in the nation. In general, it was found that Puerto Ricans and blacks had been excluded from employment in many firms and included in very small numbers in others. No black employees were found in 27 percent of the 4,249 reporting units; 43 percent of the companies had no blacks employed at the white-collar level. Several firms were employing blacks at every rung of the ladder. One major corporation reported that one third of its clerical employees were black. However, of one hundred major corporations, representing 16 percent of the GNP, fifty-six did not have a single black manager or official among their twelve thousand officials.[98]

The hearings brought out that there were 15,000 black and Puerto Rican students at the city university and that they constituted 25 percent of the enrollment in metropolitan area community colleges. Furthermore, as of October, 1966, there were 61,170 blacks enrolled in academic and vocational high schools. Chairman Alexander held that these students should be provided with opportunity to obtain a job in accordance with their skills and given a chance to move up the ladder all the way to the top according to merit. The EEOC hoped that the hearings would assist in opening the doors.[99]

Dr. Phyllis Wallace, chief of technical studies, EEOC, explained

[98] See Equal Employment Opportunity Commission, *Hearings on Discrimination in White Collar Employment, New York, N.Y., January 15–18, 1968* (Washington, D.C.: U.S. Government Printing Office, 1968), 1–2.
[99] *Ibid.*, 2.

the general conditions for minority employment in the industries surveyed. Blacks constituted 1.7 percent of officials and managers, 2.7 percent of the professionals, and 3.9 percent of the sales workers. They held 10.7 percent of the technician jobs and 8.8 percent of the clerical positions. In 1966 blacks constituted 18.2 percent of the population of New York City. Black males held 3.1 percent of the white-collar jobs in New York and black females held 9.6 percent of them.[100]

Even if blacks attained white-collar status, Dr. Wallace declared, they did not always have equal salary levels with whites in the same occupational categories. She finished by stating:

> One significant conclusion emerges from the total New York City picture: the wide variation in industry utilization suggests that substantial numbers of qualified and/or qualifiable minorities are available for white collar jobs. Clearly some industries have been more successful in locating and hiring them than others. Locating and hiring minorities may require something beyond the routine application of traditional employment practices, but this does not justify the conclusion that they are not available.[101]

Herbert Hill of the NAACP declared that he did not believe there had been any progress in race relations even though both the city and the state had anti-discrimination laws.[102] He also referred to the failure of the federal executive orders dating back to 1941 to alter the situation. Instead of enforcing these orders:

> A monumental hoax called Plans for Progress was substituted for enforcement. I've been fascinated by the fact that forty-six companies of the one hundred studied by the Commission in this series of investigations had signed the Plans for Progress agreement, some of them going back to 1962, five years ago, and interestingly enough, according to this commission, these forty-six companies lagged behind the others in Negro employment.

Hill pointed out that in spite of all the state and federal executive orders and laws, the tragedy for the black man remained unchanged:

> We are in a period that might best be described as the administrative nullification of these laws and to that degree will Negro citizens and others feel that they cannot operate within the consensual framework and that they will perhaps engage in more dramatic and less disciplined

---

[100] *Ibid.*, 5–7.   [101] *Ibid.*, 8.   [102] *Ibid.*, 491–93.

and less goal-oriented activity if their just and legitimate goals cannot be secured through the orderly procedures of law and administrative agencies.

Hill insisted that, as a result of racism in American society, voluntary plans would not work. He urged that the EEOC not permit the same thing to happen to it that had occurred in other agencies. He asked the federal government to resort to contract cancellation of those companies refusing to comply with non-discriminatory policies. He also requested that the commission:

> send formal notification of the results of these hearings to every Federal, state and municipal agency, the Federal Government, agencies of the New York state government and the New York City agencies, informing them that these corporations have broken the law, that there is a clear violation of the requirement of the law, both Federal, state, and municipal, and that some efforts will be made to cancel contracts.

In conclusion, Hill insisted that:

> We can no longer permit the obscene game of civil rights agencies and anti-discrimination commissions investigating, finding and proving that there is discrimination, while public funds are used to subsidize such discrimination. And I hope that in a long struggle to make administrative civil rights agencies work, this hearing will represent an historic breakthrough in the beginning of a whole new period, in the sense that it will lead to the vigorous withholding of public funds to subsidize racial discrimination.

In commenting on the New York City hearings one journal pointed out that even the New York *Times* was guilty of discrimination since it employed only 3 black reporters out of a total of 200, and only 1 black at the managerial level out of a total of 220. At Eastern Airlines there was only 1 black pilot out of 816, and 42 black flight attendants out of a total of 703. Finally, it was noted: "These figures are staggering when it is realized that there are more than 800,000 white collar workers in the city; that New York is the heartland of international big business; that there is always a shortage of clerical workers, salesmen, and managerial types; that city university alone has 15,500 Negro and Puerto Rican students." [103]

In its third annual report, the EEOC stated that it had taken action on 15,058 complaints of job discrimination in fiscal 1968. This was about 17 percent over the previous year with 74 percent of the

[103] "Jobs and Minorities," *New Republic*, 158 (February 17, 1968), 12.

complaints then slated for additional action. The South continued to have the most complaints and then the industrial states, but California had more than any single state.[104]

An analysis of apprenticeship programs revealed low participation by black and Spanish-surnamed Americans in the three states having the largest programs. Among 23,497 reported apprentices in New York, California, and Michigan only 4 percent were black.[105]

The EEOC met with the thirty-two largest drug firms in Washington, D.C., in October, 1967. It was noted that as of 1966, only 5.3 percent of all the jobs in the drug industry were held by blacks. This was true even including blue-collar positions, of which blacks held 10 percent; at least one half were laborers and service workers. Furthermore, while the average blue-collar workers in the drug industry had a one in four chance of being a craftsman or foreman, the average black blue-collar worker had only one chance in ten. Blacks held only 1.4 percent of the white-collar jobs in the drug industry. On the average one in seven white workers were officials or managers. However, blacks had one chance in thirty-three of holding such a position. Furthermore, blacks held 0.6 percent of salesman positions.[106]

Special efforts were made by the EEOC and the Federal Drug Administration (FDA) after the conference to improve black employment in the drug industry. Twenty-two drug companies reported to EEOC in July, 1968, that 7.4 percent of their new employees were black for the twelve month period ending January, 1967. For the next twelve months 29.4 percent of the new employees were black; and for the six months ending July, 1968, 48.7 percent of the new employees were black. For the very first time, during 1968, new black employees were distributed between white-collar and blue-collar jobs in proportions comparable to new white employees: one half in each category. Gains were especially notable in the sales category which had been traditionally closed to minority groups.[107]

As far as the effects of the New York City hearings were concerned, a number of improvements had been made. One large employer added six thousand new minority employees, many of them black. The news department of a major network had hired nine

[104] Equal Employment Opportunity Commission, *Third Annual Report* (Washington, D.C.: U.S. Government Printing Office, 1969), 4.
[105] *Ibid.*, 28.   [106] *Ibid.*, 22–23.   [107] *Ibid.*, 23.

black desk assistants. One major company whose workforce was almost entirely white collar, had established a system of offering a "bounty" to those staff members who could locate qualified or qualifiable blacks or Spanish-surnamed persons for employment. A union of publishing employees had placed a dozen blacks with five newspapers. Three other firms had hired over one hundred from minority groups—all above the clerical level.[108]

The utilities industry had been a leader in the exclusion of blacks. Blacks held 3.4 percent of all the jobs in the industry. One out of every two utility companies employed no blacks at all, and those hiring blacks largely placed them in lower-paying jobs. Blacks made up 20 percent of the service workers, 25 percent were laborers, and 25 percent were operatives. At the upper levels of employment, blacks represented 0.6 percent of the sales workers; 1.4 percent of the professionals, and 0.2 percent of all the managers and officials. Among all blacks employed with utilities, one in two hundred held managerial positions. Ninety percent of all women were no higher than the clerical category; 3.1 percent of all women were service workers, but 31.2 percent of the black women were in that category.[109]

As a consequence of this situation, in June, 1968, the EEOC and the Federal Power Commission (FPC) met with the presidents of about a hundred privately owned utilities to discuss the situation. The chairmen of the Security and Exchange Commission (SEC) and the Atomic Energy Commission (AEC) attended as observers. The EEOC made follow-up efforts to increase the hiring of blacks.[110]

There was more information about the textile industry in the Carolinas in this report. A task force had been sent by the EEOC to visit a dozen textile plants in the Piedmont area of South Carolina. It was discovered that most of the companies had never made any attempt to make contact with the black community as a source of labor supply. Most of the plants recruited workers from referrals by families of existing employees, a method which served to perpetuate the small number of blacks employed. Furthermore, entry level jobs in the manufacturing process were virtually closed to blacks, and there was practically no progression within and among job categories and departments. In order to remedy the situation the task

[108] *Ibid.*, 26.   [109] *Ibid.*, 27.   [110] *Ibid.*

force undertook efforts to establish a durable rapport with the black community. In addition, the task force made recommendations to alleviate other barriers to equal employment opportunity in the mills. Early in fiscal 1969, after the visitation in the Piedmont area, a check was made of the companies, and it was shown that black employment had increased from 19 to 25 percent. The EEOC began a new plants program in 1967 to establish fair employment practices from the start; 160 new companies were visited in May, 1967; 57 had reported that about one third of their more than five thousand new employees were from minority ranks.[111]

With regard to problems of discrimination in labor unions, the EEOC closely cooperated with the Department of Civil Rights in the AFL-CIO, holding joint conferences and exchanging information. A program called Operation Outreach was established to provide minority groups with opportunities for apprenticeship training leading to well-paid jobs in the building and construction trades. The EEOC coordinated thirty-seven Outreach projects in fiscal 1968. Federal support for the projects was $2.6 million, for the training of 2,025 young people. Also, the EEOC was cooperating with the Department of Labor in On-the-Job Training programs.[112]

In fiscal 1968, there were 6,056 charges recommended for investigation; 2,136 complaints had been deferred for state or local FEPC action, and 2,980 had been returned for more information. The bases of charges of discrimination were as follows: race, 6,650; religion, 291; sex, 2,400; national origin, 721; and unspecified, 1,110. Of the total complaints 59.5 percent were concerned with racial discrimination.[113]

In March, 1969, the EEOC held hearings in Los Angeles dealing with discrimination in employment. Though the hearings took place early in the Nixon administration, most of the conditions found dated back to the Johnson administration. The hearings dealt with some of the major industries: aerospace, motion picture production, radio/television networks, and white-collar employers.[114]

---

[111] *Ibid.*, 28, 29.   [112] *Ibid.*, 29.   [113] *Ibid.*
[114] See Equal Employment Opportunity Commission, *Hearings on Utilization of Minority and Women Workers in Certain Major Industries, Los Angeles, California, March 12–14, 1969* (Washington, D.C.: U.S. Government Printing Office, 1969).

There were seventeen major companies in the aerospace industry which accounted for 85 percent of the aerospace jobs in the area. There was a very low level of participation by minority groups in all except the lowest levels of employment in most of the major companies. Of nearly 20,000 officials and managers in 1968, there were only 177 blacks (0.9%); of nearly 53,000 professionals, only 625 (1.2%) were black; and even in the clerical category, only 1,600 (3.9%) out of 41,000 employees were blacks. In blue-collar jobs with the aerospace industry blacks were only employed at rates above all-industry averages. Table 9 shows the situation in aerospace.[115]

Table 18
RANGE OF 1968 MINORITY EMPLOYMENT AMONG 17 AEROSPACE COMPANIES

	% Mexican-American		% Black	
	Low	High	Low	High
Total Employment	2.2	32.9	1.2	15.0
White Collar	1.1	13.3	0	4.1
Blue Collar	4.3	49.1	2.8	32.0

There were about 19,000 employees in the motion picture industry in Los Angeles, of whom 13,000 were white collar. Based on 1967 statistics the industry was a very poor employer of minorities. It fell below the average rates for all industries in the metropolitan area in almost every occupational category. The percentage of black employment in 1967 was shown as follows:[116]

	SMSA*	Motion Picture Producers	Motion Picture Company Producers (excl. one company)
Total	7.4	4.2	2.1
White Collar	3.4	3.5	0.8
Officials & Managers	1.1	0.6	0.5
Professionals	2.1	7.1	0.5
Technical	4.3	0.4	0.3
Blue Collar	10.3	2.3	1.0
Craftsmen	4.9	1.5	0.4
Operatives	12.5	2.3	0.9

* Standard Metropolitan Statistical Area.
115 *Ibid.*, 350, 351.   116 *Ibid.*, 352–53.

Table 19
RANGES OF BLACK EMPLOYMENT, 1967,
AMONG MAJOR MOVIE COMPANIES [117]

	Percentage Black Low	High
Total Employment	0.6	10.4
White Collar	0.4	13.7
Professionals	0	26.9
Technicians	0	0.9
Blue Collar	0.2	5.5
Craftsmen	0	4.6
Operatives	0	6.0

The EEOC produced statistics on white-collar employment in thirty companies including banks, insurance companies, and savings and loan institutions in Los Angeles. They employed fifty thousand persons, accounting for about 65 percent of the white-collar employment in this industry group. The thirty companies exceeded the average employment of blacks in the metropolitan area only in clerical positions. Indeed ,they showed less than half of the SMSA average in every other white collar category except that of managers. The company utilizing the most black participation in managerial posts employed 2.9 percent. However, twenty-two of the thirty companies employed no black managers or officials. (See Table 20)

Table 20
PERCENTAGE OF BLACK EMPLOYMENT 1967[118]

	SMSA	30 Companies
Officials & Managers	1.1	0.6
Professionals	2.1	0.9
Technicians	4.3	1.6
Sales Workers	3.5	1.5

The data on minority employment at the major radio and television networks was also very low. The EEOC felt that in order to portray the minority groups accurately, the industry needed to employ minority personnel at all levels. While blacks held 7.4 percent of the reported jobs in the Los Angeles metropolitan area in 1967, the networks reported only 2.9 percent black employment, and this

[117] *Ibid.*, 354.   [118] *Ibid.*, 356.

figure had dipped slightly in 1968. Almost 90 percent of the employees were in white-collar occupations, and there was a decrease in the number of blacks between 1967 and 1968.

PERCENTAGE OF BLACKS, 1967 [119]
Occupation

Total White Collar	2.8
Officials & Managers	1.4
Professionals	1.6
Technicians	2.4
Sales Persons	0.0
Office & Personnel	4.8

In 1968 there was only 1 black among 499 officials and managers at the three networks combined. One network reported that 3.6 percent of its technicians were black, while another one could only show 0.9 percent. In 1968, the first network mentioned above reported blacks in 6.1 percent of its clerical jobs, and the second reported 3.6 percent.[120]

While there had been a total of 11,172 charges, of which 6,650 were based on race in fiscal 1968, in fiscal 1969 there was an increase to a total of 17,272 with EEOC jurisdiction established in 14,471, of which 9,562 (67%) were based on race. Most complaints (46 percent) continued to come from the South, and the industrial states (mid-Atlantic and Great Lakes region) had the next highest number with 28 percent of the total. Texas and Louisiana had the most complaints, while California had dropped from first in the previous year to third.[121]

In fiscal 1969 the EEOC recommended an investigation of 9,152 cases and completed the investigation of 5,543 involving 4,993 respondents. About 14 percent of the charges alleged discriminatory practices by unions or employment agencies; the other charges (86 percent) concerned employer practices of discriminatory hiring, discharges, terms of employment, job classification, conditions of employment and compensation.[122]

[119] *Ibid.*, 357.   [120] *Ibid.*, 358.
[121] Equal Employment Opportunity Commission, *Fourth Annual Report* (Washington, D.C.: U.S. Government Printing Office, 1970), 3.
[122] *Ibid.*, 4.

An outstanding case came up on August 12, 1968, when the EEOC found "reasonable cause" in a number of complaints of racial discrimination made against the Ingalls Shipbuilding Corporation, a division of Litton Industries, in Pascagoula, Mississippi. This company was charged with overt discrimination against black workers. This was the largest employer in Mississippi in an area having a black population of more than 20 percent. The findings of the commission demonstrated that the company was engaged in systematic discriminatory employment practices which violated both the Civil Rights Act of 1964 and the executive order dealing with government contracts.[123]

Richard Nathan, who was commissioned to do a study for the United States Commission on Civil Rights, evaluated the performance of the EEOC. He noted that the EEOC had 400 staff members in fiscal 1968 and 570 in fiscal 1969. The budget for the agency had been $3.25 million for fiscal 1966 (first year), $5.2 million in fiscal 1967, and $6.5 million in fiscal 1968. For fiscal 1969, President Johnson requested $11.8 million and received $8.75 million from Congress.[124] For the monumental task at hand, obviously, there was never enough money or staff to do the kind of job possible, even with the little power the commission had.

Through February, 1968, the EEOC reported that 48 percent of the conciliations attempted had been "successful," which meant a signed agreement approved by the commission. Altogether from July, 1965–February, 1968, the EEOC had successfully completed 268 conciliations involving 754 individual complaints. They had been partially successful with 72 conciliations. Nathan held that in terms of its first thirty-two months of operations, the EEOC had scarcely made a dent in relation to the nation's total labor force in improving the job position of minorities.[125]

About one half of the EEOC's racial discrimination caseload had been generated by the NAACP and the Legal Defense Fund. Civil

---

123 Hill, *Testimony Before the Ad Hoc Committee Hearings on Federal Contract Compliance, House of Representatives*, 9.

124 Nathan, *Jobs and Civil Rights*, 18–19; U.S. Commission on Civil Rights, *Federal Civil Rights Enforcement Effort*, 3. See also Equal Employment Opportunity Commission, *Fourth Annual Report*, 30, for slightly lower figures.

125 Nathan, *Jobs and Civil Rights*, 39–40.

rights organizations had been very critical of the commission, while carefully alluding to its inadequate staff, inadequate funds, and lack of authority to issue cease-and-desist orders. Nathan noted that from the point of view of its intended clientele, Title VII's route to justice was long and lumpy.[126]

Nathan also criticized the combination of racial and sex discrimination problems in the same agency. The staff of EEOC was too small to deal with both areas, and thus handling sex discrimination complaints detracted from the ability of the commission to deal with racial discrimination. Furthermore, "In even more basic terms, *wh*ere the commission is successful in opening up jobs for women, this is likely to draw into the labor force white females who do not have employment. This, in turn, may mean that jobs which minorities might otherwise obtain are unavailable." [127]

Nathan believed that the EEOC needed cease-and-desist authority as the litigation process was too slow and cumbersome. He also felt that the commission should not have to defer to states having limited and ineffective FEP agencies. Finally, he argued that the commission needed to develop an enforcement program in which it would take more initiative rather than await complaints. As far as the attorney general was concerned, Nathan charged that there had been no vigorous enforcement under Title VII. Ten cases had been filed by the end of 1967, of which five had been referred by the EEOC. As of December 31, 1967, the EEOC had sent forty cases to the Justice Department, and seventeen of these had been sent before January 1, 1967. The Civil Rights Division (CRD) of the Justice Department had accorded the lowest priority to employment discrimination cases from mid-1965 through 1967. However, in August, 1967, Attorney General Clark announced that he was assigning the highest priority to job discrimination.[128]

The Civil Rights Commission in 1970 announced that through fiscal 1969 (including the early part of the Nixon administration) the EEOC received 40,785 complaints. Of that total, 24,065 (60 percent) complaints had been recommended for investigation. By the end of fiscal 1969, the EEOC had completed its investigation of

126 *Ibid.*, 49–50.
127 *Ibid.*, 55.
128 *Ibid.*, 68, 80–81.

18,119 cases.[129] A backlog of cases had been a problem ever since the commission had begun its operations.

The Civil Rights Commission found also that by the end of fiscal 1969 the EEOC had attempted to conciliate in 3,360 cases. There had been 683 successful conciliations and relief provided for 14,304 charging parties. Termed partially successful were 276 conciliations. However, 2,027 attempts at conciliation had secured no relief at all. The rate of success had decreased over the years. In fiscal 1966, out of 68 conciliations, 56 (82 percent) were successful or partially successful; in fiscal 1967, there were 88 of 174 (51 percent) successful or partially successful cases; it was 306 out of 640 (48 percent) in fiscal 1968; and, in fiscal 1969, the figure was 376 out of 775 (49 percent).[130]

The Civil Rights Commission blamed the EEOC, at least in part, for the failure of the Justice Department to bring more suits. The EEOC had recommended thirty-five suits in fiscal 1967; twenty-six in fiscal 1968, and fifty-one in fiscal 1969. Very few of these recommendations had resulted in suits being filed by the Justice Department.[131]

In evaluating the hearings that had been held in Charlotte, North Carolina, Washington, D.C., New York City, and Los Angeles, the Civil Rights Commission charged that the results had been mixed. Although more jobs had been opened after the hearings in North Carolina, they were noticeably in the lower-paying categories and very few were available in white-collar positions. With regard to the drug companies, there had been some important gains in job opportunities for minorities, but the changes were not uniform. Indeed, some drug firms evidenced a noticeable lack of change. One year after the utilities hearings in Washington, the chairman of the EEOC described the electric utilities as "one of the poorest performers" in the field of minority employment.[132]

The hearings in New York City and Los Angeles[133] had not been followed by any concerted effort to correct the deficiencies there. After the white-collar hearings in New York, information about

[129] U.S. Commission on Civil Rights, *Federal Civil Rights Enforcement Effort*, 316.
[130] *Ibid.*, 327.   [131] *Ibid.*, 341.   [132] *Ibid.*, 364
[133] This hearing occurred early in the Nixon administration.

banking employment had been transmitted to the Treasury Department and ten EEOC charges had been filed. Though a follow-up hearing had been planned after the first one in New York, none was held. Statistics were being gathered, but that was all.[134]

The Johnson administration was very much aware of the weaknesses of the EEOC, especially its lack of power. In 1966, 1967, and 1968 Johnson requested Congress to strengthen the enforcement powers of the commission, chiefly by allowing it to initiate lawsuits, to issue cease-and-desist orders, and to order the hiring or reinstatement of aggrieved employees. All of these efforts failed.[135]

Another mechanism for dealing with job discrimination was that of the so-called Plans for Progress programs. These voluntary programs had originated in 1962 during the Kennedy administration. They called for agreements signed by companies with the President's Committee on Equal Employment Opportunity (PCEEO) whereby the signer pledged to pursue a merit employment policy that was completely non-discriminatory. By the end of 1962, 100 leading corporations had signed such agreements.[136] The PCEEO claimed that by August, 1965, there were 313 companies participating in the program and that over 100,000 blacks and other nonwhites had been hired under the agreements.[137]

Even though the PCEEO was abolished by executive order in 1965, the Plans for Progress program centered in Washington continued with policy made by a 28-member advisory council. The Department of Labor provided part of the funds for this organization. The vice-president and the secretary of labor were participants in the council, but most of the members were industrialists. By the end of 1968 there were some 441 companies which had signed nondiscrimination agreements claiming to employ some one million nonwhite employees. That figure represented a reported 10.4 percent of all their employees. There had been an increase of 72 percent

---

[134] U.S. Commission on Civil Rights, *Federal Civil Rights Enforcement Effort*, 365.

[135] *Congressional Quarterly Almanac 1969* (Washington, D.C.: Congressional Quarterly Inc., 1970), XXV, 413.

[136] Jerome Holland. *Black Opportunity* (New York: Weybright and Talley, 1969), 182. See also Harvey, *Civil Rights During the Kennedy Administration*, 46.

[137] *The Negro Handbook*, 58–59.

in nonwhite employment since 1962 among the member companies compared with a total employment increase of 37 percent. The greatest augmentation in terms of total numbers of nonwhite employment had been in the blue-collar categories. The greatest percentage increase in nonwhite employment, however, was in white-collar positions. Blue-collar employment of nonwhites was up from 12.4 percent of the total in 1962 to 15.4 percent by the end of 1968. The utilization of nonwhites in white-collar jobs was up from 3 percent in 1962 of the total to 4.9 percent of the total. The original one hundred companies were reported to have increased their minority employment by almost 100 percent as against an increase of total employment of less than 27 percent. One writer noted that these figures could have been exaggerated, however, in order to enhance the public image of the program.[138]

However, as noted elsewhere, some of the worst employers of minorities, particularly blacks, were members of the Plans for Progress Program. Herbert Hill, NAACP labor director, painted a much less rosy picture in his testimony before the House *ad hoc* committee on federal contract compliance in December, 1968. All too often the agreements had the dual effect of allowing an employer to proclaim publicly that he was following equal employment opportunity policies, while privately continuing discrimination.[139] Indeed, some companies had even decreased the number of black employees during the period. Many reports of discrimination had been filed against these same companies with the EEOC, and the Department of Justice was preparing to bring suit against some of them. Black workers had filed more than three hundred complaints against United States Steel Corporation alone, and the EEOC had found "reasonable cause" in most instances. The American Can Company in Bellamy, Alabama, which was found to be following discriminatory employment practices by the Civil Rights Commission in 1968, had signed a Plans for Progress agreement.[140]

While the Plans for Progress program was not working well, the administration made still other efforts to set up programs to put

---

[138] Holland, *Black Opportunity*, 185.
[139] Hill, *Testimony Before the Ad Hoc Committee Hearings on Federal Contract Compliance, House of Representatives*, 4.
[140] *Ibid.*, 6–9, 10.

blacks to work and provide training programs. Two analysts, Marshall and Briggs, pointed out that it had been very difficult for blacks to enter apprenticeship programs. Furthermore, apprenticeship training was not quantitatively likely to be a very important means of improving the job situation for blacks. Qualitatively, however, it could make a difference to blacks in some cities, as the only means of entering trades.[141]

For example, the Bureau of Apprenticeship and Training (BAT) administered the requirement of the Department of Labor that stipulated apprentices be selected on a non-discriminatory basis. However, it had been possible to be in compliance and still bar blacks through selection procedures—oral and written tests. Thus, in Atlanta, Georgia, every Joint Apprenticeship Committee claimed to be in compliance, but there were no black apprentices in any major program there.[142]

Title VII covered apprenticeship programs, but very few suits were undertaken and the process was very slow. As Richard Nathan wrote, it was an example of an old agency moving too slowly on the equal opportunity front. BAT administered On-the-Job Training until 1967, and then the program was transferred to the Bureau of Work Training. This change resulted at best in a shift from exclusion to tokenism. Hill of the NAACP charged that BAT had never decertified a single program as long as it operated the program. Although it was federally funded, as of March, 1967, 636 unions that controlled apprenticeship programs had not complied with anti-discrimination regulations.[143]

In general the federal government helped to fund and sponsor a number of manpower programs, the goal of which, at least in part, was to improve employment opportunities for minorities, including blacks.[144]

[141] Ray Marshall and Vernon Briggs, Jr., "Remedies for Discrimination in Apprenticeship Programs," *Industrial Relations*, 6 (May, 1967), 304.
[142] *Ibid.*, 305–306.
[143] Nathan, *Jobs and Civil Rights*, 209; Hill, *Testimony Before the Ad Hoc Committee Hearings on Federal Contract Compliance, House of Representatives*, 26–27.
[144] See Eugene P. Foley, *The Achieving Ghetto* (Washington, D.C.: The National Press, Inc., 1968), 87–88.

Manpower Programs and Equal Opportunity

1. Manpower and Development Training Program (MDTA). The program dated back to the Kennedy administration. The Labor Department furnished funds to state governments to enable state employment services to organize training programs they selected within a state. These programs called for an institutional setting. Nonwhites constituted 24 percent of the trainees in 1963; by 1968, 49 percent out of a total of 140,000 trainees were nonwhite.[145] Blacks tended to be under-represented in training for technical, professional, and skilled tasks; they were generally trained in clerical, sales, or semi-skilled occupations. In the South, black enrollment was particularly high, almost double the rate of the population as a whole.[146] The program was weak as far as job placement was concerned, particularly for blacks. There was little planning to connect the training which blacks received with jobs they might obtain.

2. On the Job Training (OJT). Under this program, the Department of Labor entered into an agreement with private employers, approved their training plans, funded part of training costs directly to employers, and paid partial subsistence to trainees. There were 125,000 apprentices in training in 1968, of whom 10,000 were black. The number of blacks doubled between the spring of 1967 and the end of 1968. In the South, blacks tended to participate at or below their proportion of the population. In spite of the MDT goals, one expert wrote:

> Placement experience of nonwhites is much less positive than the picture of nonwhite enrollments. . . . The same is evident in all but a few states, but the margin between white and nonwhite placement has been widest in the South. There appears to be considerable bias in OJT enrollments and none in institutional enrollments. The reasons for these differences between white and nonwhite enrollments and placements are unclear. Whatever the reasons, the problem is a national one, only slightly more serious in the southern states. Though there is no bias in national MDT policies, there is a national responsibility to iden-

---

145 Nathan, *Jobs and Civil Rights,* 211.
146 Garth L. Mangum, *MDTA. Foundation of Federal Manpower Policy* (Baltimore: The Johns Hopkins University Press, 1968), 97–98.

tify the reasons for the significant racial difference in the program's operation.[147]

3. The Job Corps. The Job Corps was begun in 1964. It was a residential training program conducted in urban and rural areas by the Office of Economic Opportunity (OEO) for out-of-school, out-of-work young men and women between sixteen and twenty-one years of age, and was generally operated by private or public agencies under contract to OEO.

Unfortunately, as it turned out, President Johnson had demanded "success" in the war against poverty. For that reason, written into the program were several mechanisms designed to ensure the likelihood of success. Those applicants who had serious police records or with physical disabilities were denied admission into the program. In addition, Job Corps administrators and screeners allowed only one of seven youths applying into the corps. Problem cases were automatically rejected, and thus the first year the majority of enrollees were white. The program did not ever reach the "hard core" unemployment among black teenagers as it purported to do. One evaluation charged:

> The type of training enrollees receive is another indication of the inadequacy and racism built into the Job Corps. The enrollment in 1967 was 42,032. Approximately half of these young men were sent to the ninety Conservation Centers. (There are only ten urban centers.) Activity at the Conservation Centers consists mostly of menial labor to improve National Forests and other recreation sports (for middle class vacationers). Training in skills useful for urban unemployment is virtually nonexistent. Significantly OEO reports that one-third of the graduates of work-training programs fail to find any work whatever. And of the two-thirds who do find jobs, most must settle for low-paying, unskilled labor. The Job Corps provides in its motivation training only one component of the process of social change. Because it has often failed to take seriously the need for special skills and job openings, the Job Corps is an inauthenic response to the problems of unemployment.[148]

Samuel Yette, former special assistant for civil rights in OEO, called the Job Corps part of a giant pacification program for blacks,

---

147 *Ibid.*, 97–99.
148 Louis L. Knowles and Kenneth Prewitt (eds.), *Institutional Racism in America* (Englewood Cliffs, N.J.: Prentice-Hall, Inc., 1969), 124–25.

one which was at the same time very profitable for many businesses engaged in the program. He stated that large corporations trained about two thirds of the enrollees and only a few private nonprofit organizations were involved such as Alpha Kappa Alpha sorority, the Texas Foundation, Inc., and the National Board of the YWCA. Finally, Yette charged that the OEO never held a compliance review of the training programs to determine if they were following nondiscriminatory policies.[149]

In 1968, 59 percent of the trainees were black. Those who completed this program continued to have trouble finding employment.

4. The Neighborhood Youth Corps (NYC). It was run by the Department of Labor under the poverty program. The NYC provided full- and part-time work experience in a trainee's neighborhood and enabled him to remain at school or improve his employability. This program tended to be highly regarded by civil rights groups, but Richard Nathan felt that other kinds of manpower programs would generally achieve better long-range results.[150]

5. The Adult Basic Education Program. HEW ran this program of basic education for adults. No statistics were available as to the total numbers involved or the number of blacks involved or what it accomplished in placing blacks in jobs.

6. The Work Experience Program. The Welfare Administration of HEW provided funds to states, counties, and local communities for on-the-job training, basic literacy classes, and vocational instruction and counseling.

7. Model Cities Programs. They were supposed to draw a large part of their labor supply from the areas being rebuilt. There were no figures available of black employment down to the end of the Johnson administration.

8. JOBS. This program was intended only for "disadvantaged" workers, and it had centers in fifty of the largest urban centers. The

149 Yette, *The Choice*, 41–44.
150 Nathan *Jobs and Civil Rights*, 211.

workers were hired first and then trained afterwards. The National Association of Businessmen (NAB) was formed to enlist the support of businessmen for the program. The cooperating companies provided jobs and training, while paying for the normal cost of training and recruiting. Additional funds for counseling, remedial education, and prevocational training were provided by the Department of Labor. By early 1969, over 100,000 workers were placed in these programs, and as of November, 1968, 75 percent of the JOBS workers were blacks. The goal of the program was to place 500,000 "disadvantaged" in jobs by June, 1971.[151]

9. United States Employment Service (USES) and state employment services (federally funded). When examining this program for the Civil Rights Commission Nathan charged that many state employment agencies lacked a vigorous equal employment stance and a record which corresponded. Both USES and the state employment officials tended to be pro-employer rather than client-oriented. Though the federal government insisted that state offices of USES serve fair employers only, many state agencies continued to cater to unfair employers at public expense, possibly in violation of the Fifth and Fourteenth Amendments to the United States Constitution.[152]

In summary, though considerable funds and efforts had been expended, relatively little progress was made by blacks on the employment front, considering the magnitude of the problem. Even less progress was made on the housing front. A breakthrough had occurred with the passage of the Civil Rights Act of 1968 and the Supreme Court decision in *Jones* v. *Mayer*. However, the end of the Johnson administration came too soon to determine their impact. In general, it might be said that the president's primary focus was on Vietnam. This left little attention to domestic problems, including housing and employment needed by blacks. The president appeared to give relatively little time even to the enforcement of existing laws and executive orders and seemed unwilling to prod a reluctant bureaucracy.

[151] Kovarsky and Albrecht, *Black Employment*, 124.
[152] Nathan, *Jobs and Civil Rights*, 207; Kovarsky and Albrecht, *Black Employment*, 63.

CHAPTER VI

Voting and Education

VOTING

The major effect of the voting section in the Civil Rights Act of 1964 had been to remove some of the delays in litigation experienced under the acts of 1957 and 1960. The 1964 law provided for a hearing before a three-judge federal district court with a direct appeal to the United States Supreme Court.[1]

The Voting Rights Act of 1965 was more far-reaching. Southern critics expressed outrage since "illiterates" were being permitted to vote. In many parts of the Deep South, especially Mississippi, Alabama, and Louisiana, voting was a right accruing to a white person automatically at the age of maturity. Though there had been some exceptions, "tests and devices" had not been serious obstacles to poorly educated whites when they wanted to register to vote. The effect of the Voting Rights Act of 1965, if fully enforced, would be to permit poorly educated blacks to register in the same way as poorly educated whites.[2]

Shortly before he had signed the 1965 act into law, President Johnson, through a White House aide, contacted John Doar, assistant attorney general in charge of the Civil Rights Division of the Justice Department, to request information as to how many federal examiners should be sent into southern counties. Doar notified the White House that he would recommend that examiners be sent to twenty counties. He based his recommendation on four considerations: (1) data already gathered by the CRD about the twenty counties; (2) the government's capability of sending in federal examiners; (3) areas where both voluntary compliance and open defiance

[1] Thorne McCarty and Russell B. Stevenson, "The Voting Rights Act of 1965: An Evaluation," *Harvard Civil Rights—Civil Liberties Review*, 3 (Spring, 1968), 361.

[2] Donald S. Strong, *Negroes, Ballots, and Judges: National Voting Rights Legislation in the Courts* (University: University of Alabama Press, 1968).

were unlikely; and (4) the rapidity with which the operation could be undertaken. The assistant attorney general also insisted that "we wanted to show that the appointment of examiners was out of the realm of politics . . . we wanted to get voluntary compliance." [3]

Apparently in an effort to placate white southerners, Doar wanted the operations implemented in such a fashion that "people would say that the Department of Justice . . . was fair." He also described the method of selecting counties as "rational and objective." The reason for this approach, Doar claimed, was that his staff had "to justify our means—we worked like hell." His office sent the names of the counties to Attorney General Katzenbach, who in turn "selected ten to fifteen." [4] The question as to how many examiners would be sent and where they would go was to be a source of continual disagreement between the Justice Department and civil rights groups throughout the balance of the Johnson administration.

On August 7, 1965, the Justice Department filed suit in federal court at Jackson, Mississippi, seeking a ruling that those sections of the Mississippi Constitution pertaining to the poll tax be held in violation of the Fourteenth and Fifteenth Amendments to the United States Constitution. A few days later, on August 10, similar suits calling for the abolition of the poll tax were filed against the states of Texas, Alabama, and Virginia.[5] On August 7 literacy tests were suspended in Alabama, South Carolina, Alaska, Georgia, Louisiana, Mississippi, twenty-eight counties in North Carolina, and one county in Arizona.

Moreover, on August 9, 1965, Katzenbach designated nine counties and parishes where federal voting examiners were to be sent. The chairman of the Civil Service Commission, John Macy, sent examiners to the following areas: Dallas (Selma), Hale, Lowndes, and Morengo counties in Alabama; East Carroll, East Feliciana, and Plaquemines parishes in Louisiana; and LeFlore and Madison counties in Mississippi. By August 12 the Justice Department claimed

[3] Wolk, *The Presidency and Black Civil Rights*, 75.

[4] *Ibid.*

[5] Poll taxes in state and local elections were ended by a decision of the United States Supreme Court in *Annie Harper, et al.* v. *Virginia State Board of Elections, et al.* (1966).

that the examiners had already registered 2,881 blacks. This was said to represent 165 percent of the total previous registration of blacks in the areas.[6]

In August, 1965, over the opposition of the Ku Klux Klan, Mississippi voters approved an amendment to the state constitution wiping out some of the traditional barriers to black voting. This amendment removed from the constitution a requirement that a voter had to write an interpretation of any of the 285 sections of the document, write an essay "on duties and obligations of a citizen under a republican form of government," and "be of good moral character." The decision on those three qualifications had been in the hands of the county voter registrar. Moreover, under the leadership of Governor Paul Johnson the legislature passed ten bills which, along with the amendment, were said by state leaders to have placed the state essentially in compliance with the Voting Rights Act of 1965.[7]

In spite of the alleged changes in Mississippi, more federal examiners were sent there as well as to other southern states. On August 19, 1965, two more counties in Alabama were added to the list, two more in Mississippi, and another parish in Louisiana. One month later, on September 24, five additional counties in Mississippi had federal examiners. Another Alabama County joined the list on October 11, 1965. By late October, 1965, twelve counties were added which by then made a total of thirty-two counties having federal examiners. These new areas were the following: Jefferson, Neshoba, Hinds, DeSoto, Holmes, and Walthall counties in Mississippi; Antauga, Elmore, and Greene counties in Alabama; Clarenda and Dorchester counties in South Carolina; and West Feliciana Parish in Louisiana.

No more counties or parishes were added in 1965. By the end of the year the Justice Department claimed that local officials had added about 160,000 new black voters in these five states—Alabama, South Carolina, Mississippi, Georgia, and Louisiana. Moreover, federal examiners had registered 79,593. Therefore, there had

---

[6] "Voting Rights," *Congressional Quarterly Weekly Report,* 23 (August 13, 1965), 1595.

[7] New York *Times,* August 18, 1965, p. 21.

been a 40 percent increase in black registration since the enactment of the Voting Rights Act of 1965.[8]

Despite these gains, the Commission on Civil Rights took note of the violent acts committed against persons in Mississippi who were engaged in civil rights activities, including voter registration drives. These acts were largely committed against blacks, and Mississippi's law enforcement institutions and officials were criticized for their failure to protect persons engaged in exercising civil rights. Other state officials in the South—Alabama, Florida, and Georgia—were similarly faulted. Indeed, the said officials themselves stood accused of abusing those engaged in civil rights activities. The commission called for a strong federal presence in these regions in order to prevent continued violation of federal rights. Moreover, it was recommended that more blacks be appointed by the attorney general to law enforcement agencies and courthouse staffs "and that state and municipal governments be made liable to persons found to be victims of police misconduct." Finally, the commission urged the enactment of a new federal criminal law to protect persons engaged in civil rights activities.[9] This report and other information would lead eventually to the section of the Civil Rights Act of 1968 dealing with additional federal protection of such rights.

The Commission on Civil Rights also made a study of the voting rights situation after the first few months the act had been in existence. It noted that there were still many abuses and efforts to evade the act which prevented blacks from registering and voting. At the end of the report the commissioners made some recommendations. First, they recommended that federal examiners be appointed in all remaining areas covered by the act in which applicants were being turned away by reason of inadequacy of state registration facilities, or in which applicants were disqualified for failure to meet literacy requirements. Second, the Civil Service Commission should initiate, within the counties where examiners were placed, programs de-

[8] *Congressional Quarterly Almanac,* XXI (1965), 564.

[9] U.S. Commission on Civil Rights, *Law Enforcement. A Report on the Equal Protection of the Law in the South* (Washington, D.C.: U.S. Government Printing Office, 1965), 174–77; *The Negro Handbook* (Chicago: Johnson Publishing Company, 1966), 59. See also "Findings in Commission's Equal Protection Report," *Congressional Quarterly Weekly Report,* 23 (November 23, 1965), 2362–65.

signed to inform unregistered persons about qualifications required for registration, and times and places at which they might be enrolled. Third, new affirmative programs should be established to encourage persons to register to vote by disseminating information about the right to vote and requirements of registration, and by education and training to further a better understanding of citizenship and the importance of voting. Fourth, the commissioners recommended that federal officials be effectively prepared for the possible invoking of all enforcement provisions under the Voting Rights Act, including the announcement of intent to apply sanctions and the appointment of poll watchers.[10]

In November, 1965, a panel of three judges in Montgomery, Alabama, ruled that the Voting Rights Act of 1965 had to be preserved to be constitutional, and that state court injunctions against the enrollment of federally registered voters in six Alabama counties were "null and void, and of no effect." [11] In Mississippi and Louisiana state courts barred state officials from enrolling federally certified voters. In 1966 efforts to impede the enforcement of the Voting Rights Act of 1965 were dealt a legal blow as a result of the Supreme Court's decision in *South Carolina* v. *Nicholas deB. Katzenbach* (383 U.S. 301, 1966).

In the meantime, on November 30, 1965, a meeting occurred between a number of civil rights leaders and cabinet members in the federal government. Among other things, the civil rights spokesmen were concerned about the "administrative repeal" of the Voting Rights Act of 1965 as a result of lack of enforcement. After the conference Roy Wilkins of the NAACP said that the parties had agreed that the Justice Department would concentrate on enforcement and "private civil rights agencies would work in areas where registration was low and stimulate activity." [12]

In January, 1966, Wilkins in a press interview stated that civil rights leaders were still not satisfied with federal enforcement of civil rights laws. He insisted that blacks still lacked access to the ballot box in the South. On Lincoln's birthday, February 12, 1966, Presi-

---

[10] U.S. Commission on Civil Rights, *The Voting Rights Act . . . the First Few Months* (Washington, D.C.: U.S. Government Printing Office, 1965), 4.
[11] New York *Times*, November 24, 1965, p. 1.
[12] *The Negro Handbook*, 60.

dent Johnson appeared more optimistic. He stated that since the 1965 act had become law federal examiners had been sent to thirty-seven southern counties and had registered 100,000 new black voters. He also said: "Even more encouraging, however, is the voluntary compliance by local voting officials, who had registered nearly 200,000 Negro citizens in those same Southern states in the same period of time." [13]

On February 28, 1966, Attorney General Katzenbach spoke in Atlanta, Georgia, at the opening meeting of the new South-wide Voter Education Project. He declared that he expected more than one half of the eligible blacks to vote in the 1966 elections. Katzenbach insisted that it was the major responsibility of private organizations rather than the federal government to make sure that more blacks were registered. His speech drew only mild applause, and Dr. Martin Luther King, Jr., and John Lewis lodged complaints that not enough federal examiners had been sent to the South.[14]

The Southern Regional Council published voter registration figures (black and white) for the South in the summer of 1966.[15] These figures are shown in Table 21.

Regionally, the difference between black and white voter statistics was significant in 1966. There were more black voters only in Texas, and the reason was that Mexican-Americans (with low registration) were included with whites in the figures. The gap between black and white registration figures was greatest in the Deep South states of South Carolina, Louisiana, Mississippi, Georgia, and Alabama.

A dramatic incident connected with voting occurred in Mississippi in June, 1966. One May 31, 1966, James Meredith announced that he would march from Memphis, Tennessee, to Jackson, Mississippi, in order "to encourage the 450,000 unregistered Negroes in Mississippi to go to the polls and register." At the same time, he stated that he wanted to "point up and to challenge the all-pervasive and overriding fear that dominates the day-to-day life of the Negro in the United States—especially in the South and particularly in Mis-

[13] New York *Times,* January 16, 1966, IV, p. 5; *ibid.,* February 13, 1966, p. 1.
[14] *Ibid.,* March 1, 1966, p. 43.
[15] *The Negro Almanac* (New York: Bellwhether Publishing Co., Inc., 1967), 447.

Table 21

NEGRO VOTER REGISTRATION BY STATE, SUMMER, 1966

State	Negro Voting Age Population	Estimated Number Registered	Percentage of Age-Eligible Registered
Ala.	481,320	248,000	51.5
Ark.	192,672	105,000	54.5
Fla.	470,306	288,000	61.3
Ga.	612,910	272,000	44.4
La.	514,589	243,000	47.2
Miss.	422,256	139,000	32.9
N.C.	550,929	280,000	50.8
S.C.	373,104	187,000	50.4
Tenn.	313,873	225,000	71.7
Tex.	649,412	400,000	61.6
Va.	421,051	205,000	48.6
Totals	5,000,422	2,592,000	51.9

WHITE REGISTRATION BY STATE, SUMMER, 1966

State	White Voting Age Population	Estimated Number Registered	Percentage of Age-Eligible Registered
Ala.	1,353,038	1,176,000	86.9
Ark.	850,643	583,000	68.5
Fla.	2,617,438	2,092,000	79.9
Ga.	1,797,062	1,340,000	74.6
La.	1,289,216	1,072,000	83.1
Miss.	788,266	472,000	62.9
N.C.	2,005,955	1,654,000	82.5
S.C.	895,147	715,000	79.9
Tenn.	1,779,018	1,375,000	77.3
Tex.	4,884,769	2,600,000	53.3
Va.	1,812,154	1,159,000	64.0
Totals	20,032,706	14,237,000	71.0

sissippi." [16] On June 6, just south of Hernando, Mississippi, Meredith was shot and wounded while walking along Highway 51. He had begun his march from Memphis in order to urge blacks to register and vote. He suffered from buckshot wounds in the back of his head, back, and leg, but recovered within a short time. The gun had been fired by Aubrey Jones Norvell who was arrested. Dr. Martin Luther King, Jr., and other civil rights leaders completed Meredith's march to Jackson.[17]

In a special message to Congress on February 15, 1967, President Johnson claimed that black voter registration in the five Deep South states had increased from 715,099 to 1,174,569 since the passage of the Voting Rights Act of 1965. He said that federal officials had registered 125,000 black voters in forty-seven counties.[18]

By early June, 1967, federal examiners had been sent to sixty southern counties. They were sent as follows: thirteen to Alabama, four to Georgia, nine to Louisiana, thirty-two to Mississippi, and two to South Carolina. However, the Justice Department refused to send any examiners to Sunflower County, home of Senator James Eastland of Mississippi. Only a very small percentage of blacks were registered there, although if many more had been they could have controlled the politics of the county.[19]

In the spring of 1968 the Commission on Civil Rights issued a report on an investigation of the participation by blacks in the electoral and political processes in ten southern states since the enactment of the Voting Rights Act of 1965. The findings were summarized as follows:[20]

1. Black voter registration and political participation in the Deep South had increased substantially since 1965. Black voter registra-

[16] New York *Times*, June 1, 1966, p. 24.

[17] "Civil Rights Leader Shot," *Congressional Quarterly Weekly Report*, 24 (June 10, 1966), 1242.

[18] Special Message to the Congress on Equal Justice, Rebruary 14, 1967, *Public Papers of the Presidents. Lyndon B. Johnson, 1967* (2 books; Washington, D.C.: U.S. Government Printing Office, 1968), I, 184.

[19] Robert Sherrill, *The Accidental President* (New York: Grossman Publishers, 1967), 195.

[20] U.S. Commission on Civil Rights, *Political Participation* (Washington, D.C.: U.S. Government Printing Office, 1968), 171–79. See also Monroe Berger, *Equality by Statute. The Revolution in Civil Rights* (Garden City, N.Y.: Doubleday & Co., 1967), 48.

tion had more than doubled, which was a little over one half of those eligible. In 1966 and 1967 hundreds of thousands of blacks voted for the first time. Blacks had been appointed to serve as polling officials and poll watchers in areas where resistance to the exercise of the vote by blacks had been exceptionally strong. Over 1,000 blacks had run for election to state and local government posts; about 250 had been elected to public office and a number of others had been selected for party posts.

2. Black voter registration and political participation still lagged behind in some localities. There were still 185 counties in six southern states covered in whole or in part by the Voting Rights Act of 1965 which still had not been designated for federal examiners by the attorney general. Despite the progress made in many areas and the lack of "massive resistance" since 1965, black candidates and voters had experienced hostility on the part of whites. They had also encountered many types of discrimination practiced by state and local governments, political parties, and public and party officials, primarily in areas of heavy black population in the Deep South and in isolated cases in states outside the Deep South.

3. The commission charged that political party committees and state legislatures in Mississippi and Alabama had adopted rules or laws since the act of 1965 became law which had either the purpose or effect of diluting the ballots of the new black voters. Among the charges made were: switching to at-large elections where black voting strength was concentrated in certain election districts; facilitating the consolidation of predominantly black and predominantly white counties; and redrawing the boundaries of legislative districts in order to divide heavy concentrations of black voters. In other southern states, full slate voting laws passed before the 1965 act had the effect of requiring blacks, where a full slate of their own candidates were not running for office, to dilute their votes by voting for competing candidates too.

4. Since the act of 1965 had become law it was charged that the Alabama and Mississippi legislatures had passed measures designed to prevent or having the effect of preventing blacks from either becoming candidates or obtaining office. In Georgia, Mississippi, Alabama, and Arkansas party and public officials as well as private corporations had engaged in acts or issued rules with the same effect

or purpose. Some of these actions were: (a) abolishing the office sought; (b) extending the term of the white incumbent; (c) withholding important information from black candidates; (d) making former elective offices appointive; (e) raising filing fees; (f) otherwise increasing the requirements for being on the ballot; (g) imposing barriers to the assumption of office by successful black candidates; and (h) withholding certification of the nominating petitions of black candidates.

5. It was charged that election officials had discriminated against black voters in some parts of the South by: (a) omitting names of registered blacks from official voter lists; (b) harassing black voters; (c) failing to provide adequate polling places in areas with increased black voter registration; and (d) failing to permit or provide adequate assistance to illiterate black voters.

6. The commission charged that in 1966 and 1967 there were instances of exclusion and interference with black poll watchers in parts of Mississippi, South Carolina, Georgia, and Alabama.

7. Voting fraud was charged against officials in a few counties of the Deep South in efforts to prevent black candidates from obtaining offices.

8. It was held that there was widespread discrimination by party and public officials in the selection of polling officials in South Caroline, Mississippi, Georgia, and Alabama. Such discrimination had been reduced in Mississippi in 1967, but in some Mississippi counties even though black party officials were selected, they were prevented from assisting illiterate black voters.

9. The commission charged that intimidation had occurred in some areas of Louisiana, Mississippi, Alabama, Georgia, South Carolina, and Virginia in 1966 and 1967. Black candidates, their poll watchers, and their campaign workers, black voters, and persons active in urging blacks to register and vote, were subjected to harassment and intimidation.

10. It was charged that blacks who were economically dependent, especially sharecroppers and farmers, were deterred from voting at all, voting for candidates of their choice, or from running for office. Moreover, black school teachers were sometimes afraid of being dismissed if they decided to run for office.

11. It was found that comparatively few blacks held party office

in either political party at the county or state level, and none in most instances. It was held that:

> The Mississippi statute requiring adherence to party principles coupled with provisions of the Mississippi Republican and Democratic platforms endorsing segregation of the races, requires Mississippi Negroes to endose racial segregation as a condition of voting or running as candidates in primary elections. Although not legally enforceable, the test is a deterrent to Negro participation in party elections and activities.

In conclusion, the commission noted that while progress had been made, there was still a long road to travel before blacks were fully enfranchised. It proposed that the following steps be taken: (1) that existing laws be broadened and their enforcement strengthened; (2) that national political parties take measures to eliminate discrimination at the state and local levels of party organization; (3) that the federal government aid in the elimination of illiteracy and in providing information and assistance which would enable citizens to exercise fully the rights and duties of citizenship; and (4) that the federal government take action to overcome the problems of economic dependency since citizens could never be free to exercise their political rights if they had to fear economic reprisals for their political activities.

Some of the same findings were made by McCarty and Stevenson in their study of effects of the Voting Rights Act of 1965.[21] They contended that while federal examiners had helped some in the South, black registration generally increased when the examiners were reinforced by voter registration drives.

The following statistics told part of the story:

State	Counties With Examiners and Drives	Counties With Examiners	Counties With Drives	Neither
Ala.	69.5%	63.7%	57.6%	45.2%
Miss.	51.7%	41.2%	34.9%	24.2%
S.C.	67.0%	71.4%	51.6%	48.8%

McCarty and Stevenson also claimed that it was some small progress that George Wallace had used the term Negro in the 1966 elec-

[21] See McCarty and Stevenson, "The Voting Rights Act of 1965: An Evaluation," 357–411.

tion campaign. Furthermore, the state Democratic party in Alabama had struck "white supremacy" from its slogan. More courtesy was being shown blacks, streets were being paved in the black communities, driveways were being graveled, and culverts were being installed. Like the United States Commission on Civil Rights, McCarty and Stevenson urged that more federal examiners be sent into more counties. They recommended that the offices of the examiners be set up in the black communities, since blacks were often reluctant to enter "white man's territory."

In evaluating the role of election observers from the civil service, McCarty and Stevenson charged there had been dubious results as almost all were white and most of them were southerners. Though a screening process was supposed to have taken place, they charged that some observers gave the appearance of being overt racists. For instance, it was said that in Mississippi some observers told "nigger jokes" and made derogatory remarks about blacks in the presence of black voters. Even their presence—being white—caused fear among blacks to vote against the "white man's candidate." Although the observers may have served as a deterrent, they were generally of no benefit in making elections fairer. It was suggested that federal observers have a name tag, and that in the future they come from the Civil Rights Commission or the Justice Department and that there be more blacks and more from the North. Federal observers should also assist illiterates rather than state officials.

As for litigation, Stevenson and McCarty charged that the Justice Department seemed apathetic in view of the widespread violations of the act of 1965. The department had been involved in twenty-eight cases involving the law, none of which were affirmative actions to redress election fraud or to enjoin intimidation. In some instance, the department had intervened only after private litigants had brought suit. No suits had been brought by the department under the punitive sections of the Voting Rights Act of 1965.

In addition, McCarty and Stevenson charged that although the need had been great, only recently had Sunflower County in Mississippi been declared eligible for federal registrars. They also pointed out that the Mississippi legislature continued to place obstacles in the paths of black voters.

Evidently black voters faced many obstacles in the South. Although completely accurate figures were not available, the Southern Regional Council published voter registration statistics in the summer of 1968 (See Table 22).

While an increase in the number of black voters and black elected officials had occurred in the South, there was still much remaining to be done. The administration had not pushed enforcement of the Voting Rights Act of 1965 as much as it might have. The president had succeeded in obtaining the enactment of the law, but he seemed to fail when it came to full implementation. The Justice Department, including the attorneys general and the heads of the CRD, never saw it as their task to "directly go out and get the voters to the polls." [23] Though some progress had been made, "In 1968 there were still many Black Belt counties without a single Negro officeholder—a witness to racial prejudice. Indeed, as recently as 1968, there were still five Deep South counties which had yet to register the first black. There were 65 other counties in which less than a third of the voting age blacks had been registered." [24]

Even so, acquisition of the vote and electing some black officials, while important, would not magically transform conditions for blacks in the South. They were trapped in too many ways for the vote and some officeholders alone to provide all the answers. [25]

BLACKS AND THE DESEGREGATION
OF PUBLIC ELEMENTARY AND SECONDARY EDUCATION

Although the United States Supreme Court had declared segregated schools unconstitutional in *Brown* I in 1954, means of delay had been provided in *Brown* II by leaving the federal district court with the determination of the rate of speed with which desegregation would proceed. In the South, this situation meant very little desegregation by the time Lyndon Johnson assumed the presidency, since most federal judges in the region were products of the dominant culture there and adherents to its basic tenets, e.g., segregation of

[23] For a good discussion of the views of Katzenbach, Clark, Doar, and Pollak, see Wolk, *The Presidency and Black Civil Rights*, 76–84.

[24] Harrell R. Rodgers and Charles S. Bullock III, *Law and Social Change: Civil Rights Laws and Their Consequences*, (New York: McGraw-Hill Book Co., 1972), 43.

[25] See Keech, *The Impact of Negro Voting*, for a good discussion on the limitations of the ballot.

Table 22
NEGRO-WHITE VOTER REGISTRATION IN THE SOUTH
Spring-Summer, 1968 [22]

State	White Voting Age Pop.	Negro Voting Age Pop.	White Reg.	Negro Reg.	Percent White Reg.	Percent Negro Reg.
Ala.	1,353,058	481,320	1,117,000*	273,000*	82.5	56.7
Ark.	850,643	192,626	640,000	130,000	75.2	67.5
Fla.	2,617,438	470,261	2,195,000	292,000	83.8	62.1
Ga.	1,797,062	612,910	1,524,000	344,000	84.7	56.1
La.	1,289,216	514,589	1,133,000	305,000	87.9	59.3
Miss.	748,266	422,256	691,000	251,000	92.4	59.4
N.C.	2,005,955	560,929	2,579,000	305,000	78.7	55.3
S.C.	895,147	371,873	587,000	189,000	65.5	50.8
Tenn.	1,779,018	313,873	1,448,000	228,000	81.3	72.8
Tex.	4,884,765	649,512	3,532,000	548,000	72.3	83.1
Va.	1,876,167	436,720	1,256,000	255,000	67.0	58.4
Totals	20,096,735	5,016,100	15,702,000	3,112,000	78.1	62.0

Miss., Ala., and Ga. have large numbers not registered by race—divided on the basis of V.E.P. estimates, numbers are cumulative and do not reflect names removed by purging. Likely to make some inflation of figures, particularly with white voter registration.
* Reflects estimates. More recent than county-by-county table.
Note: Voting age population figures are from the 1960 census.

[22] Voter Education Project, *Voter Registration in the South* (Atlanta: Southern Regional Council, 1968), n.p.

schools. Most southern whites were very wary of the close kind of relationship with blacks called for with desegregation of the schools. They were fearful above all, however unrealistically, of any prolonged physical contact which might lead to miscegenation.[26] Many whites, of course, had never thought much about the fact that "race-mixing" on the white man's terms had gone on for a long time in the South.

In the 1963–1964 school year, when Johnson became the president, only about 9.3 percent of the black public school pupils in the South and border region were attending elementary and secondary schools with whites. The eleven former confederate states had but 1.06 percent of the black public school enrollment in biracial schools, 30,798 out of a total of 2,901,671. Blacks made up 26.8 percent of the total public school enrollment in the South. While 33.5 percent of the black children attended schools in desegregated districts, only 1.06 percent attended schools with whites. In the six border states (Missouri, Maryland, West Virginia, Kentucky, Delaware, and Oklahoma) and Washington, D.C., 14.6 percent of the enrollment was black and 96.6 percent of the blacks were in desegregated districts, but only 56.2 percent of the black pupils attended public schools with whites. The South had 85 percent of the total black enrollment in the South and border region, but of the 318,038 blacks attending desegregated schools, only 9.7 percent were in the South.

In one state, Mississippi, there was not a single black student attending school with whites.[27] A person who participated in civil rights activities in the sixties noted that the Supreme Court's decision in 1954 had not altered anything in Mississippi, and that "the only response to 'separate but equal' was the hasty building of Negro schools in some communities where no schools had existed at all."[28]

---

[26] Rodgers and Bullock, *Law and Social Change*, 64. It should be noted that this fear has abated very little if at all. This form of racism is not confined to the South, however.

[27] See "Only Nine Percent of Southern, Border Negroes in School with Whites," *Congressional Quarterly Weekly Report*, 22 (January 3, 1964), 2. See also "Revised Figures Show More Negroes in Biracial Schools," *Southern School News*, 10 (January, 1964), pt. 1, 14.

[28] Tracy Sugarman, *Stranger at the Gates: Summer in Mississippi* (New York: Hill and Wang, 1966), 14.

A minor breakthrough occurred in Mississippi on July 29, 1964, when a federal district judge, Sidney Mize, approved a plan for desegregation of the first grade in the fall for the public schools of Jackson, Biloxi, and Leake Counties. After that first school year, at least one grade a year was to be desegregated. The NAACP challenged the plan as being vague and below the standards of the United States Supreme Court. Judge Mize did not accept the NAACP position, but allowed for a reconsideration of the plan by continuing the hearing on the NAACP's motion until January, 1965.[29]

In the meantime, the Civil Rights Act of 1964 was enacted into law, but HEW, given the major responsibility for dealing with schools, claimed that it needed time to set up guidelines and enforcement machinery. HEW enforcement efforts did not really get under way until the 1965–1966 school year. During the fall of 1964 the number of black children attending public schools with whites almost doubled. The percentage was still only 2.25 percent in the South. For the region (South, border states, and Washington, D.C.) there was an increase from 9.2 percent in May, 1964, to 10.8 percent in the fall of 1964. Even Mississippi, which had no black students attending schools with whites in 1963–1964, had 58 in 1964–1965.[30]

On April 9, 1965, HEW announced that the public schools should plan to eliminate all segregation by the fall of 1967 and were to make "a substantial good faith start" toward desegregation in the fall of 1965. The schools were to comply with this policy in order to continue receiving federal financial assistance.[31] The guidelines that were issued set up minimum standards a school had to follow in order to receive federal funds. The standards were as follows: a school system desegregating for the first time had to show a good faith start by desegregating at least four grades and possibly five in 1965; all twelve grades had to be desegregated by the fall of 1967; faculties had to be desegregated but not necessarily during the first

[29] New York *Times*, July 30, 1964, p. 12.

[30] "Negroes Double Enrollment with Whites," *Southern School News*, 11 (December, 1964), 1; *Congressional Quarterly Almanac*, XXI (1965), 569.

[31] "HEW Calls for Full Desegregation by 1967," *Southern School News*, 11 (May, 1965), 1.

year; and school districts were permitted to desegregate in a variety of ways, which included the use of attendance zones and freedom of choice plans.[32] The grades desegregated had to include the first and any other lower grade, the first and last year of the high school grades, and the lowest grade of junior high where schools were so organized.[33] Furthermore, a school could qualify for federal funds if it did at least one of the following: (1) filed an assurance of compliance; (2) was under a federal court order to desegregate and promised to obey; or (3) submitted an acceptable plan to the commissioner of education.

The new guidelines were very conservative at best. Jack Greenberg of the NAACP Legal Defense and Education Fund described them as very weak. He felt that the southern school system had been led to believe that "they can drag their feet and nobody will make them desegregate." He was especially critical of "freedom of choice" which he insisted meant the maintenance of the status quo. Greenberg explained his view by insisting that: "A Negro family in rural Mississippi or Alabama will have no freedom of choice. The South knows just what intimidation and habit will do. Freedom of choice means the status quo." [34]

Even the weak guidelines, however, brought complaints from the South. On May 18, 1965, eight southern governors met with their states' congressional delegations in an attempt to bring about a relaxation of Title VI criteria pertaining to the possible withdrawal of federal funds. They charged that the Office of Education had gone beyond the Civil Rights Act of 1964 in drafting desegregation requirements.[35]

By the time classes had begun in the fall of 1965, some 89 percent of the school districts in the southern and border states had integrated at least four classes, making them eligible to receive federal funds. In October, 1965, black enrollment in integrated schools in the area had increased by 56 percent over the previous year. How-

---

[32] Wolk, *The Presidency and Black Civil Rights*, 118.
[33] *Congressional Quarterly Almanac*, XXI, 568.
[34] "NAACP Official Says Regulations are Weak," *Southern School News*, 11 (June, 1965), 3.
[35] *Ibid.*

ever, the figures were misleading since many of the newly integrated schools and districts had only a few blacks attending schools with whites. Therefore, though the percentage of integrated school districts was high, the actual number of children attending integrated classes was low.[36] Moreover, another problem was arising that would continue as schools were desegregating: the firing or demoting of black teachers and administrators.[37] Table 23 told part of the story of school desegregation.

HEW announced that black enrollment with whites increased from 2.25 percent in 1964–1965 to 7.5 percent in 1965–1966 in the eleven southern states. However, some non-governmental organizations claimed that the figure was lower, perhaps 5 percent. Moreover, some blacks counted as attending integrated schools were enrolled in predominantly black schools with a few white students.[39]

During September, 1965, Francis Keppel, commissioner of education, deferred funds and sent hearing notices to sixty-five school districts charging that they were not in compliance with Title VI of the Civil Rights Act of 1965. All of the sixty-five districts were located in six southern states: Mississippi, Georgia, Arkansas, Louisiana, Alabama, and South Carolina. On October 26, 1965, Covington County, Mississippi, became the first school district to have a hearing in Washington, D.C. Its spokesmen denied that there was any discrimination in the district.[40] Four of the sixty-five districts were dropped from the list after hearings. There were fifteen districts from Mississippi, thirty-one from Louisiana, three from Georgia, three from Alabama, eight from Arkansas, and one from South Carolina.

By late 1965, 97 percent of the southern and border school districts had had their desegregated plans accepted. The 166 districts not complying included 97 that had submitted unacceptable plans and 69 that had not offered any plan. Mississippi had 17 school districts which had not submitted a plan; there were 35 districts in Louisiana that had refused to submit plans; Arkansas and Alabama

---

[36] *Congressional Quarterly Almanac,* XXI, 568.
[37] "Desegregation," *Southern Education Report,* 1 (July–August, 1965), 31.
[38] *Ibid.,* 569.
[39] *Ibid.*

Table 23
PUBLIC SCHOOL DESEGREGATION COMPLIANCE WITH
TITLE VI OF THE CIVIL RIGHTS ACT OF 1964[40]

State	No. of Districts	HEW 441's Accepted	Court Orders Accepted	Voluntary Plans Accepted	Total Districts Accepted	% Districts Accepted
Ala.	119	1	11	82	94	79
Ark.	410	193	5	160	358	88
Del.	61	26	0	35	61	100
Fla.	67	2	17	45	64	96
Ga.	197	5	8	140	153	78
Ky.	204	139	5	59	203	99
La.	67	0	20	0	20	30
Md.	24	6	0	18	24	100
Miss.	149	0	17	63	80	54
Mo.	688	670	0	14	684	99
N.C.	170	3	5	99	107	63
Okla.	1,090	975	0	68	1,043	96
S.C.	105	0	6	56	62	59
Tenn.	152	13	17	112	143	93
Tex.	1,350	697	14	536	1,247	92
Va.	136	7	10	77	94	69
W.Va.	55	48	2	5	55	100
Total	5,044	2,785	137	1,569	4,491	89%

[40] *Congressional Quarterly Almanac*, XXI, 568.

had five each; Georgia had three; South Carolina had two; and Oklahoma and Texas had one each.[41]

During the 1965–1966 school year there was not a single black teacher assigned to where there were white teachers in the three southern states of Alabama, Louisiana, and Mississippi. In the South as a whole 1,800 black teachers were assigned to biracial facilities; whereas in the border states 51 percent of the black teachers worked with white teachers. As black students were being transferred to former all-white schools, black teachers often lost their jobs. Several methods were used to reduce the "excess" of teachers:[42] failure to renew contracts; use of the standard teacher examination with a higher passing score required than the average black teacher's score; and use of black teachers as "aides" in integrated classrooms. As a law journal pointed out: "Since the Office of Education is now concerned with desegregation of teachers and assignment of teachers under Title VI of the Civil Rights Act of 1964, it would seem to be the obvious agency to undertake elimination of discriminatory hiring and firing of teachers. All that is needed is the appropriate enabling legislation by Congress." [43]

Early in 1966 figures were published on compliance with the 1965 guidelines.[44] (See page 175)

In the meantime, the legality of the HEW guidelines for 1965 was upheld in *Singleton* v. *Jackson Municipal Separate School District* (348 F. 2d 729) and *Price* v. *Davison Independent School District Board of Education* (348 F. 2d 1010) by the Fifth Circuit Court of Appeals. The grade-a-year stair-step desegregation plans were held to be constitutionally inadequate. The federal district courts were directed to order the schools to submit desegregation plans substantially in accord with the requirements of the HEW guidelines. The circuit court reiterated in *Singleton* that the "all de-

---

[41] "Desegregation," *Southern Education Report,* 1 (November–December 1965), 30,32.

[42] A number of private academies were appearing in the South for white students whose parents did not want their children attending schools with blacks.

[43] "Notes: Desegregation of Public School Faculties," *Iowa Law Review,* 51 (Spring, 1966), 681–85.

[44] "Desegregation," *Southern Education Report,* 1 (January–February, 1966), 28–32.

liberate speed" command of *Brown* II did not allow for community hostility to change, but was based on anticipated administrative problems in making the transition to a single desegregated school system.

A major piece of legislation, the Elementary and Secondary Education Act, was signed into law on April 11, 1965. It was the first general federal school aid bill in history and was to operate in conjunction with Title VI of the Civil Rights Act of 1964.[45] The major aim of the bill was to meet the educational needs of "educationally deprived" children, a large percentage of whom included, as defined,

State	Percentage of Districts in Compliance	Percentage of Pupils Covered by Desegregation Plans	Percentage of Negroes Enrolled with Whites
Ala.	88	77	.43
Ark.	98	99	4.38
Fla.	100	100	9.76
Ga.	97	89	2.66
La.	49	71	.69
Miss.	79	69	.59
N.C.	98	94	5.15
S.C.	80	88	1.46
Tenn.	99	91	16.31
Tex.	99	99	17.18
Va.	91	86	11.49
South	95	90	6.01
Del.	100	100	83.22
Ky.	100	100	78.37
Md.	100	100	55.60
Mo.	100	100	75.12
Okla.	99	99	38.25
W.Va.	100	100	79.85
Border	99.8	93	68.90
Region	97	93	15.89

[45] See John H. McCord, *With All Deliberate Speed: Civil Rights Theory and Reality* (Urbana: University of Illinois Press, 1969), 48–49.

blacks. Private schools were also to benefit under the act. Title I of the measure provided federal funds to the states on the basis of the number of children from low-income (under $2,000 a year) families and 50 percent of a state's average expenditure per school child. No exact criteria were provided for spending the funds at the local level except that the needs of low-income children were to be paramount. Title II provided grants to states for textbooks and other library materials. Title III authorized a five-year program of grants for supplementary community-wide centers to provide services which individual schools could not provide; Title IV authorized a five-year program of grants for new research and training in teaching methods; and Title V authorized a five-year program to strengthen state departments of education.

The basic thrust toward desegregation was aimed at the South; however, an event of some significance took place in 1965 in attempting to deal with segregation in a northern school district—in Chicago. A supplementary appropriation bill had been enacted by Congress to finance the Elementary and Secondary Education Act passed earlier in 1965. The Chicago public school system requested thirty-two million dollars under the program. Although the funds were intended by Congress to assist in the education of children from low-income families, the Chicago school administration apparently intended to use the money for those children from the middle-income and largely white families. A complaint charging racial discrimination was filed to HEW by the Chicago Community Council, a coalition of about seventy-five civil rights groups. On September 30, 1965, Francis Keppel, commissioner of education, wrote a letter to the Illinois superintendent of public instruction directing him to defer any further grants to the Chicago schools. The next day, Keppel publicly announced that the funds were being withheld on the grounds of racial discrimination in violation of Title VI of the Civil Rights Act of 1964. This action was taken without consulting President Johnson, although Douglass Cater, a member of the White House staff, had been shown the letter being sent to the Illinois superintendent of public instruction and had not objected.[46] John Gard-

---

[46] Gary Orfield, *The Reconstruction of Southern Education: The Schools and the 1964 Civil Rights Act* (New York: John Wiley & Sons, 1969), 181–84. See also *Congressional Quarterly Almanac*, XXI, 569.

ner, secretary of HEW, and attorneys for the Justice Department, had not been warned of the action in advance.

Pressure was quickly applied by Mayor Richard Daley, members of Congress from Illinois, and city school officials. Senator Dirksen threatened a Senate investigation of the matter.[47] Faced with this opposition, the president, although he did not directly order HEW to restore the funds, let it be known that he wanted the matter quickly settled and "wanted funds to flow with Chicago commitments and compromises." [48] Gardner then sent Wilbur Cohen, under-secretary of HEW, to work out a compromise with Frank M. Whiston, president of the Chicago Board of Education. A "compromise" was worked out, but the chief losers were the poor and black children.

The Chicago incident helped to undermine the credibility of the school desegregation effort by HEW. Another result was the hiring of Peter F. Libassi as special assistant on civil rights to the HEW secretary. His main task was to keep the White House informed and to convince the White House that what HEW was doing in the area of school desegregation was correct.

In February, 1966, the Commission on Civil Rights issued a report concerning school desegregation in the seventeen southern and border states. It found that a "very small" number of black children attended public schools with white children in the region. The commission pointed out that under "freedom of choice" very little integration occurred and the dual school system was maintained. The reasons given were: (1) inertia in both the white and black communities; and (2) fear of reprisal among blacks if they transferred to a white school. Very few white students ever transferred to a black school. The commission also found that the Office of Education lacked the staff and procedures to monitor effectively the enforcement of desegregation policies. The office accepted at face value whatever the school districts claimed they were doing and made very little effort to check on the verity of the school districts' statements. The commission recommended a tightening of procedures by the Office of Education. It also recommended that Congress enact a law empowering the attorney general and victims to bring civil suits to

[47] "Leaning on HEW," *Newsweek*, 66 (October 18, 1965), 98.
[48] Wolk, *The Presidency and Black Civil Rights*, 130.

enjoin persons from harassing or intimidating black parents and children who sought to exercise their rights under desegregation plans approved by the Office of Education.[49]

Late in January, 1966, Harold Howe II, commissioner of education, HEW, requested suggestions from various groups concerning desegregation guidelines for the 1966–1967 school year. A number of civil rights and human relations groups in the South had attacked the 1965 guidelines as being "too timidly drawn and too timidly enforced." [50] They planned meetings in five Deep South states to attempt to persuade the federal government that it should carry out a "massive school desegregation program."

As a result of pressures, primarily from the Commission on Civil Rights, on March 7, 1966, HEW issued somewhat stronger guidelines for grades to be desegregated in 1966, and 1967 remained the deadline for all grades.[51] The beginning of faculty desegregation, where it had not already begun, was also required. School districts were to report on their progress to HEW by April 15, 1966. Though school districts might use the freedom of choice approach, it was to be evaluated as to whether or not real desegregation occurred as a result.

The so-called freedom of choice approach was the one most frequently adopted by southern school systems as it retained the dual school system largely intact. Because of this situation of producing very little desegregation and the fact that white students almost never elected to attend an all-black school, the guidelines set up standards which had to be met for plans to be acceptable. Under freedom of choice, each student had to choose annually which school he wished to attend. Furthermore, a choice period had to meet certain requirements: that notice be given to students and parents of the existence and details of the proposed plan, and that the notice be published.[52]

Furthermore, a freedom of choice plan was acceptable only if

[49] See *Congressional Quarterly Almanac*, XXII (1966), 479.

[50] *School Desegregation 1966: The Slow Undoing* (Atlanta: Southern Regional Council, 1967), 94.

[51] See Erwin Knoll, "There's Room for Negotiations," *Southern Education Report*, 1 (May–June, 1966), 4.

[52] Martin L. Cooper, "The New School Desegregation Guidelines," *Harvard Civil Rights–Civil Liberties Review*, 2 (Fall, 1966), 89–90.

certain conditions were found in the school district. The burden for creating the necessary conditions was on the school officials. Both the majority and minority members of the community had to be convinced that school officials were sincere and that all would operate smoothly.[53] Certain criteria had to be met to determine if desegregation was actually occurring in a school district. These criteria were as follows: (1) If a significant percentage—8 to 9 percent—had transferred from segregated schools in 1965–1966, at least double that amount would be normally required for 1966–1967; (2) If a small percentage—4 to 5 percent—had transferred in 1965–1966, at least three times that amount would be expected in 1966–1967; (3) If a still lower percentage had transferred in 1965–1966, then the ratio would normally be more than three times in 1966–1967; (4) If no students had transferred in 1965–1966, a very substantial beginning would be expected for 1966–1967.[54]

At first, there seemed to be a reluctant acceptance of the new guidelines in much of the South. However, strong opposition was soon forthcoming from Mississippi, Alabama, and Georgia. In a speech delivered before an audience at the University of South Carolina, Attorney General Katzenbach called the guidelines "moderate, perhaps even tardy benchmarks. . . . They contain no sudden surprises nor do they in themselves break new ground." [55]

One writer commented:

> To say that there is growing concern about the role of the federal government in education is to understate the case. There seems to be a groundswell of disquiet. The continuing controversy over the withholding of funds from the Chicago public schools is just one example of an upsetting interaction between an agency of the federal branch of government, a state department of education, and a local system of schools (albeit the third largest public system in the nation). It is but one of the many that has occurred recently, involving chiefly the administration of Title VI of the Civil Rights Act of 1964. From the perspective of the local school board administrator and school board member it appears that the federal government has flexed its muscles and violated the sacred principle of the preamble to all federal aid bills which stipulated at considerable length, the control features in the laws. It appears that the U.S. Office of Education and its series of "able young commis-

[53] *Ibid.*, 90.　　　　　　　[54] *Ibid.*
[55] *School Desegregation 1966: The Slow Undoing,* 9.

sioners" has trespassed upon the sacred presence of state and local responsibility for education.[56]

Meanwhile, as the April 15 deadline neared, there were charges in much of the southern press that the new guidelines imposed a formula for racial balance and that immediate faculty desegregation was being demanded by HEW. By April 19, 1966, only one school district in Louisiana and four in Alabama had filed a compliance form. At the end of April, 1,193 of the 1,900 concerned school districts had filed the compliance forms. Faced with this situation HEW extended the deadline to May 6 in the hope of increasing the number of complying districts.

On May 5 the Office of Education ordered that the payment of federal funds be delayed for any new school projects in districts that did not meet the May 6 deadline. Nevertheless, some 255 districts had not filed compliance forms by May 7. Human Relations Councils in eight southern states then urged that funds be withheld from all school districts "flagrantly disobeying guidelines." [57] By mid-May some 1,475 out of 1,893 districts were judged by HEW to have adequate plans. Over 200 school districts still had not even filed the necessary forms. A few weeks later, in June, 21 school districts were reported as refusing to follow the guidelines, and many others still had not filed with HEW. At this point, the House of Representatives, with its strongly entrenched white southern contingent, reduced HEW's plans for compliance budget, which meant that instead of 348 staff members there would be but 70. Many southern congressmen complained that the 1966 guidelines were illegal.

In the meantime, on May 13, 1966, eighteen southern senators (the ones from Texas and Tennessee did not sign) wrote to President Johnson protesting the guidelines and urging the president to use his executive power to revoke them.[58] The president replied to Senator Russell that the guidelines were "fair," and that the "percentage requirements were for administrative procedures," and that

---

[56] Luvern L. Cunningham, "Federal Role Arouses Growing Concern Among School Officials," *American School Board Journal*, 152 (May, 1966), 64.

[57] *School Desegregation 1966: The Slow Undoing*, 14.

[58] Reg Murphy and Hal Gulliver, *The Southern Strategy* (New York: Charles Scribner's Sons, 1971), 31.

the guidelines still permitted freedom of choice without requiring any busing or racial balance.[59]

At a meeting of the Southern Regional Education Board held at Miami Beach, Florida. Governor George Wallace of Alabama tried to line up unified opposition to the guidelines. While other southern governors and educators agreed that the guidelines went too far, they rejected his plea for open defiance.[60] As time passed, individual school districts were able to secure concessions from the Office of Education after they complained. The school districts were aided by pressure continually exerted by southern congressmen. All of this activity, of course, resulted in a weakening of the guidelines.[61]

In the meantime, the Coleman report was issued in July, 1966. It was the result of a study called for in the Civil Rights Act of 1964. The report pointed out that most children in the country attended segregated schools. Among minority groups, black pupils were the most segregated; however, combining all groups together white students were the most segregated. Accordingly, "about 80 percent of all white pupils in the 1st grade and 12th grade attend schools that are from 90 to 100 percent white, and 97 percent at grade 1, and 99 percent at grade 12, attend schools that are 50 percent or more white." [62]

For black pupils segregation was most nearly complete in the South, but it was extensive elsewhere whenever the black population was concentrated. More specifically,

> More than 65 percent of all Negro pupils in the first grade attend schools that are between 90 and 100 percent Negro. And 87 percent at grade 1, and 66 percent at grade 12, attend schools that are 50 percent or more Negro. In the South most students attend schools that are 100 percent white or Negro.

Concerning teachers:

> For the nation as a whole, the average Negro elementary pupil attends a school in which 65 percent of the teachers are Negro; the average

[59] *School Desegregation 1966: The Slow Undoing,* 14.
[60] *Ibid.,* 16.
[61] Jim Leesen, "Guidelines, A Repeat Performance," *Southern Education Report,* 2 (October, 1966), 28–30.
[62] James S. Coleman, et al., *Equality of Educational Opportunity* (2 vols.; Washington, D.C.: U.S. Government Printing Office, 1966), I, 3.

white pupil attends a school in which 97 percent of the teachers are white. White teachers are most predominant at the secondary level, where the corresponding figures are 59 and 97 percent.[63]

The same trend was evident with regard to principals. White and black students usually had white principals. At the elementary level only 1 percent of the white pupils had a black principal. Racial matching was most complete in the South. However, while white teachers taught blacks, black teachers seldom taught white pupils.

In terms of achievement, by grade twelve both white and black students in the South scored below their counterparts in the North. Southern blacks scored further below southern whites than northern blacks scored below northern whites.[64] The authors of the Coleman report stated that it appeared that variations in curricula and facilities of schools accounted for relatively little variation in pupil achievement in so far as it could be measured by standardized tests. However, schools were more important for minority children than for whites. The least difference was noted for white children; somewhat more difference was noted among blacks. The quality of teachers appeared to be more important for minority achievement than for that of whites. Pupils' achievements were held to be strongly related to the educational background and aspiration of the other students in the school. Family background was held to be especially important. Minority children, except for Orientals, had less conviction that they could affect their environment and future. When such minority children had such convictions, however, their achievement level was higher than that of whites with no such convictions. It was held that blacks in schools with a higher proportion of whites had a greater sense of control.[65]

A re-analysis was made of the report by staff members and outside consultants who prepared the United States Commission on Civil Rights' Report on Racial Isolation in the Public Schools, by members of the Harvard University Seminar, and the Center for Educational Policy. While there were said to have been some important errors in the original report, the main conclusion of the Coleman re-

---

[63] *Ibid.* [64] *Ibid.*, 21

[65] *Ibid.*, 22. See also James S. Coleman, "The Concept of Equality of Educational Opportunity," *Harvard Educational Review*, 38 (Winter, 1968), 7–22, for a discussion of environmental influence, especially that of the family.

port was held to have been correct. Christopher Jencks argued that in particular, and contrary to what critics had thought, the net effect of the report's errors was to underestimate the importance of family background and overestimate the importance of school in determining achievement.[66]

However, there were those who were in fundamental disagreement with the Coleman report. One such critic, Deborah Meier, noted that Coleman who was pro-integrationist, and the advocates of black power and white racism who were anti-integrationist, placed great emphasis on family and home surroundings. While Coleman emphasized that blacks should have as little contact with their own as possible, advocates of black power insisted that blacks have as little contact as possible with other than their own kind.[67]

Meier challenged the Coleman report on its notion that the quality of educational facilities had little impact on educational achievements, and that racial integration was an important factor in improving the achievements of black pupils. Black students could learn to read and do arithmetic without being around white students. At the same time, however, she listed three reasons why she felt school integration was important. First of all, it needed to be made clear to blacks that society was repudiating its long effort at separation in order to keep blacks in an inferior position. Second, as long as blacks were politically less powerful than whites, the threat of integration, or better yet actual integration, forced whites to make improvements in black education. Finally Meier wrote: "our insistence on integrated education should rest on the contention that an integrated education and classroom is an important tool for producing the kind of learning that is most needed in our society today." [68]

While educational circles were arguing the pros and cons of the Coleman report, the battle in the schools continued. As the fall of 1966 came around, some school districts, mainly in the Deep South, decided to forego federal funds rather than desegregate. The largest increase in desegregation occurred in the large cities which were

[66] Charles E. Silberman, *Crisis in the Classroom: The Remaking of American Education* (New York: Vintage Books, 1971), 72–73.

[67] Deborah Meier, "The Coleman Report," *Integrated Education*, 5 (December, 1967–January, 1968), 37.

[68] *Ibid.*, 38–42.

already under court orders to desegregate. In Alabama, the legislature even passed an anti-guidelines act, declaring the guidelines illegal. However, a number of Alabama school districts proceeded to ignore them.[69] Ironically, George Wallace, Jr., entered Bellingrath Junior High School in Montgomery on September 6. That school was being desegregated for the first time as sixteen black children entered the school.[70] As a partial defiance of federal policy, Virginia, Mississippi, and South Carolina ended compulsory school attendance. In Grenada, Mississippi, grown men armed with chains and clubs assaulted black children as they entered desegregated schools. Over in Louisiana, Leander Perez reacted to a court order for Plaquemines Parish to desegregate by establishing private schools. Indeed, private schools set up to avoid desegregation were dotting the map in much of the Deep South.

On December 29, 1966, the controversy over the legality of the 1966 guidelines was settled by a three-judge panel in a decision of the Fifth Circuit Court of Appeals in New Orleans. The case was *United States* v. *Jefferson County Board of Education* which was affirmed en banc (372 F. 2d 836). The decision was that "the only desegregation plan that meets constitutional standards is one that works. By helping public schools to meet that test, by assisting the courts in their independent evaluation of school desegregation plans, and by accelerating the progress but simplifying the process of desegregation, the HEW Guidelines offer new hope to Negro school children long denied their constitutional rights." This decision clearly placed those using freedom of choice plans on notice. It was also held that the guidelines which also called for faculty integration operated within the congressional mandate and were consistent with the decisions of federal courts. Moreover, as for freedom of choice, it was not a goal, but disestablishment of the dual system was. Freedom of choice was merely a means and if it did not work, something else had to be devised. The full court upheld this decision in March, 1967, and directed each state within the fifth circuit area to take all necessary action to bring about a unitary system with no racial de-

---

[69] "Civil Rights," *Congressional Quarterly Weekly Report,* 24 (September 9, 1966), 1963; Jim Leesen, "The Crumbling Legal Barriers to Desegregation," *Southern Education Report,* 2 (October, 1966), 11.

[70] "Civil Rights," 1964.

segregation. In October, 1967, the United States Supreme Court refused to review the case.

In spite of the stronger guidelines, the Southern Regional Council charged that very little desegregation occurred during the fall of 1966. While many school districts had not turned in acceptable guarantees of compliance, federal funds were terminated in only 39 of them. Of the remainder, action to terminate had begun in 64 districts and was anticipated in 47 others. The Southern Regional Council charged that what was called "massive" desegregation amounted to very little, in the Deep South especially. The council pointed out: "In short, enforcement of Title VI had not touched most southern school districts with financial sanctions. And southern schools were far short of Title VI demands for the elimination of discrimination." [71] The Southern Regional Council reached a number of conclusions in its late 1966 report. They were as follows:

1. Segments of the southern political and educational establishment successfully avoided significant desegregation in 1966.

2. The guidelines would not have ended dual schools even if perfectly applied and accepted.

3. The poor performance of the South in the second year of the implementation of Title VI for school desegregation remained the strongest rebuttal of the southern complaint that the Office of Education had been overzealous.

4. Congress had intended to end dual schools despite a prohibition against enforced racial balances.

5. Political pressure on administrators, fears of a white backlash, and confusion about the intent of Congress in Article VI had weakened counter-pressures for strong enforcement. There was also a lack of enthusiasm for the guidelines by civil rights groups who regarded them as too weak.

6. The situation could be retrieved if attention were focused on ending the dual school system.

7. Southern schools were still overwhelmingly segregated. Black students who entered formerly all-white schools under freedom of choice plans were confronted with force and violence.[72]

[71] *School Desegregation 1966: The Slow Undoing,* 21.
[72] *Ibid.,* 43.

The Southern Regional Council noted that the tragic consequences of the continued failure of many southern schools and public officials to live up to the basic duties of American citizenship and the common decencies observed by all mankind in the rearing of children could not be counted. The patience of black southerners could not be expected to continue indefinitely under such conditions.

> The schools in the South by all statistical standards are the worst in the nation. Part of the reason for this is the extravagant waste of dual systems of segregated schools. Another part is waste of administrative and executive energy on attempts to preserve these systems that might better be spent in improving the education of a generation which faces the complexity of a new and baffling era of the scientific age.[73]

The Commission on Civil Rights published certain statistics for the seventeen southern and border states which were gathered from the Office of Education as of December 9, 1966.[74] (See Table 24)

A somewhat different set of statistics was published by the Southern Education Report for the seventeen southern and border states and Washington, D.C.[75] (See Table 25)

There were no figures as yet, but it was reported that most southern schools had begun to desegregate their faculties.[76]

The United States Commission on Civil Rights reported the following findings in its study of school desegregation during 1966–1967:[77]

1. The number of black children attending schools not all black had more than doubled. However, over 80 percent of the black children in eleven southern states and over 90 percent of black children in the Deep South states attended all-black schools.

2. In one half of the border states, a great majority of black children attended schools less than 80 percent black. Relatively few black children attended all-black schools in those states. In the other

[73] *Ibid.,* 44.
[74] U.S. Commission on Civil Rights, *Southern School Desegregation, 1966–67* (Washington, D.C.: U.S. Government Printing Office, 1967), 167. See also *Congressional Quarterly Almanac,* XXII, for slightly different figures.
[75] Jim Leesen, "Guidelines and a New Count," *Southern Education Report,* 2 (January–February, 1967), 31.
[76] *Ibid.,* 32.
[77] U.S. Commission on Civil Rights, *Southern School Desegregation 1966–67,* 141–45.

Table 24

	Negro Pupils Attending Schools Less Than 95% Negro		Negro Pupils Attending Schools 95–99% Negro		Negro Pupils Attending Schools 100% Negro	
	%	Number	%	Number	%	Number
All States (17)	17.3	589,680	7.0	237,990	75.7	2,537,190
Southern States	12.5	363,350	4.3	124,380	83.2	2,411,650
Ala.	2.4	6,750	2.3	6,300	95.3	260,900
Ark.	14.5	17,200	0.6	700	84.9	100,300
Fla.	14.7	41,120	6.1	17,060	79.2	221,550
Ga.	6.6	22,610	3.3	11,300	90.1	308,450
La.	2.6	6,850	.9	2,370	96.5	254,050
Miss.	2.6	6,840	.6	1,580	96.8	254,700
N.C.	12.8	44,850	2.8	9,810	84.4	295,650
S.C.	4.9	12,120	1.1	2,720	94.0	232,550
Tenn.	21.9	40,600	9.8	18,170	68.3	126,550
Tex.	34.6	117,050	12.7	42,760	52.7	178,250
Va.	20.0	47,540	4.8	11,410	75.2	178,700
Border States	45.1	226,330	22.7	113,610	32.2	161,540
Del.	84.8	20,440	15.2	3,660	0	0
Ky.	88.5	28,230	0	0	11.5	4,980
Md.	40.5	88,980	23.5	51,630	36.0	79,150
Mo.	26.7	24,710	37.5	48,750	35.8	46,540
Okla.	40.5	24,950	15.2	9,360	44.3	27,290
W.Va.	83.4	19,020	.9	210	15.7	3,580

Table 25
STATUS OF PUBLIC SCHOOL DESEGREGATION, 1966–1967

	School Total	Districts Funds Cut-Off	Cut-Off Requested Funds Deferred	In Compliance	Enrollment in Thousands White	Enrollment in Thousands Negro	Negroes in Schools With Whites Number	Negroes in Schools With Whites %
Ala.	118	2	51	65	571.2	273.8	12,900	4.7
Ark.	407	4	10	393	316.5	118.2	17,900	15.1
Fla.	65	—	1	64	980.4	279.7	58,150	20.8
Ga.	196	2	37	157	731.2	342.5	34,050	9.9
La.	67	17	4	46	557.3	263.4	9,350	3.5
Miss.	148	11	42	95	321.8	263.2	8,500	3.2
N.C.	169	—	10	159	833.3	350.4	54,750	15.6
S.C.	107	1	19	87	395.1	247.3	14,750	6.0
Tenn.	151	—	2	149	688.9	185.4	58,850	31.7
Tex.	1,314	—	2	1,312	2,224.8	338.3	160,050	47.3
Va.	135	—	7	128	765.4	237.7	59,000	24.8
South	2,877	37	185	2,655	8,385.9	2,899.9	488,250	16.8
Del.	56	—	—	56	88.5	24.1	24,100	100.0
D.C.	1	—	—	1	13.4	133.3	114,976	86.3
Ky.	200	—	—	200	631.3	43.2	38,220	88.5
Md.	24	—	—	24	571.2	219.7	140,550	64.0
Mo.	689	—	—	689	833.8	130.0	83,460	64.2
Okla.	996	—	—	996	536.8	61.6	34,310	55.7
W.Va.	55	—	—	55	398.2	22.8	19,220	84.3
Border	2,021	0	0	2,021	3,073.2	634.7	454,836	71.7
Region	4,898	37	185	4,676	11,459.1	3,354.6	943,086	26.7

half of the border states over one third of the black pupils attended all-black schools and a majority attended schools over 95 percent black.

3. During 1966–1967, there was no, or only token, desegregation of full-time teachers in the southern states.

4. Throughout the entire region most schools were desegregated under free choice plans.

5. There was serious doubt about the viability of free choice as a means of abolishing the dual school system.

6. Freedom of choice plans required affirmative actions by black and white parents and pupils before disestablishment of the dual system could be achieved. A number of deterring factors were mentioned: (a) a fear of retaliation and hostility from whites; (b) in some parts of the South black children attending formerly all-white schools under freedom of choice were targets of violence, crime, threats of violence, and economic reprisals by whites, and harassment of black children by white classmates; (c) in some areas public officials improperly influenced black parents to keep their children in black schools and excluded black children attending formerly all-white schools from official functions; (d) poverty kept many black families in the South from choosing all-white schools; and (e) improvements in equipment and facilities had been made in all-black schools in some districts to discourage blacks from choosing white schools.

7. The Equal Educational Opportunities program in the Office of Education made for an improvement in its administration of the Title VI program.

8. Many school districts fell far short of meeting the guidelines. The Office of Education did not enforce the guidelines as written. Although most school districts in South Carolina, Georgia, Mississippi, Alabama, and Louisiana did not meet the standards in the guidelines governing transfers from segregated schools, only a small fraction of them were subjected to enforcement efforts. Many specific prohibitions set forth in the guidelines were not enforced.

9. Procedures employed by HEW in tabulating vital statistical information on desegregation were initiated late and remained inadequate.

10. There were still many school districts desegregated under

court orders imposing standards less rigorous than those imposed by the guidelines in districts desegregating under voluntary plans.

11. Many private schools attended exclusively by whites had been established in the South in the wake of desegregation. In some places these schools had drained off from the public schools most or all of the white pupils and many white teachers. The Internal Revenue Service had approved some of these private schools for the receipt of tax benefits and others had requests for such benefits pending before the I.R.S.

The Civil Rights Commission ended its report with conclusions and recommendations. It insisted that not only were the HEW guidelines legal, but they represented a minimum standard. It recommended:[78]

1. For 1967–1968 each district operating under voluntary free choice should be required to fulfill the percentage expectations set forth in the 1966 guidelines.

2. For 1968–1969 and each year thereafter, HEW should require all districts which had not achieved substantial desegregation throughout the system to have a significant increase in the percentage of black students attending desegregated schools. Freedom of choice plans should not be accepted unless there had been no harassment or intimidation of black parents or children in making their choices.

3. By 1968–1969 HEW should require that schools no longer be racially identifiable on the basis of the racial composition of the staff. Substantial progress should be required toward that end.

4. All other sections of the guidelines should be firmly and consistently enforced, and any failure or refusal to comply should result in prompt beginning of enforcement proceedings if efforts to obtain voluntary compliance failed.

5. HEW needed to review the enforcement procedures related to all aspects of desegregation to insure that desegregation requirements were strictly applied and that districts similarly circumstanced be treated alike.

6. The attorney general ought to request the federal courts to revise school desegregation orders to comply with standards already established.

[78] *Ibid.*, 149–60.

7. HEW should review procedures for obtaining school desegregation statistics and adopt uniform procedures in order to expedite the collection of relevant statistics in a form easily usable to HEW and readily available to all interested governmental agencies and private individuals.

8. Congress ought to appropriate sufficient funds to meet the estimated manpower requirements for Title VI enforcement.

9. Congress should pass legislation authorizing any black child, and his parents, to bring civil action for injunctive relief and damages against private persons who harassed or intimidated him because of his race or his enrollment or attendance at any public school, or to discourage or prevent him because of his race or any other person or class of persons of a certain race, from participating in such activity. The attorney general needed to be authorized to sue in behalf of such a victim for injunctive relief. Criminal sanctions ought to be imposed against any persons, whether acting under color of law or otherwise, engaging or attempting to engage in intimidation or harassment.

10. The secretary of the treasury ought to solicit an opinion from the attorney general as to whether or not Title VI of the Civil Rights Act of 1964 or the Internal Revenue Code authorized or required the IRS to require that racially segregated private schools be desegregated as a condition to the receipt of tax benefits, or whether an act of Congress was necessary to achieve that result. The attorney general ought to consider whether, as a result of these benefits, the federal government was so significantly involved in private school segregation as to justify legal action to enjoin the continued operation on a discriminatory basis of schools receiving tax benefits. If the attorney general decided his authority was inadequate he should then recommend to the president that he introduce appropriate legislation.

Southerners continuously complained that for political reasons the desegregation guidelines were being enforced only in the South and not in the North and West. David S. Seeley, assistant commissioner for equal educational opportunities, Office of Education, HEW, addressed himself to the problem by noting that in the North and West school segregation largely resulted from housing patterns rather than law and school policy, as in the South. He wrote:

To be quite frank, neither the Office of Education nor the school officials in the North or West know how to overcome this *de facto* seg-regation in its more extreme forms. We do not even know how to define the problem of discriminate *de facto* segregation with sufficient preci-sion to determine under what circumstances it contravenes Title VI.

This does not mean that we are shrugging our shoulders over *de facto* segregation and concluding that it must be tolerated forever. It does mean that the circumstances, the course and conditions of North-ern school segregation and discrimination are so complex and elusive that they do not lend themselves easily to a legal solution. More impor-tant, local school officials in many cities are developing desegregation plans which in their ingenuity and imagination surpass any ideas OE could offer.[79]

On January 1, 1967, John Gardner announced new guidelines which were not much changed from March, 1966. They called gen-erally for another doubling of black pupils attending classes with whites in 1967–1968. School districts were informed as to what per-centages were expected in order to continue to receive federal funds. The guidelines provided a reprieve for freedom of choice for another year, however. They also stipulated that the thirty-day choice could be anytime between January 1 and April 1, instead of from March 1 to April 30. Civil rights groups immediately attacked the guide-lines for leading to very little desegregation.[80] In discussing the new guidelines, the Southern Regional Council alluded to the notion that the administration era was almost over. Moreover,

> Negro parents, target of every trick known to a national minority ac-customed to working its will on the nation in matters of race, were getting tired. Negro children, in all too many instances, were disillu-sioned. Private agencies' field workers, who had often been Negroes' only assurance that all of white America was not hostile, that their children were not totally alone, were reluctantly pulling out.[81]

On February 9, 1967, the United States Commission on Civil Rights presented another report on the schools to the president. He

[79] David S. Seeley, *Desegregation Guidelines: Do They Go Far Enough?* (Washington, D.C.: U.S. Government Printing Office, 1967), n.p.

[80] *Congressional Quarterly Almanac*, XXIII (1967), 802; Jim Leesen, "Re-prieve for Freedom of Choice," *Southern Education Report*, 2 (March, 1967), 30–31.

[81] Glenda Bartley, "Full Circle of Failure," *Lawlessness and Disorder: Fourteen Years of Failure in Southern School Desegregation* (Atlanta: South-ern Regional Council, 1968), 5.

had requested such a report on November 17, 1965. Its findings were as follows: [82]

1. Racial isolation in the public schools was extensive throughout the nation: 75 percent of the black elementary students in the cities attended schools with nearly all black enrollments (90 percent or more); and 83 percent of the white students attended all-white schools.

2. A high level of racial separation in city schools existed whether the city was large or small, and whether the city was located in the North or South.

3. The high level of racial separation in the city schools was increasing. Once a school became almost half or majority black, it tended to become nearly all black.

4. In the southern and border states a rising black enrollment, combined with only a slight degree of desegregation, had proceeded with a considerable increase in the number of blacks attending all-black schools (although the proportion of blacks in all-black schools had decreased since 1954).

5. The nation's metropolitan area populations were growing and were increasingly separated by race.

6. The following trends were reflected among school age children: (a) By 1960 about four of every five nonwhite school children in metropolitan areas lived in the central cities, while nearly three of every four white children lived in the suburbs. (b) Black school children were increasingly attending central city schools and white children, suburban schools. (c) A large number of major cities had elementary school enrollments that were over half black.

The report concluded that black children had been largely "untouched" by compensatory programs in their schools and would continue to suffer academically unless they attended integrated schools.[83] The commission had taken a position against those who thought the answer was to pour more federal funds into the ghetto

---

[82] See U.S. Commission on Civil Rights, *Racial Isolation in the Public Schools* (2 vols.; Washington, D.C.: U.S. Government Printing Office, 1967) I, 199–200. See also Jim Leesen, "The Attention Now Turns to Balance," *Southern Education Report*, 2 (March, 1967), 12.

[83] New York *Times*, February 20, 1967, p. 1.

schools. Confronted with these findings, the commission made the following recommendations: [84]

1. Congress should establish a uniform standard for the elimination of racial isolation in the public schools.

2. Congress should vest in each of the states responsibility for meeting the standard it creates and should allow state flexibility in devising appropriate remedies.

3. The legislation ought to include programs of substantial financial assistance to provide for construction of new facilities and improvement in the quality of education in all schools.

4. Congress ought to provide adequate time in which to fulfill the legislation.

The goals of equal educational opportunity and equal housing opportunity were inseparable. Therefore, the commission recommended that the president and Congress consider legislation that would:

5. Prohibit discrimination in the rental or sale of housing.

6. Expand programs of federal assistance designed to increase the supply of housing throughout metropolitan areas within the means of low- and moderate-income families.

The Commission also recommended that HUD:

7. Require as a condition of application for low- and moderate-income housing projects that the sites be selected and the projects planned in a non-discriminatory manner that would contribute to the reduction of residential racial concentrations and the elimination of racial isolation in schools.

8. Require as a condition of approval of urban renewal projects that relocations be planned in a non-discriminatory way that would contribute to the reduction of residential racial concentrations and the elimination of racial isolation in schools.

While there was criticism of the racially isolated school, a leading black political scientist wrote the following in discussing the need for black people to direct their own strategies:

[84] U.S. Commission on Civil Rights, *Racial Isolation in the Public Schools*, 209–12; "The Disadvantaged: Remedies for Racial Isolation," *Education Digest*, 32 (April, 1967), 1–4; Leesen, "The Attention Now Turns to Balance," 15.

Take the issue of school integration. Pursuing a principle of integration to overcome legal segregation and discrimination, many integrationists (Black and White) simply never come to grips with the problem of what was to happen to those Black children sitting in the previously all-white classrooms. The thinking was that if Black children got into those schools and received the same education as the white children were receiving, things would be substantially better. But there was little attention given to the fact that those classrooms were educationally (i.e., substantially) racist. What good is structural integration, if the same racist materials and teachers are used? I suggest the Black children will be even more crippled. How much thought went into the desire to have Black parents involved in the schools? [85]

In March, 1967, two branches of the federal government were placed in political conflict in *Lee* v. *Macon County* (267 F. Supp. 458, M.D. Ala., 1967). The court placed 99 of Alabama's 118 districts under court order. They had formerly operated under HEW guidelines. During the summer of 1967 HEW held that the Lovett, Alabama, school district was not in compliance with the 1967 guidelines and was ineligible for federal funds. The school officials protested that they were under a court order, and the court held that it had the responsibility to determine whether the school systems were complying, and since they had agreed to comply, HEW requirements were satisfied. Over 80 black schools were closed following the orders. While urging HEW to continue its investigation and report any failures to comply, the court warned HEW that it could do nothing without the court's approval.[86] If freedom of choice did not work, it would be replaced by something that did. Simultaneously, the court declared the Alabama tuition grants designed to help white students attend segregated private institutions unconstitutional.

At the same time, with House southerners mostly in the background, Representative Edith Green of Oregon fought their segregation battles. She, supported by southerners, succeeded in requiring HEW to apply the guidelines to all fifty states and to cite statutory authority under which it was decided to withhold federal funds from

[85] Charles V. Hamilton, "Black Americans and the Modern Political Struggle," *The Black World*, 19 (May, 1970), 8.

[86] See James Bolner, "The Supreme Court and Racially Imbalanced Schools in 1967," *Journal of Negro Education*, 38 (Winter, 1969), 131–32, for a discussion of the dissenting views of Judge Harold Cox.

non-complying school districts. Southern civil rights organizations perceived the action as a diversionary tactic to weaken HEW's compliance efforts in southern states.[87]

Southern officials gained another victory in 1967 when Senator Richard Russell led an attack in the Senate which resulted in a statement from Secretary Gardner, pledging that HEW would give school districts notice of any possible termination of federal funds six months before the beginning of the school year.[88]

Meanwhile, on May 10, 1967, Peter Libassi, special assistant in civil rights to Secretary Gardner, was named as director of HEW's Office of Civil Rights. There had been pressure in Congress for several years to centralize civil rights enforcement activities. Finally, an ultimatum was given to HEW by Representative David Flood of Pennsylvania: centralize or face large budget cuts. Flood had also requested clarification on two others matters: (1) were the guidelines "directed exclusively at the Southern states and not at similar practices in the North?" (2) had the Office of Education "gone beyond the intent of the law" by requiring racial balance which had been expressly prohibited by the very terms of the Civil Rights Act of 1964? On May 9 Gardner had surrendered. He wrote Flood that: (1) the groundwork had been laid for the centralization of civil rights efforts; (2) Title VI applied to the entire nation; and (3) "we will continue to adhere faithfully to the statutory prohibition requiring racial balance." After his new appointment, Libassi announced that his goal for the South in 1967–1968 was that 25 percent of the region's blacks would be attending schools with whites and that considerable faculty desegregation would occur. Libassi also spoke of turning north to the urban centers.[89]

Opponents of desegregation in the South received still another boost on August 2, 1967, when the Internal Revenue Service announced that it had approved the applications of forty-two private segregated schools for tax benefits. This step was taken in spite of the fact that the Civil Rights Division of the Justice Department in a memorandum had taken the stand that such institutions could not be

[87] Robert E. Anderson, Jr., "The Congress, the Courts and the National Will," *Lawlessness and Disorder*, 17–18.

[88] *Ibid.*, 18.

[89] William Steif, "The New Look in Civil Rights Enforcement," *Southern Education Report*, 3 (September, 1967), 4–5.

regarded as being operated for educational or charitable purposes within the meaning of the Internal Revenue Code. The CRD also cited Title VI of the Civil Rights Act of 1964 contending there was a clear national policy in education condemning segregation. Nevertheless, the IRS ruled otherwise.[90]

In September, 1967, when the public schools opened, 86 percent of the southern black students still attended segregated schools. Figures for the Deep South were most depressing: Alabama, 94.6 percent; Louisiana, 93.3 percent; Mississippi, 96.1 percent; South Carolina, 90.1 percent; and Georgia, 90.1 percent.[91]

The Southern Regional Council claimed that the administrative defeat of school desegregation had occurred for a number of reasons. The acceptance of the freedom of choice approach had proved to be a fatal blunder as it had not worked in desegregating schools. Furthermore, Title IV, which prohibited busing to achieve racial balance, had proven an insurmountable obstacle in attempting to deal with *de facto* segregation caused by housing patterns. Whether a school district set up pairing, combination pairing-zoning, or educational parks, there were limits to what these could accomplish to end the dual school system. Indeed, the restriction on busing automatically eliminated the possibility of making viable zoning plans which would destroy the designation of white and black schools. Moreover, the ultimate weapon—the termination of federal funds—had proven ineffective. After all, Title I funds were generally spent on black schools and when termination occurred it was generally the black students who suffered in black schools.[92]

As 1968 began officials at HEW were praising instead of condemning southern educators in solving school desegregation problems. The compliance section of HEW-OCR under Libassi (Mrs. Ruby Martin, a black woman, replaced him in 1968) was in the process of establishing policies to end the dual school system in 1969. Civil rights groups believed that southern educators had merely changed their techniques of defiance, and they considered the HEW approach too moderate. Civil rights leaders interpreted the new policy as one providing a two-year delay and insisted "that the Negro community is becoming disillusioned about the possibility of integra-

90 *Federal Civil Rights Enforcement Effort*, 563.
91 Bartley, "Full Circle of Failure," *Lawlessness and Disorder*, 5.
92 *Ibid.*, 6–7.

tion and is returning to the concept of improving their racially separate schools." [93]

It was felt in many quarters that the change in approach was based on presidential and congressional politics in 1968. Libassi told a group of Georgia educators that HEW "will not get as much involved as we have in the past in a counting numbers and percentage game." He continued, however, "I don't mean to say we're not going to be interested in the results, because we are. But the result that we're looking for is not number of children but a plan for the full and total elimination of the dual system." Jean Fairfax, of the NAACP Legal Defense and Education Fund stated that she perceived a general watering down of intent, regulations, and the machinery of HEW.[94]

New policies were issued in March, 1968, and revised ones again in June, 1968. For the first time, an actual deadline was set for the end of the dual system. The guidelines also, for the first time, applied to southern and nonsouthern schools alike. All school districts were required to be completely desegregated by 1970–1971; however, in most cases the deadline was either 1968 or 1969. The only districts eligible to delay until 1970–1971 were those containing black majorities or having construction troubles. Furthermore, if a 1970–1971 terminal date were accepted, the school district had to take enough steps in the interim period to assure that it would meet the deadline. These interim steps would normally include the desegregation of one or more grade levels. Under ideal circumstances, each school population would eventually "reflect the same ratio as the population of the school system as a whole." [95]

In April, 1968, the Department of Justice filed its first desegregation suit in the North. It charged that a Cook County, Illinois, school district was promoting discrimination. This was the 157th school suit filed by the department under the Civil Rights Act of 1964.

[93] Jim Leesen, "Desegregation: A New Approach, A New Deadline," *Southern Education Report*, 3 (January–February, 1968), 14.

[94] *Ibid.*, 15, 17.

[95] Horace Barker, *The Federal Retreat in School Desegregation* (Atlanta: Southern Regional Council, 1969), 6–7. See also *Civil Rights Progress Report 1970* (Washington, D.C.: Congressional Quarterly Inc., 1971), 50; Jim Leesen, "A Popular and Precise Phrase," *Southern Education Report*, 3 (June, 1968), 13–15.

By 1968 it had become abundantly clear that the freedom of choice approach would not result in more than token desegregation. In May, after a delay of many months, the Office of Civil Rights in HEW announced that some 14 percent of the black students in eleven southern states were attending desegregated elementary and secondary schools in 1967–1968. This figure applied only to black students attending schools that were at least 50 percent white. However, there were errors in the computations and not all school districts were included.[96] Progress in the desegregation of faculties was still slow and steps were being taken through the federal district courts to deal with the problem in Mississippi, Alabama, and Louisiana.[97]

Information about the schools in the eleven southern states was furnished by OCR in May, 1968 (See Table 26).

In the wake of the very slow move toward desegregation in the South, the United States Supreme Court came to grips with the freedom of choice issue in May, 1968. This policy which was being followed by a rural Virginia county school board was struck down in *Green et al.* v. *County School Board of New Kent County, Va., et al.* (88 S. Ct. 1689, 1968). In effect, the Supreme Court held that continued delays were no longer acceptable in those southern and border states still maintaining dual school systems. Freedom of choice plans were declared to be inadequate if they did not terminate school segregation as rapidly as other methods would. School authorities were charged with the affirmative responsibility to take whatever steps were necessary to end racial discrimination "root and branch." Although not all freedom-of-choice plans were ruled unconstitutional per se by the decision, as they had generally been prepared, such plans were invalid.[98] Northern de facto segregation was not involved in this decision.[99]

[96] John Morsell, "Racial Desegregation and Integration in Public Education," *Journal of Negro Education*, 38 (Summer, 1969), 277–78.

[97] Jim Leesen, "Desegregating Faculties," *Southern Education Report*, 3 (May, 1968), 27.

[98] See H. C. Hudgins, "Desegregation: Where Schools Stand with the Courts as the New Year Begins," *American School Board Journal*, 156 (January, 1969), 21–25, for a summary of the effects of federal court decisions on school boards and administrators.

[99] See James C. Harvey and Charles H. Holmes, "Busing and School Desegregation," *Phi Delta Kappan*, 53 (May, 1972), 540–41.

Table 26

PUPIL DESEGREGATION IN 11 SOUTHERN STATES[100]

Schools omitted from the survey were 1,119 districts assuring OCR they were in full compliance and containing less than 3,000 pupils (some 16.5 percent of the total).

State	Districts Reporting	Enrollment		Desegregation	
		Total	Negro	Negro Students	% Negro Students
Ala.	113	690,343	232,021	12,528	5.4
Ark.	144	288,277	105,443	17,746	16.8
Fla.	66	1,296,208	301,752	54,391	18.0
Ga.	163	850,956	274,302	26,086	9.5
La.	46	663,543	259,637	17,344	6.7
Miss.	117	422,915	199,772	7,817	3.9
N.C.	137	1,179,373	338,876	55,905	16.5
S.C.	93	543,194	219,262	14,045	6.4
Tenn.	108	746,115	162,693	29,954	18.4
Tex.	381	1,866,484	313,388	81,767	26.1
Va.	114	986,567	244,156	49,879	20.4
Total	1,482	9,534,025	2,651,302	367,512	13.9

[100] Jim Leesen, "Few Statistics—No Summary," *Southern Education Report*, 4 (December, 1968), 11.

Meanwhile, the House Appropriations Committee reported the Labor-HEW appropriations measure for fiscal 1969. This bill included two amendments added in the committee by Representative Jamie Whitten of Mississippi. One amendment prohibited the use of funds to force the busing of students, to force abolishment of any school, or to force any pupil to attend a particular school against the wish of his parents. The other amendment prohibited the withholding of federal funds from a state or school district in order to force the attendance of a pupil at a certain school, or the busing of any pupil, or the abolishment of any school. The basic purpose of the amendments was to prevent the withholding of funds from school districts using freedom of choice plans. The bill passed the House without change, including Whitten's amendments. However, there was a modification in the Senate. The new version of the Whitten amendments provided that attendance of pupils at a particular school, busing of pupils, or abolishment of schools could not be forced "in order to overcome racial imbalance." This change had the effect of limiting the Whitten amendment provisions to northern schools since "racial imbalance" traditionally was applied to de facto segregation only. The bill with the new change passed the Senate and was accepted in conference by the House.[101]

In the meantime, a black-consciousness movement was developing and a trend toward separatism, as there was widespread disillusionment with integration. That seemed to be the dominant view among the new breed of black college students who perceived themselves as bound ever-closer to the black community. Charles Hamilton in speaking of this new mood declared: "I think we're turning out a cadre of people who can't be the same—who are going to effect a new way of living in the black community. I just can't see all those kids coming out as Little Black Samboes, which might mean—and I don't want to say this too loudly—that we are laying the foundation for a different kind of rapprochement between black and white later on." [102]

Preston Wilcox, a former professor of social work at Columbia, echoed a similar theme. He declared that few whites believed that a school could be all black and succcessful. He insisted:

[101] *Civil Rights Progress Report, 1970,* 36–37.
[102] See Robert F. Campbell, "Community Control," *Southern Education Report,* 4 (July–August, 1968), 19.

There is a whole rhetoric in this country that segregated education cannot be quality education, and usually when they say that they mean black segregated schools, not white segregated schools. Our contention is that if we can get the white racists out of our way, that is, if we can get them out from any control of the cities of black people we can effectively develop quality education. . . . Neither white education nor integration holds any interest for the black community. We happen to feel that white education in this country is bankrupt and that the large number of whites are not taught social responsibility in terms of their society, nor are they educated to respect the black people as people. . . . We also feel that integration in this country has essentially been a subterfuge for white supremacy. It has not been based on bringing co-equals together but in most cases is an attempt to subsidize white people for being nice to black people.[103]

During the summer of 1968 and as the new school year approached, many blacks, reflecting the concept of "black awareness," came to feel that school desegregation was no longer relevant. They asked: "Why don't they ever transfer to our schools? Why should we be the ones to do all the sacrificing?" Some of them voiced the attitude that if "quality education" could be achieved in an all-black school, why should black children suffer the cruelty, estrangement, and pain by attending a "previously all-white school." "Separate but equal" had never been achieved when it was the law of the land, and it had now become "a sour goal of the disappointed, the disillusioned and the betrayed." [104]

As the end of 1968 neared, Pat Watters of the Southern Regional Council noted that the effect of school desegregation in the South had been largely a failure. The mistakes of the past were being repeated. To make matters worse, he did not believe that the nation was aware that there had been a failure.[105] Meanwhile, the United States Commission on Civil Rights reported that many southern school districts favored freedom of choice because it did not work. There was white resistance to any other approach, and school boards reacted accordingly. Furthermore, a number of federal district courts continued to permit the path of least resistance.[106]

[103] Jim Leesen, "Time and Variations," *Southern Education Report,* 4 (July–August, 1968), 5.

[104] See Betty Fancher, *Voices from the South: Black Students Talk About Their Experience in Desegregated Schools* (Atlanta: Southern Regional Council, 1970), 1.

[105] "Enforcing Civil Rights Laws: The Full Circle of Failure," *Current,* 102 (December, 1968), 33.

[106] Bartley, "Full Circle of Failure," *Lawlessness and Disorder,* 11–14.

Typical of this situation was a case in Mississippi. On July 6, 1968, in spite of *Green*, Judge William Keady, northern district of Mississippi, ruled that freedom of choice was the only practical way of accomplishing school desegregation in Holly Springs, Marshall County, Mississippi. In *Anthony* v. *Marshall County Board of Education* (Civil Action No. WC6819, 1968) Judge Keady contended that his decision was based on evidence submitted by the school board that other methods considered—pairing and zoning—would have led to immediate integration. The judge added: "This appears from the uncontroverted evidence in this case. There is no assault made by the plaintiffs upon those realistic, hard facts." He then found that the presence of black pupils in schools attended by whites would "necessarily lower" the quality of education. Needless to say, then, the best method was freedom of choice, since it provided the least integration. Later, in 1969, the Fifth Circuit Court of Appeals overruled Keady's decision and ordered the school district to develop a more effective means of desegregation (409 F. 2d 1287, 1969).[107]

In spite of growing disenchantment over the rate of desegregation by civil rights groups, HEW claimed the largest gains ever in terms of 1968–69 school desegregation progress. Figures for the degree of desegregation are shown in Table 27.[108]

Table 27

PERCENTAGE OF NEGRO STUDENTS ATTENDING
DESEGREGATED SCHOOLS IN SEVEN SOUTHERN STATES

State	1968–1969 School Year % of All Negro Students
Ala.	7.4%
Ga.	14.2%
La.	8.8%
Miss.	7.1%
N.C.	27.8%
S.C.	14.9%
Va.	25.7%
All States	16.1%

[107] See U.S. Commission on Civil Rights, *Federal Enforcement of School Desegregation* (Washington, D.C.: U.S. Government Printing Office, September 11, 1969), 15.

[108] *Ibid.*, 31, 35.

The pace of desegregation was faster in districts operating under HEW guidelines than those acting under court orders. The statistics were as follows:

Table 28
PERCENTAGE OF NEGRO STUDENTS ATTENDING
DESEGREGATED SCHOOLS IN SEVEN
SOUTHERN STATES, FALL, 1968

State	% in Districts Under Court Order	% in Districts Operating Under Voluntary Plans (HEW Guidelines)	Total % for All Districts
Ala.	7.4	0	7.4
Ga.	7.9	18.4	14.2
La.	8.6	24.0	8.8
Miss.	4.3	12.0	7.1
N.C.	24.1	27.3	27.8
S.C.	7.5	15.4	14.9
Va.	13.9	25.6	25.7
All States	9.4%	21.0%	16.1%

HEW reported that the overall percentage of black students enrolled in schools with a majority of whites in the eleven southern states was about 18 percent in 1968–69. Parenthetically, while desegregation was increasing at a slow pace in the South, it was decreasing in the North, particularly in cities.[109] Also, in 1968–69, 68 percent of the black students still attended all-black schools in the eleven southern states.[110] Moreover, by then a significant portion of the white children in the South, particularly in the Deep South, had fled to segregated private schools.[111]

A southern political scientist, James Prothro, had this to say about the progress made in school desegregation in the South:

> By 1968, school desegregation in the South looked massive compared with the modest level of the early 1960's. Compared with an ab-

[109] William Van Til, "The Great American Cop-Out," *Phi Delta Kappan*, 54 (October, 1972), 128.
[110] James Cass, "How Much Progress is Enough?," *Saturday Review*, July 17, 1971, 41.
[111] See John C. Walden and Allen D. Cleveland, "The South's New Segregation Academies," *Phi Delta Kappan*, 53 (December, 1971), 234.

solute ideal of integration, on the other hand, it still looked like tokenism. The amount of desegregation achieved depends in part, of course,
on the operational definition of segregation that is employed. Our focus
is on the percentage of blacks in integrated schools. In order not to
count a school as integrated if several hundred blacks are attending a
school that has only three or four white pupils, we have used a twenty
percent cut-off point. If 20 percent or more of the pupils in a school
are white, then the blacks attending that school are counted as attending a desegregated school. Applying this standard to the 894 counties
of the South from which more recent (1968) data are available, 28
counties still did not have a single black in an integrated school. Five
percent or less of the black pupils were attending integrated schools in
25 percent of the counties, ten percent or less in 40 percent of the
counties. At a level approaching genuine integration, 90 percent or
more of the black pupils were reported to be attending integrated
schools in 20 percent of the counties. For all southern counties, the
median attending integrated schools was 15.6 percent.[112]

One educational writer when looking at the nation as a whole,
charged that schools were more segregated in 1968–1969 than they
had been before the *Brown* decision. He argued that this was largely
the consequence of the white flight to the suburbs from the cities and
their replacement by increased concentrations of blacks and various
Spanish-speaking minorities in some instances. He pointed out that
this development was not confined to the South but increasingly in
the North and was not immediately reachable by the Civil Rights Act
of 1964. Thus, blacks in the North, to remedy the situation, had had
to rely more heavily upon the courts and state legislatures than federal authority. He stated that in 1968 desegregation efforts were
under way in such places as Evansville and Kokomo, Indiana; Ni-
agara Falls, New York; Grand Rapids, Michigan; Berkeley and San
Mateo, California; South Holland, Illinois; Providence, Rhode Island; and Waterbury, Connecticut.[113]

Some progress had been made toward desegregation of the
schools in the South, and a beginning had been made in the North
in terms of physical presence. However, as already noted, the North
had become more segregated as whites fled to the suburbs. In the
South, blacks had paid a heavy price for the token gains made. Black

[112] James W. Prothro, "Stateways Versus Folkways Revisited: An Error in
Prediction," *Journal of Politics*, 34 (May, 1972), 356–57.
[113] Morsell, "Racial Desegregation and Integration in Public Education,"
279.

students," black teachers, and black administrators[114] suffered as never foreseen in the euphoria of earlier years by those favoring integration. Perhaps down the road, things would get better, but in the process a lot of disenchantment had set in in the black community. It was the black students who had to do the integrating; and black teachers and administrators were often dismissed or demoted when desegregation occurred. Genuine integration was still a long way off at the end of the Johnson administration.

The president had generally not interfered with the operations of the Office of Education, except in the Chicago case. Yet, he could be faulted for not giving the kind of genuine support needed to aid HEW in its efforts. It can be explained in part, perhaps, by the growing involvement in Vietnam which diverted much of his time and interests.

This view is shared by Thomas Cronin who pointed out that John Gardner, secretary of HEW from 1965 to 1968, had enjoyed good relations with the White House during the middle sixties when the major health and educational legislation was being passed and put into operation. He noted that "when the Vietnam war began overshadowing all else and causing more and more of the President's time and potential budget increases, White House communications with HEW's Gardner began to resemble those of most other cabinet members—less frequent and less supportive." [115]

The president needed southern support for the war effort as opposition in the rest of the country began to mount. Of course, one cannot overlook the entrenched positions of white southern congressmen in important committees which gave them leverage to prevent the strong enforcement of Title VI by HEW in the field of education. Moreover, the recalcitrance among white school boards, administrators, and the white community in general should also be noted.

Therefore, though more black students were physically present in former all-white schools, there remained much to be done. Improvements had also been made in the number of blacks registered and

---

[114] See John Egerton, "When Desegregation Comes, the Negro Principals Go," *Southern Education Report*, 3 (December, 1967), 8–12.

[115] Thomas E. Cronin, "Everybody Believes in Democracy Until He Gets to the White House . . . ; An Examination of White House-Departmental Relations," *Law and Contemporary Problems*, 35 (Summer, 1970), 605.

voting, and running for office and winning. There were still parts of the South, however, where blacks were deprived of voting rights and candidates for public office still encountered many obstacles. Furthermore, taking part in political activities had very limited possibilities as far as improving the lot of black people was concerned.

CHAPTER VII

Health and Welfare Services

Health and welfare services were very discriminatory toward black people in many parts of the country at the time of the passage of the Civil Rights Act of 1964. Both services were affected by Section 601 of Title VI of the act, which provided: "No person in the United States shall, on the ground of race, color, or national origin, be excluded from participation in, be denied the benefits of, or be subjected to discrimination under any program or activity receiving Federal financial assistance."

On March 9, 1964, even before the passage of the Civil Rights Act of 1964, the administration, through Secretary of HEW Anthony Celebrezze, informed Congress that it had taken a step to bar any federal construction funds from hospitals that insisted on maintaining segregated facilities. This was after a Supreme Court decision upheld a lower court ruling from the Fourth Circuit Court of Appeals that hospitals built with federal funds could not segregate patients or staff and thus held unconstitutional the "separate but equal" provisions of the Hill-Burton Hospital Construction Act of 1946. Celebrezze stated that assurances of non-discrimination would be required of all hospital projects constructed with federal money.[1]

In 1965 the United States Commission on Civil Rights staff visited facilities in eleven southern and border states and then published a report of its investigation. It found that two hospitals in Maryland had been substantially desegregated before the passage of the Civil Rights Act of 1964. Out of the other thirty-seven hospitals visited, the commission found that in only eleven hospitals had there been any considerable amount of desegregation one year after the act had been signed into law. In about two thirds of the hospitals there was a large degree of noncompliance in that no substantial change had occurred in patient admissions or assignment to rooms and wards. Although in most cases black wings or floors had been eliminated in

[1] New York *Times*, March 10, 1964, p. 20.

the hospitals, integration of patients within wards was less frequent and biracial assignments to two-bed rooms was the most difficult step for hospital administrators to take.[2]

The commission staff members found that in some of the public health centers they visited there were very great differences in the patient loads, even though there were blacks and whites in large number eligible for such services. In a few cases, heart and cancer clinics had predominantly white clienteles. They found that the dental clinic in one county served only white children and three fourths of the patients were white in another county dental clinic. They also noted that in some communities prenatal and well-baby clinics were all or predominantly black.[3]

The commission reported that in Selma (Dallas County), Alabama, where the numbers of black and white families with incomes below the poverty level were about equal, the health officer stated that only blacks were involved in the prenatal program. He also declared that he did not know where poor white women went for their prenatal care. However, according to the commission:

> Although it is not known how poor white women receive prenatal care in Selma, it was apparent that the care they receive outside the public health program results in the birth of their babies in hospitals with a physician in attendance. On the other hand, the federally assisted program which provides care only for Negroes, resulted primarily in the birth of babies outside hospitals attended only by untrained midwives.[4]

Dental care had been limited to whites in Dallas County, Alabama, prior to 1965. Early in the summer of 1965 a black youngster had had a tooth repaired by a dentist on duty there at the time. A few days later several black youngsters sought dental care at the health center. At that point, the county health officer adopted a new policy for treating children on a school-by-school basis. The children were treated at schools rather than clinics. This procedure assured that the treatment would be largely segregated because the schools were.[5]

Some of the health clinics and departments tried to comply with

---

[2] See U.S. Commission on Civil Rights, *Title VI . . . One Year After the Survey of Health and Welfare Services in the South* (Washington, D.C.: U.S. Government Printing Office, 1966), 14.

[3] *Ibid.*, 15.   [4] *Ibid.*, 15–16.   [5] *Ibid.*, 16.

Title VI by removing racial signs from waiting rooms, entrances, and other public facilities. Still others abolished separate treatment days for black and white patients. However, segregated practice continued as whites and blacks segregated themselves. One example was the Hinds County Health Clinic in Jackson, Mississippi, where racial signs were removed from drinking fountains, restrooms, entrances, and waiting rooms, but a mason partition was retained which divided the main waiting room. In the Tuberculosis Clinic in Dallas County Health Center blacks and whites sat in separate alcoves according to race although the old racial signs had been removed.[6]

There was an investigation of medicare programs under the public welfare category. At that time, the staff found that several states were financing medical care for their patients on a segregated basis. The programs utilized the services of private physicians who had segregated offices, scheduled different treatment days for blacks and whites, and referred patients to hospitals on a racial basis. The Mississippi State Welfare Department had just prepared a non-discrimination clause to be inserted in the statements regularly signed by doctors who served welfare clients. The form was to be used as of September, 1965. The state director told the staff that segregated health care by physicians was fairly widespread in Mississippi.[7]

Under the public welfare category there was a substantial failure of a number of hospitals to comply with Title VI. Four Mississippi agencies, including the State Welfare Department, all of which purchased hospital care for clients, issued a joint statement explaining to cooperative hospitals the need for non-discriminatory treatment. Out of 250 hospitals 30 refused to sign the pledge and thereby were excluded from the program. When asked by the staff of the commission the welfare administrator stated that she did not know how much change had occurred in the practices of the hospitals that had signed the pledge. In Louisiana, Arkansas, Tennessee, and Georgia many of the hospitals had signed assurances with state departments, but there was no familiarity with the actual practices of the hospitals. A few hospitals had been dropped for failing to sign a pledge. However, in Memphis, the welfare director listed the Methodist Hospital as a vendor, but no assurance of non-discrimination had been given.[8]

[6] *Ibid.*, 16–17.   [7] *Ibid.*, 19–20, 21.   [8] *Ibid.*, 21.

Nursing homes and child care institutions showed quite extensive segregation. Some nursing homes excluded blacks and some were designated for blacks. In Americus, Georgia, elderly white welfare clients accounted for one half of the patients at the Magnolia Nursing Home. Neither the one at Magnolia nor any other nursing home at Magnolia admitted blacks. In Milledgeville, Georgia, the welfare director did not know if Title VI had caused any nursing homes to change their racial exclusion policies. She also declared that the maternity homes were still segregated.[9]

Segregation in Local Offices. Most local public welfare officers visited by the staff had segregated public facilities or waiting rooms, and four offices were located in segregated courthouses. In Texas, Mississippi, and North Carolina officials indicated that there would have to be some changes in the buildings before compliance could be completed. In Shreveport, Louisiana, although the welfare office had removed its signs designating separate waiting rooms, the rooms were divided by a partition with blacks and whites sitting apart. When questioned about it, the director claimed that the clients preferred segregated waiting rooms.[10]

Administrative Procedure of State Agencies. Local county units had not been involved by state welfare departments in the process of securing compliance pledges from vendors. Most state agencies emphasized the signing of papers from vendors instead of the achievement of any half-meaningful change in discriminatory practices. The welfare department in Texas had set a cut-off date for child care institutions failing to comply with "nondiscriminatory requirements in extending care and services to clients." The commission did not find that local welfare directors had been instructed on the matter of referrals or assistance to Negro clients who sought service from vendors for the first time.[11]

Vocational Rehabilitation. The commission staff found wide variations in achieving non-discrimination. The Mississippi Rehabilitation Division of the State Welfare Department had instructed its staff to make checks to guard against discriminatory practices in its

---

[9] *Ibid.,* 22.   [10] *Ibid.*   [11] *Ibid.,* 23.

programs. Certain kinds of discrimination were forbidden and staff members were required to use courtesy titles in correspondence with clients. However, at the time of the investigation in September, 1965, the commission staff found that whites and blacks worked in different departments at the Mississippi Industries for the Blind in Jackson. After learning about Title VI requirements early in 1965, the manager said that he assigned a black woman to the plant's all-white sewing department and she had been warmly received.[12]

The Louisiana vocational rehabilitation program, in contrast to the one in Texas, at the time of the visit had not established any procedures for informing vendors about Title VI requirements, and it had not told its district staff either. An interview with a public welfare official in Shreveport, who used the same vendors as the Vocational Rehabilitation Program, revealed that hospitals, private physicians, and schools still practiced segregation and racial discrimination in their offices and buildings.[13]

In summary, the commission concluded that no positive efforts had been made by state rehabilitation agencies to desegregate services except in Texas. In the main, state agencies—except in Texas —permitted individual vendors to determine their own methods and pace of complying with Title VI.[14]

The Commission on Civil Rights reported the following findings:

1. Written agreements to comply with Title VI had been secured for most federally assisted programs. There had also been progress in eliminating the most overt kinds of segregation such as separate hospital wings and segregated public facilities and waiting rooms. There had even been a few instances of rapid and complete hospital desegregation.

2. There continued to be widespread segregation or exclusion of blacks in federally assisted programs at the state and local levels in the areas visited:

a. Some state operated hospitals and training facilities remained segregated.

b. Some local hospitals had eliminated separate black wings or buildings in response to the requirements of Title VI, but black

---

[12] *Ibid.*, 26.   [13] *Ibid.*   [14] *Ibid.*, 30.

patients in most hospitals were still assigned to rooms or wards occupied only by blacks.

c. Blacks were still excluded from many nursing homes, child care institutions, and training facilities which were providing service for a fee to whites under federally assisted programs. Local officials of some federally assisted programs were not referring blacks to services previously denied them.

d. Some federally assisted local health programs were racially segregated or exclusive.

e. Some physicians who were providing services to clients of federally assisted programs continued to segregate patients in their offices and to make racial distinctions in referring patients to hospitals.

3. HEW, which often drafted and issued regulations and formal documents required thereunder, had failed to take steps to achieve compliance. For example:

a. Consistent and uniform standards had not been applied to state programs.

b. States had not been required to report on the steps they had taken to achieve compliance.

c. Except for complaint investigations, field inspections had not been undertaken to ascertain the amount of noncompliance in state programs.

d. No enforcement action had been taken even in instances where negotiations had not led to the elimination of violations of the law.

4. Since HEW had not adopted adequate review and compliance procedures, the department did not know whether discrimination was being eliminated or not.

5. HEW had not provided state and local directors and administrators of federally assisted programs with the support, leadership, and information needed to facilitate compliance with Title VI.[15]

To remedy these weaknesses the commission made the following recommendations to HEW:

1. Proceed immediately to apply sanctions in cases where negotiations had not ended violations of Title VI.

[15] *Ibid.*, 45–46.

2. Conduct immediate surveys and thorough inspections to determine the extent to which discrimination continued to exist in federally assisted programs.

3. Establish for its programs the affirmative goals of actual participation on a desegregated basis in all benefits made available.

4. Inaugurate regular reporting systems and program evaluation sufficient to identify areas of noncompliance and racial differentials in benefits received in each facility and program.[16]

Although many state agencies resisted and delayed the submission of statements of compliance with Title VI, only Alabama decided to defy and put to a test the legal authority to establish certain requirements and impose certain conditions under Title VI.[17] As early as August 17, 1965, U.S. Commissioner of Welfare Ellen Winston had notified Alabama that it was not in compliance with Title VI. Months later, on April 6, 1966, a hearing examiner had recommended that federal assistance to Alabama be terminated. After months of futile negotiations with Alabama, on January 12, 1967, John Gardner, secretary of HEW, finally announced that federal funds would be cut off on February 28 unless assurance of compliance was given. Alabama requested a delay but Secretary Gardner stated that he could not justify a delay any longer.[18] The matter involved $96 million a year in welfare funds. The federal government contributed 80 percent of the welfare funds in the state.[19]

George Wallace, special assistant to his wife, Lurleen, then governor of Alabama, went to Washington to appeal to members of the Senate Finance Committee for support. He called the federal government's action an arbitrary and illegal exercise of power. All members of the committee, including the chairman, Russell Long of Louisiana, except Senator Vance Hartke of Indiana, promised that they would exert whatever pressure they could to reverse the administration's decision.[20]

The state of Alabama took the case to court in the federal district court of northern Alabama, and there a preliminary injunction was

16 *Ibid.*, 47.

17 U.S. Commission on Civil Rights, *HEW and Title VI* (Washington, D.C.: U.S. Government Printing Office, 1970), 23–24.

18 New York *Times*, January 25, 1967, p. 33.

19 *Congressional Quarterly Almanac*, XXIII (1967), 802.

20 New York *Times*, January 26, 1967, p. 20.

issued to prevent the termination of funds. HEW then appealed to the Fifth Circuit Court in New Orleans, and a three-judge panel held that the federal requirements for Alabama's compliance with the Civil Rights Act of 1964 were valid and had to be upheld. Furthermore, the district court's preliminary injunction was invalidated on the grounds of lack of jurisdiction.[21] Alabama then appealed to the United States Supreme Court.

In January, 1968, the Supreme Court announced its refusal to review the decision of the lower court in New Orleans which had upheld HEW's authority to cut off Alabama's federal welfare funds. Following this adverse decision, Alabama's Commissioner of Pensions and Security, Ruben King, announced that his agency had signed a new qualified agreement with HEW to comply with Title VI. Under the agreement, King announced that Alabama institutions and physicians had to certify to the state that their services were in full compliance with Title VI before they would be paid by a state agency for treating welfare patients. He placed conditions in the agreement to the effect that "nothing in the statement of compliance shall obligate the state to more than try, persuade, negotiate, or act in good faith in accordance with the language of the federal court." [22] There was no news about whether or not HEW accepted the conditions, but apparently it did and that ended the controversy.

Meantime, after the criticism by the Civil Rights Commission, HEW made a review of welfare practices in Mississippi. Eighteen staff members visited ten counties. Their study made it appear that there was no difference between blacks and whites with regard to access to welfare aid; that with the exception of the "putative" father rule, there was insufficient evidence to demonstrate unequal treatment with respect to eligibility; that there were no clear-cut differences between black and white recipients as far as average payments were concerned; and that most allegations of discrimination were very difficult "to factualize one way or the other." Each allegation of the HEW staff was refuted by both the NAACP and the Civil Rights Advisory Committee of Mississippi. Both reported widespread violations of almost every aspect of the state's welfare program and recommended corrective measures. The Mississippi Ad-

[21] *Ibid.*, August 30, 1967, p. 24.
[22] *Ibid.*, January 20, 1966, p. 20.

visory Committee held hearings in Jackson February 17–18, 1967, and numerous witnesses told of discriminatory treatment there.[23]

Despite the findings by the HEW staff members, the full Mississippi report which was completed in December, 1966, was never published. Welfare Commissioner Ellen Winston did state in a letter to the Mississippi Commissioner of Public Welfare that public welfare programs in Mississippi had to be viewed within the context of the economic and cultural setting within which the program was being administered. Seen within that framework, she concluded that Mississippi was largely in compliance with Title VI in spite of some evidence of discrimination. The Civil Rights Commission charged that the statement did not truly reflect the extent of discrimination found in the report. The commission formally requested a copy of the report on March, 1967, but was told that the study was already out of date and "more work was needed." The commission concluded that HEW had decided that the withholding of funds was not the best way to deal with the situation, and noted that a full-time investigator was assigned from the Atlanta office of HEW to spend several weeks in Mississippi.[24] It was indeed reprehensible, however, that the Mississippi report was simply filed away.

By February 8, 1966, the Public Health Service had terminated new assistance to 54 hospitals and had initiated enforcement proceedings involving 53 more of the 7,450 hospitals in the nation. On March 7, 1966, at the same time HEW was issuing guidelines for school desegregation, it also set up requirements for the desegregation of hospitals and medical facilities.[25] HEW began in July, 1966, an effort to pressure hospitals receiving federal aid to comply with desegregation guidelines under threat of termination of that assistance. Such institutions had been given until July 1, 1966, to comply; if they did not, they could receive a 48-hour notice that they were not in compliance and that procedures were under way that could lead to termination of funds. They were given 48 hours to reply as to their plans for ending discriminatory practices. By September 8,

[23] "Comment: Title VI of the Civil Rights Act—Implementation and Impact," 975–76. See also Richard A. Cloward and Frances Fox Piven, "Mississippi: Starving by the Rule Book," *Nation*, 204 (April 3, 1967), 429–31.

[24] U.S. Commission on Civil Rights, *HEW and Title VI*, 51.

[25] *Congressional Quarterly Almanac*, XXII (1966), 477.

1966, 24 hospitals had received such letters: 4 in Alabama, 3 in Georgia, 3 in Louisiana, 6 in Mississippi, 4 in Texas, 3 in South Carolina, and 1 in Virginia. No funds had been terminated up to that point.[26]

On September 1, 1966, the Justice Department took the additional step of filing the first suit charging racial discrimination in a hospital. It was filed in the federal district court in Jackson, Mississippi, against Marion County and the trustees and administrators of the Marion County General Hospital located in Columbia, Mississippi. The hospital was charged with acting in violation of Title III of the Civil Rights Act of 1964, which required that public facilities owned or operated by or on behalf of any government be desegregated. It was alleged that the hospital maintained segregated waiting rooms, snack bars, wards, rooms, and other facilities.[27] This was a different approach from that of Title VI.

The Commission on Civil Rights took another look in 1970 at recent trends in eliminating discrimination in health care and welfare. The medicare program had been enacted into law in 1965, and in 1966 HEW's Office of Equal Health Opportunity (OEHO) undertook a massive effort with a staff of nearly five hundred to determine whether the requirements of Title VI were being met. As of June 30, 1966, over 2,700 compliance reviews were held of hospitals, nursing homes, and extended care facilities; some 1,329 institutions were brought into compliance by negotiations. From July 1, 1966, to January 1, 1967, there were 4,142 compliance reviews. As a result, 2,167 institutions were found to be in compliance and 1,875 were not. Anxious to obtain federal funds many hospitals abolished such practices as refusing to admit black patients or of segregating them in assignment to wards, wings, and rooms in order to qualify. As of June 30, 1967, six hospitals had had their funds terminated and seven more received notices of hearings. Moreover, eleven more hospitals had had at least an initial determination of noncompliance by a hearing examiner. By January 1, 1968, HEW reported that 97 percent of the nation's hospitals were committed to nondiscriminatory practices. It was said that over 3,000 health facilities

[26] "Civil Rights," *Congressional Quarterly Weekly Report*, 24 (September 9, 1966), 1964.
[27] *Ibid.*

and hospitals had changed their previous practices and policies to comply with Title VI. By then, also, only twelve hospitals had lost funds for failure to comply with Title VI. However, the commission sounded a pessimistic note when it noted that there had been no review of many hospitals since 1966 and there were reports that many of them had resumed discriminatory practices. Apparently also, extended care facilities were not being examined carefully.[28]

In March, 1968, enforcement activities in Health and Welfare were brought together in a Health and Welfare branch within the Office of Civil Rights in HEW. Throughout the remainder of 1968 field work was completed in seventeen state agency reviews with a final visitation of 1,500 facilities and agencies. Final written reports had been completed for Florida, Maryland, Arkansas, and Connecticut by the end of 1968. In January, 1968, a final report was ready for South Carolina. As far as Mississippi was concerned, as an aftermath of the earlier review, some steps were taken by the Bureau of Family Services and the Office of Commissioner of Welfare Services to remedy deficiencies in the implementation of Title VI.

The commissioner and bureau directed themselves to the following: (1) insurance of prompt decisions on welfare applications (30 days); (2) enforcement of requirements of fair hearings for welfare denial or termination (fair notice, advice as to right of appeal, proper instructions for carrying out appellate procedures and hearings); (3) periodical review of the administration of welfare programs; (4) use of courtesy titles to welfare recipients; (5) improvements of hitherto strained federal-state relations in order that Title VI policies might be better implemented; (6) recruitment and employment of blacks in previously segregated welfare agency staffs; (7) integration of Title V work-training programs; and (8) instruction of both state and local agencies against the practice of requiring that welfare payments be spent in restricted manners.[29]

An important case with civil rights overtones arose in Alabama in the 1960s. Mrs. Sylvester Smith was a black woman who lived in

[28] U.S. Commission on Civil Rights, *Federal Civil Rights Enforcement Effort*, 32–33; U.S. Commission on Civil Rights, *HEW and Title VI*, 47; "Comment: Title VI of the 1964 Civil Rights Act—Implementation and Impact," 983.
[29] "Comment: Title VI of the 1964 Civil Rights Act—Implementation and Impact," 976.

Dallas County. Her first husband had died and left her with three children. She married again and had another child but was soon deserted by her second husband. She requested and received support from the aid-to-dependent-children program. In 1964 Alabama issued a "substitute" father regulation. Aid would be denied to the children of a mother who "cohabited" in or outside her home with an able-bodied male, a "substitute" father being considered a nonabsent parent and thus responsible for them. Soon Mrs. Smith's eldest child, Ida Elizabeth, thirteen, had an illegitimate child. When this happened, the aid for her was prohibited. In the meantime, too, Mrs. Smith had been living with a man on occasion who was already married and had nine children. After learning about this situation, the caseworker asked Mrs. Smith to end her relationship with the man. She refused to do so and on October 11, 1966, she was notified that the state was cutting off payments to her family under the aid-to-dependent-children program.[30] All she had for her family was sixteen to twenty dollars a week she earned as a cook and waitress after that.

She took the matter to court and a three-judge panel called the "substitute" father rule arbitrary, discriminating, and in violation of the equal protection clause of the Fourteenth Amendment by allowing Alabama to pick and choose the women and children to whom it would give aid in accordance with no rational basis. It also held that the "substitute" father had no responsibility to support children under Alabama law and thus aid could not be denied on the basis of a "substitute" father. The state of Alabama appealed the case to the United States Supreme Court. The Supreme Court in *King, Commissioner, Department of Pensions and Security, et al.* v. *Smith, et al.* (392 U.S. 309, 1968) affirmed the decision of the lower court without going as far as the lower court did. It declared: "We hold today only that Congress had made at least this one determination: that destitute children who are legally fatherless cannot be flatly denied federally funded assistance on the transparent fiction that they have a "substitute" father."

The decision was said to have affected 21,000 children in Alabama and perhaps 400,000 in the country. Although there were

[30] See Walter Goodman, "Victory for 400,000 Children, The Case of Mrs. Sylvester Smith," *New York Times Magazine*, April 25, 1968, 28–29.

more white poor than black poor in the nation as a whole, a higher percentage of the poor were black than white and thus civil rights was involved in the decision. Furthermore, one might speculate that blacks of whatever circumstances received less courteous treatment than whites.

On the surface, and as far as physical facilities were concerned, considerable progress was made during the Johnson administration in desegregating health and welfare services. Of course, as the Civil Rights Commission pointed out, the affected institutions and persons were not monitored enough. Paper compliance was too often the case, it seems. The subtler forms of racism, often referred to as institutional racism, unquestionably remained despite the efforts of the federal government to improve the treatment of black persons. The president himself, as far as the public record showed, took no important steps to prod the federal bureaucracy into moving strongly to enforce Title VI requirements. He referred to the health and welfare conditions of blacks quite often in his public speeches, but it was unlikely that these problems occupied a very high place in his priorities for urging the implementation of federal policies on a desegregated basis.

CHAPTER VIII

Epilogue

Overall, more gains were made in desegregating some of America's major institutions during the Johnson administration than in any previous ones of the modern presidency. Furthermore, the three major civil rights bills enacted during his five years of office were more far-reaching than the ones passed in 1957 and 1960 which were confined to weak efforts in the area of voting. The Civil Rights Act of 1964 was truly an omnibus bill covering many different areas. The Voting Rights Act of 1965 dealt with voting, and it was a comparatively strong bill. The Civil Rights Act of 1968 was concerned with several policy areas, but the housing section was the most important covering in theory around 80 percent of the nation's housing after it went through the three stages of implementation.

President Johnson was aware that there was still much left to be done to bring black people into the mainstream as he was about to leave office. On December 6, 1968, he received the first achievement award of the United Negro College Fund for "distinguished leadership and significant achievements in the field of education and civil rights." In accepting the award, the president stated that he intended to encourage future presidents to continue "the very long march" for civil rights. He also declared that he hoped that his administration's efforts in civil rights might represent a small step or two forward in that long march in the years ahead.[1]

On December 17, 1968, several hundred black federal government officials held a farewell reception for the president at the Federal City Club in Washington, D.C. He again referred, in language that must have sounded patronizing to some blacks, to the long march ahead when he declared: "What we've got to learn is that we've got a long way to walk, and there are going to be a lot of bruised and bloody feet. You're just like a grandson. You've just learned to walk." He claimed that the civil rights legislation passed

[1] New York *Times*, December 7, 1968, p. 31.

during his administration had opened the chance of a "marvelous future." [2] However, he said:

> We waste our time, and we defraud ourselves if we look back on what we've accomplished. Those accomplishments were infinitesimal in the face of the tasks still to be completed and good just to pep us up for the work ahead.
>
> You are the vanguard. Behind you there are millions of others who are proud that a Negro is a Justice of the Supreme Court . . . yet these millions of Americans cannot get a decent job. These are the Negroes who are locked in poverty, locked in ill paying jobs, locked out of American promise.
>
> Some of these millions, especially the young, want a place in the prosperous democracy that they cannot find. Some of them feel that their only course is to attack the institutions of this society and all who made it.
>
> The quality of life in America five years from now or 10 years from now will depend on how the nation responds to the needs and desires of these millions of impoverished Negroes.
>
> If we turn a deaf ear to them, or if we try to patronize them, or if we simply try to suppress their impatience and deny its causes then we are not going to solve anything. All we are going to do is just compound our troubles. [3]

Just before leaving office, President Johnson made the following remarks in his last State of the Union address on January 14, 1969:

> The Nation's commitments in the field of civil rights began with the Declaration of Independence. They were extended by the 13th, 14th, and 15th amendments. They have been powerfully strengthened by the enactment of three far-reaching civil rights laws within the past five years, that this Congress, in its wisdom, passed. On January 1 of this year, the Fair Housing Act of 1968 covered over 20 million American houses and apartments. The prohibition against racial discrimination in that Act should be remembered and it should be vigorously enforced throughout the land.
>
> I believe we should also extend the vital provisions of the Voting Rights Act for another 5 years. [4]

The three major civil rights bills that passed during Johnson's term of office, though important, chiefly benefited the black middle

[2] *Ibid.*, December 18, 1968, p. 1.

[3] *Ibid.*, p. 31.

[4] "President's State of the Union Message," January 14, 1969, *Congressional Quarterly Almanac*, XXV (1969), 3A; *Public Papers of the Presidents: Lyndon B. Johnson, 1968–69*, 1266.

class. They had little or no effect on the black masses located in the ghettos or in rural poverty areas. What good was it to be able to eat or sleep at the Holiday Inn if one could not afford it? Of what importance was it to the black man without a job to find out that if he could afford it he might possibly be able to purchase a home in the plush suburbs? As one writer, Donald H. Smith, pointed out, none of the legislation had "begun to show any appreciable difference in the ghettos of our huge urban complexes. A man who lives in a slum tenement, who has no job, and who has lost his self-respect because he must accept charity, finds little comfort in the knowledge his Southern brother can now vote and sleep in white hotels. In fact, the more he hears on television how much better off he is, and how much conditions have changed, the more bitter he becomes." [5]

Yet, in spite of these serious deficiencies, in a certain sense many blacks would be concerned about civil rights for a long time to come, though the civil rights movement, coinciding with the push for major legislation, seemed to many people by the late 1960s to be dead. As Alice Walker, a brilliant young black writer, noted, many of the white liberals and civil rights sponsors were disenchanted in seeing that relatively little if anything had been accomplished. Moreover, she wrote:

> The movement is dead to the white man because it no longer interests him. And it no longer interests him because he can afford to be uninterested; he does not have to live by it, with it, or for it as Negroes must. He can take a rest from the news of the beatings, killings and arrests that reach him from the North and South—if his skin is white. Negroes cannot now and will never be able to take a rest from the injustices that plague them for they—not the white man—are the target.
> What good was the civil rights movement? If it had just given this country Dr. King, a leader of conscience once in our lifetime, it would have been enough. If it had just taken black eyes off white television stories, it would have been enough.
> If the civil rights movement is "dead," and if it gave us nothing else, it gave us each other forever. It gave us some bread, some of us shelter, some of us knowledge and pride, all of us comfort. It gave us our chil-

---

[5] Donald Hugh Smith, "Civil Rights: A Problem of Communications," *Phylon*, (Winter, 1966), 385. See also Robert L. Allen, *Black Awakening in Capitalist America* (Garden City, N.Y.: Anchor Books, Inc., 1969), 26; and Richard L. Worsnop, "Black Pride," *Editorial Research Reports*, 2 (September 11, 1968), 671.

dren, our husbands, our brothers, our fathers, as men reborn and with purpose for living. It broke the pattern of black servitude in this country. It shattered "the phony promise" of white soap operas that sucked away so many pitiful lives. It gave us history and men better than Presidents. It gave us houses, unselfish men of courage and strength, for our little boys to follow. It gave us hope for tomorrow. It called us to life. Because we live, it can never die.[6]

In summary, it is difficult to evaluate the accomplishments of the Johnson administration in any absolute sense. True, the statistics showed more black employment, more school desegregation in the South; more blacks could vote in the South; they had gained more access to public accommodations such as restaurants and motels. Moreover, more major civil rights bills (three) had been pushed through than during any of the previous modern administrations.

However, the groundwork for the act of 1964 was laid by the Kennedy administration, and in a sense its passage was a tribute to Kennedy's memory more than anything accomplished by Johnson. The Voting Rights Act of 1965 came largely as a reaction to the events in Alabama. In the case of the Civil Rights Act of 1968 with its housing section, Clarence Mitchell deserves more credit for its passage than Johnson himself. However, the president did utilize a number of levers at his disposal to assist in the passage of these laws, including the following: public addresses, messages to Congress, meetings with interested groups, private communications with key congressmen, and the like.

Nevertheless, if President Johnson is to be faulted it is not so much in his role as a legislator but in that of administration. No president can ever merely issue an order and assume that it will be carried out. However, if he is persistent in his demands on the bureaucracy he will be heard. It seems as though once a bill had been passed into law, he gave its enforcement relatively little attention. Needless to say, without his pressure and support the bureaucracy was often unable or unwilling to cope with the counter-pressures of strategically placed southern congressmen and the recalcitrance of their white constituents in opposition to the implementation of civil rights laws. Moreover, many members of the vast bureaucracy were at best in-

[6] Alice Walker, "Civil Rights Movement: What Good Was It?" *The American Scholar*, 36 (Autumn, 1967), 550–51, 554.

different, if not hostile, to the cause of civil rights for black people. This problem merely compounded some of the weaknesses in the bills, such as the inadequate authority given to the Economic Employment Opportunity Commission in the Act of 1964.

Southern political leaders, with the backing of their white constituents, often used the language of federalism and states' rights to buttress white supremacy in their states. As one black political scientist, Hanes Walton, Jr., pointed out:

> For the most part, the problems of federalism for blacks started through reluctance of the federal government to move in and vigorously defend the rights of blacks because of the possibility of interfering with the doctrine of states' rights. Whether the problem is simply the national government's deference to the rights of states, or whether it is the ability of states to use the least invasion of their sovereignty to embarrass the federal government by crying authoritarianism and forcing the federal government to move slowly, cautiously, or not at all is irrelevant. Moreover, whether or not southerners have more power in Congress and more influence with presidential candidates, though significant in the final analysis, is not sufficient. The fact remains that the major problem of American federalism is neither the system itself, not its inbred weaknesses, but its unwillingness, because of entrenched racism, to effectively establish and protect black rights. . . . The cry of states losing their rights to the federal government has become in many instances only a smoke screen to deny blacks their full civil rights.[7]

To overcome the tendency of states' rights to hurt the cause of civil rights for black people, strong presidential leadership was needed. It never was forthcoming.

President Johnson missed a golden opportunity when he dismantled the vehicle he had established early in 1965 for a centralized coordination of civil rights efforts under the chairmanship of Vice-President Humphrey. If he had retained that instrumentality and given it his full support there would have been much greater progress than there was in implementing civil rights. However, Johnson decided for unknown reasons not to maintain this coordinated effort. One can only speculate that he gave in to southern pressures in return for support of an increasingly unpopular war. Moreover, he may not have wished to magnify the image of the vice-president as

[7] Hanes Walton, Jr., *Black Politics: A Theoretical and Structural Analysis* (Philadelphia: J. P. Lippincott Co., 1972), 31–32.

a champion of civil rights. In any case, the major responsibilities for coordination were turned over to the attorney general—for the all-important Title VI enforcement; but there was never the emphasis needed in the Justice Department to make the programs work. The same general statement can be made about the other agencies dealing with civil rights enforcement other than under Title VI. Diffusion of authority meant civil rights would suffer.

One can agree with Dick Gregory who often said that he did not want his civil rights "on an installment plan." Afterall, why should black people have to struggle so hard for rights as American citizens which should be automatically theirs? They have the responsibilities, e.g., paying taxes and serving in the armed forces. Blacks should, therefore, also have the rights of citizenship. However, there is another dimension of the problem. No matter what civil rights laws were passed and implemented by the Johnson administration, these measures did not deal adequately with the cold hard facts of being poor and black. Civil rights, to be fully fruitful, have to be supplemented with adequate jobs and incomes. They are so intertwined that adequate jobs and income should be regarded as civil rights. The efforts made to deal with the war on poverty were pitifully inadequate in the Johnson administration. Much as the president discussed the possibility of having both "guns and butter" and being able to wage a battle against poverty as well as fight in Vietnam, the domestic front always took the back seat. Congress never funded the civil rights and poverty programs adequately. Top priority went to the war abroad, and despite some splendid rhetoric at times on the part of the president, the war to eliminate poverty and racism at home never seriously got off the ground. As so often mentioned before, the black middle class fared somewhat better, but at the end of the Johnson administration the black masses were if anything in some respects worse off than before. This is not to say, however, that all blacks did not still suffer from discrimination.

UNITED STATES GOVERNMENT PUBLICATIONS

Coleman, James S., *et al. Equality of Educational Opportunity.* 2 vols.; Washington, D.C.: U.S. Government Printing Offiice, 1966.

Equal Employment Opportunity Commission. Equal Employment Opportunity Report No. 1, *Job Patterns for Minorities and Women in Private Industry 1966.* 3 pts.; Washington, D.C.: U.S. Government Printing Office, 1968.

————. Equal Employment Opportunity Report No. 2, *Jobs for Minorities and Women in Private Industry 1967.* 2 pts., Washington, D.C.: U.S. Government Printing Office, n.d.

————. *Fourth Annual Report.* Washington, D.C.: U.S. Government Printing Office, 1970.

————. *Hearings on Discrimination in White Collar Employment, New York, N.Y., January 15–18, 1968.* Washington, D.C.: U.S. Government Printing Office, 1968.

————. *Hearings on Utilization of Minority and Women Workers in Certain Major Industries, Los Angeles, California, March 12–14, 1969.* Washington, D.C.: U.S. Government Printing Office, 1969.

————. *Second Annual Report, June, 1967.* Washington, D.C.: U.S. Government Printing Office, 1968.

————. *Third Annual Report.* Washington, D.C.: U.S. Government Printing Office, 1969.

Executive Order 11246, September 24, 1965, *Federal Register,* XXX (September 30, 1965).

Executive Order 11247, September 24, 1965, *Federal Register,* XXX (September 30, 1965).

Hill, Herbert. *Testimony of Herbert Hill, National Labor Director, National Association for the Advancement of Colored People Before the Ad Hoc Committee Hearings on Federal Contract Compliance, House of Representatives.* Washington, D.C.: U.S. Government Printing Office, December 5, 1968.

Nathan, Richard P. *Jobs and Civil Rights.* Washington, D.C.: U.S. Government Printing Office, 1969.

The President's Committee on Urban Housing. *A Decent Home.* Washington, D.C.: U.S. Government Printing Office, 1968.

Public Papers of the Presidents: Lyndon B. Johnson 1963–1969. Washington, D.C.: U.S. Government Printing Office, 1964–70.

Seeley, David S. *Desegregation Guidelines. Do They Go Far Enough?* Washington, D.C.: U.S. Government Printing Office, 1967.

U.S. Civil Service Commission. *Preliminary Report of Minority Group Employment 1969.* Washington, D.C.: U.S. Government Printing Office, 1969.

————. *Study of Minority Group Employment in the Federal Government.* Washington, D.C.: U.S. Government Printing Office, 1967.

U.S. Commission on Civil Rights. *Equal Opportunity in Farm Programs: An Appraisal of the Services Rendered by Agencies of the Department of Agriculture.* Washington, D.C.: U.S. Government Printing Office, 1965.

————. *Federal Civil Rights Enforcement Effort.* Washington, D.C.: U.S. Government Printing Office, 1970.

————. *Federal Enforcement of School Desegregation.* Washington, D.C.: U.S. Government Printing Office, 1969.

————. *For all the People: A Report on Equal Opportunity in State and Local Government Employment.* Washington, D.C.: U.S. Government Printing Office, 1969.

————. *Hearings before the U.S. Commission on Civil Rights, Jackson, Mississippi, February 16–20, 1965.* Washington, D.C.: U.S. Government Printing Office, 1965.

————. *HEW and Title VI.* Washington, D.C.: U.S. Government Printing Office, 1970.

————. *Law Enforcement. A Report on the Equal Protection of the Law in the South.* Washington, D.C.: U.S. Government Printing Office, 1965.

————. *Political Participation.* Washington, D.C.: U.S. Government Printing Office, 1968.

————. *Racial Isolation in the Public Schools.* 2 vols.; Washington, D.C.: U.S. Government Printing Office, 1967.

————. *Southern School Desegregation 1966–67.* Washington, D.C.: U.S. Government Printing Office, 1967.

————. *Title VI . . . One Year After the Survey of Health and Welfare Services in the South.* Washington, D.C.: U.S. Government Printing Office, 1966.

————. *Voting in Mississippi.* Washington, D.C.: U.S. Government Printing Office, 1965.

————. *The Voting Rights Act . . . The First Few Months.* Washington, D.C.: U.S. Government Printing Office, 1965.

U.S. Department of Labor. *Manpower Report of the President Including a Report on Manpower Requirements, Resources, Utilization and Training 1968.* Washington, D.C.: U.S. Government Printing Office, 1968.

————. *Statistics on Manpower. A Supplement to the Manpower Report to the President.* Washington, D.C.: U.S. Government Printing Office, 1969.

SECONDARY WORKS

BOOKS

Allen, Robert L. *Black Awakening in Capitalist America*. Garden City, N.Y.: Anchor Books, Inc., 1969.

Barker, Horace. *The Federal Retreat in School Desegregation*. Atlanta, Ga.: Southern Regional Council, 1969.

Becker, Joseph J., ed. *In Aid of the Unemployed*. Baltimore: The Johns Hopkins University Press, 1965.

Berger, Monroe. *Equality by Statute. The Revolution in Civil Rights*. Garden City, N.Y.: Doubleday & Co., 1967.

Berman, William C. *The Politics of Civil Rights During the Truman Administration*. Columbus: Ohio State University Press, 1970.

Blaustein, Albert P. and Robert L. Zangrando. *Civil Rights and the American Negro*. New York: Trident Press, 1968.

Blumrosen, Alfred W. *Black Employment and the Law*. New Brunswick, N.J.: Rutgers University Press, 1971.

Bond, Julian. *A Time to Speak. A Time to Act. The Movement in Politics*. New York: Simon and Schuster, 1972.

Carmichael, Stokeley and Charles V. Hamilton. *Black Power*. New York: Random House, 1967.

Chester, Lester, *et al. The Presidential Election of 1968*. New York: The Viking Press, 1969.

The Civil Rights Act of 1964. Washington, D.C.: Bureau of National Affairs, 1964.

Civil Rights Progress Report 1970. Washington, D.C. Congresssional Quarterly, Inc., 1971.

Congressional Quarterly Almanac. Washington, D.C.: Congressional Quarterly, Inc., 1964–1970. Vols. XIX–XXV.

Cosman, Bernard. *Five States for Goldwater*. University: University of Alabama Press, 1966.

Cousens, Frances Reisman. *Public Civil Rights Agencies and Fair Employment. Promise vs. Performance*. New York: Frederick A. Praeger, Publishers, 1969.

Dalfiume, Richard M. *Desegregation of the U.S. Armed Forces*. Columbia: University of Missouri Press, 1969.

Davis, John P., ed. *The American Negro Reference Book*. Englewood Cliffs, N.J.: Prentice-Hall, 1966.

Drenan, William D., ed. *The Fourth Strike: Hiring and Training the Disadvantaged*. New York: American Management Association, Inc., 1970.

Eisenhower, Dwight D. *The White House Years: Waging Peace 1956–1961*. Garden City, N.Y.: Doubleday & Co., 1965.

Evans, Roland and Robert Novak. *Lyndon B. Johnson: The Exercise of Power*. New York: The New American Library, 1966.

Fancher, Betty. *Black Voices in the South: Black Students Talk About Their Experience in Desegregated Schools.* Atlanta: Southern Regional Council, 1970.

Flax, Michael J. *Blacks and Whites: An Experiment in Urban Indicators.* Washington, D.C.: The Urban Institute, 1971.

Foley, Eugene P. *The Achieving Ghetto.* Washington, D.C.: The National Press, Inc., 1968.

Fourteen Years of Failure in Southern School Desegregation. Atlanta, Ga.: Southern Regional Council, 1968.

Freeman, Linton C. and Morris H. Sunshine. *Patterns of Residential Segregation.* Cambridge, Mass.: Schenkman Publishing Co., 1970.

Friedman, Lawrence M. *Government and Slum Housing: A Century of Frustration.* Chicago: Rand McNally & Co., 1968.

Goldman, Eric F. *The Tragedy of Lyndon Johnson.* New York: Alfred A. Knopf, 1969.

Greer, Edward. *Black Liberation Politics: A Reader.* Boston: Allyn and Bacon, Inc., 1971.

Grier, George and Eunice. *Equality and Beyond: Housing and the Goals of the Great Society.* Chicago: Quadrangle Books, 1966.

Harvey, James C. *Civil Rights During the Kennedy Administration.* Hattiesburg, Miss.: University & College Press of Mississippi, 1971.

Henderson, William L. and Larry C. Lidebur. *Economic Disparity: Problems and Strategies for Black Americans.* New York: The Free Press, 1970.

Holland, Jerome. *Black Opportunity.* New York: Weybright and Talley, 1969.

Hughes, John Emmet. *The Ordeal of Power: A Political Memoir of the Eisenhower Years.* New York: Atheneum Publishers, 1963.

Johnson, Lyndon Baines. *The Vantage Point: Perspectives of the Presidency, 1963–1969.* New York: Holt, Rinehart and Winston, 1971.

Johnson, Sam Houston. *My Brother Lyndon.* New York: Cowles Book Co., Inc., 1969.

Jones Charles O. *An Introduction to the Study of Public Policy.* Belmont, Calif.: Wadsworth Publishing Co., Inc., 1970.

Keech, William R. *The Impact of Negro Voting: The Role of the Vote in the Quest for Equality.* Chicago: Rand McNally, 1968.

King, Donald B. and Charles W. Quick, eds. *Legal Aspects of the Civil Rights Movement.* Detroit: Wayne State University Press, 1965.

King, Martin Luther, Jr. *Where Do We Go From Here?* New York: Harper & Row, Publishers, 1967.

Kovarsky, Ivor and William Albrecht. *Black Employment: The Impact of Religion, Economic Theory, Politics, and Law.* Ames, Iowa: The Iowa State University Press, 1970.

Konvitz, Milton R. *Expanding Liberties: Freedom's Gains in Postwar America.* New York: The Viking Press, 1966.

Krislov, Samuel. *The Negro in Federal Employment: The Quest for Opportunity.* Minneapolis: University of Minnesota Press, 1967.

Kvoraceus, William, *et al. Poverty, Education and Race Relations.* Boston: Allyn and Bacon, 1968.

Lincoln, C. Eric. *Sounds of the Struggle: Persons and Perspectives in Civil Rights.* New York: William Morrow & Co., 1967.

MacNeil, Neil. *Dirksen: Portrait of the Public Man.* New York and Cleveland: World Publishing Co., 1970.

McCord, John M. *With All Deliberate Speed: Civil Rights Theory and Reality.* Urbana: University of Illinois Press, 1969.

Mangum, Garth L. and Lewell M. Glenn. *Employing the Disadvantaged in the Federal Civil Service.* Washington, D.C.: University of Michigan, Wayne State University and National Manpower Policy Task Force, 1969.

Mangum, Garth L. *MDTA: Foundations of Federal Manpower Policy.* Baltimore: The Johns Hopkins University Press, 1968.

Morgan, Ruth. *The President and Civil Rights: Policy-Making by Executive Order.* New York: St. Martin's Press, 1970.

Murphy, Reg. and Hal Gulliver. *Southern Political Strategy.* New York: Charles Scribner's Sons, 1971.

National Committee Against Discrimination in Housing. *Model Cities and Metropolitan Desegregation.* New York: National Committee Against Discrimination in Housing, 1967.

The Negro Almanac. New York: Bellwether Publishing Co., 1967.

The Negro Handbook. Chicago: Johnson Publishing Co., 1966.

Northrup, Herbert R. and Richard L. Rowan. *The Negro and Employment Opportunity: Problems and Practices.* Ann Arbor: The University of Michigan Press, 1965.

Orfield, Gary. *The Reconstruction of Southern Education. The Schools and the 1964 Civil Rights Act.* New York: John Wiley & Sons, 1969.

Peeks, Edward. *The Long Struggle for Black Power.* New York: Charles Scribner's Sons, 1971.

Race Relations in the USA, 1954–68. New York: Charles Scribner's Sons, 1970.

Report of the National Advisory Commission. *The Kerner Report.* New York: Bantam, 1968.

Revolution in Civil Rights. Washington, D.C.: Congressional Quarterly, Inc., 1968.

Rodgers, Harrell R. and Charles S. Bullock III. *Law and Social Change: Civil Rights Laws and their Consequences.* New York: McGraw-Hill Book Co., 1972.

Ross, Arthur and Herbert Hill, eds. *Employment, Race, and Poverty.* New York: Harcourt, Brace & World, Inc., 1967.

School Desegregation, 1966: The Slow Undoing. Atlanta: Southern Regional Council, 1967.

Schussheim, Morton J. *Toward New Housing Policy.* New York: The Committee for Economic Development, 1969.

Sharkansky, Ira. *Public Administration: Policy-Making in Government Agencies.* Chicago: Markham Publishing Co., 1972.

Sherrill, Robert. *The Accidental President.* New York: Grossman Publishers, 1967.

Silberman, Charles E. *Crisis in the Classroom: The Remaking of American Education.* New York: Vantage Books, 1971.

Sinfield, Adrian. *The Long-Term Unemployed.* Paris: Organization for Economic Cooperation and Development, 1968.

Sovern, Michael I. *Legal Restraints in Racial Discrimination in Employment.* New York: Twentieth Century Fund, 1966.

Stillman III, Richard. *Integration of the Negro in the U.S. Armed Forces.* New York: Frederick A. Praeger, 1968.

Strong, Donald S. *Negroes, Ballots, and Judges: National Voting Rights Legis'ation in the Courts.* University: University of Alabama Press, 1968.

Sugarman, Tracy. *Stranger at the Gates: Summer in Mississippi.* New York: Hill and Wang, 1966.

Sundquist, James L. *Politics and Policy: The Eisenhower, Kennedy and Johnson Years.* Washington, D.C.: The Brookings Institution, 1968.

Voter Education Project. *Voter Registration in the South.* Atlanta: Southern Regional Council, 1968.

Walton, Hanes, Jr. *B!ack Politics: A Theoretical and Structural Analysis.* Philadelphia: J.P. Lippincott Co., 1972.

Watters, Pat. *Encounter with the Future.* Atlanta, Ga.: Southern Regional Council, 1965.

White, Theodore H. *The Making of the President, 1964.* New York: Atheneum Publishers, 1965.

Wirt, Frederick W. *Politics of Southern Equality: Law and Change in a Mississippi County.* Chicago: Aldine Publishing Co., 1970.

Witherspoon, Joseph Parker. *Administrative Implementation of Civil Rights.* Austin: The University of Texas Press, 1968.

Wolk, Allan. *The Presidency and Black Civil Rights.* Cranbury, N.J. Fairleigh Dickinson University Press, 1971.

Wright, Nathan, Jr. *Black Power and Urban Unrest.* New York: Hawthorn Books, Inc., 1967.

Yette, Samuel F. *The Choice: The Issue of Black Survival in America.* New York: Berkley Publishing Corporation, 1971.

PERIODICALS AND NEWSLETTERS

"After Alabama . . . Negro's Next Battleground." *U.S. News & World Report,* 58 (April 5, 1965), 37–38.

Anderson, Frederick D. "Civil Rights and Fair Employment." *Business Lawyer,* 22 (January, 1967), 513–31.

"Armed Forces: The Integrated Society." *Time,* 88 (December 23, 1966), 22.

Bachelder, Alan B. "Decline in the Relative Income of Negro Men." *Quarterly Journal of Economics,* 78 (November, 1964), 525–48.

"Backlash Jitters." *The New Rrpublic,* 155 (October 22, 1966), 5–6.

Benewitz, Maurice C. "Coverage Under Title VII of the Civil Rights Act." *Labor Law Journal,* 17 (May, 1966), 285–91.

Berg, Richard. "Title VII: A Three Years View." *Notre Dame Lawyer,* 44 (February, 1969), 311–44.

Bennett, Lerone, Jr. "What Negroes Can Expect from President Lyndon Johnson." *Ebony,* 19 (January, 1964), 81–84.

Bickel, Alexander M. "The Belated Civil Rights Legislation of 1968." *New Republic,* 15 (March 30, 1968), 11–12.

————. "Civil Rights' Dim Prospects." *New Republic,* 155 (September 17, 1966), 17–18.

Bolner, James. "The Supreme Court and Racially Imbalanced Schools in 1967." *Journal of Negro Education,* 38 (Winter, 1969), 125–34.

Brimmer, Andrew. "Employment Patterns and the Dilemma of Desegregation." *Integrated Education,* 5 (October–November, 1965), 17–23.

Brooke, Edward, *et al.* "Non-Discrimination in Sale or Rental of Property: Comments on Jones v. Alfred H. Meyer Co. and Title VII of the Civil Rights Act of 1968." *Vanderbilt Law Review,* 22 (April, 1969), 455–502.

Campbell, Robert F. "Community Control." *Southern Education Report,* 4 (July–August, 1968), 19f.

Carmichael, Stokeley. "Toward Black Liberation." *Massachusetts Review,* 7 (Autumn, 1966), 639–51.

Cass, James. "How Much Progress is Enough?" *Saturday Review,* July 17, 1971, 41.

"Civil Rights." *Congressional Quarterly Weekly Report,* 24 (September 9, 1966), 1964.

"Civil Rights." *Time,* 88 (September 30, 1966), 21.

"Civil Rights Leader Shot." *Congressional Quarterly Weekly Report,* 24 (June 10, 1966), 1242.

"Civil Rights Lobbying." *Congressional Quarterly Weekly Report,* 24 (August 5, 1966), 1713.

"Civil Rights Act Signed Into Law." *Congressional Quarterly Weekly Report,* 22 (July 3, 1964), 1331.

Clark, Henry. "Desegregated Housing: Still Worth Waiting For." *Social Action,* 33 (May, 1967), 8–14.

"Cloture on Civil Rights Breaks a 26-Year Precedent." *Congressional Quarterly Weekly Report,* 22 (June 12, 1964), 1169–72.

Cloward, Richard A. and Frances Fox Piven. "Mississippi: Starving by the Rule Book." *The Nation,* 204 (April 3, 1967), 429–31.

Coleman, James S. "The Concept of Equality of Educational Opportuntiy." *Harvard Educational Review,* 38 (Winter, 1968), 7–22.

"Comment; Title VI and the 1964 Civil Rights Act—Implementation and Impact." *George Washington Law Review,* 36 (May, 1968), 824–993.

"Controversy Over Public Housing: Pro and Con." *Congressional Digest,* 45 (November, 1966), 257–88.

"Civil Rights." *Congressional Quarterly Weekly Report,* 24 (August 12, 1966), 1719.

Cooper, Martin L. "The New School Desegregation Guidelines." *Harvard Civil Rights-Civil Liberties Review,* 2 (Fall, 1966), 86–109.

Cronin, Thomas E. "Everybody Believes in Democracy Until He Gets to the White House . . . : An Examination of White House-Departmental Relations," *Law and Contemporary Problems,* 35 (Summer, 1970), 573–625.

Cunningham, Luvern L. "Federal Role Arouses Growing Concern Among School Officials." *American School Board Journal,* 152 (May, 1966), 7, 63–64.

"Democratic Platform Seeks Wider Voter Appeal." *Congressional Quarterly Weekly Report,* 22 (August 28, 1964), 1964.

"Desegregation." *Southern Education Report,* 1 (July–August, 1965), 31.

"Desegregation." *Southern Education Report,* 1 (November–December, 1965), 30.

"Desegregation." *Southern Education Report,* 1 (January–February, 1966), 28–32.

"Dirksen Amendments." *New Republic,* 150 (June 6, 1964), 3–4.

" 'The Disadvantaged' Remedies for Racial Isolation." *Education Digest,* 32 (April, 1967), 1–4.

Egerton, John T., "When Desegregation Comes, the Negro Principals Go," *Southern Education Report,* 3 (December, 1967), 8–12.

"Employment of Negroes in the Federal Government." *Monthly Labor Review,* 88 (October, 1965), 1222.

"Enforcing Civil Rights Laws: The Full Circle of Failure." *Current,* 102 (December, 1968), 33.

"Fair Housing Again in Rights Bill." *U.S. News & World Report,* 62 (February 27, 1967), 69.

"The Federal Fair Housing Requirements: Title VIII of the 1968 Civil Rights Act." *Duke Law Journal* (August, 1969), 733–71.

Fein, Rashi. "Relative Income of Negro Men: Some Recent Data." *Quarterly Journal of Economics,* 80 (May, 1966), 336.

"Final House Bill on Civil Rights Scheduled." *Congressional Quarterly Weekly Report,* 22 (June 27, 1964), 1273–77.

"Findings in the Commission's Equal Protection Report." *Congressional Quarterly Weekly Report,* 23 (November 23, 1965), 2262–65.

Fleming, Harold C. "The Federal Executive and Civil Rights: 1961–1965." *Daedalus,* 94 (Fall, 1965), 921–48.

Goodman, Walter. "Victory for 400,000 Children: The Case of Mrs. Sylvester Smith." *New York Times Magazine*, April 25, 1968, 28–29f.

"Government Hiring More Negroes—But in Low Paid Jobs." *Congressional Quarterly Weekly Report*, (February 14, 1969), 263.

Grier, George W. "The Negro Ghettos and Federal Housing Policy." *Law and Contemporary Problems*, 32 (Summer, 1967), 550–60.

Grove, Gene. "The Army and the Negro." *New York Times Magazine.* July 24, 1966, 4–5f.

Hamilton, Charles V. "Black Americans and the Modern Political Struggle" *The Black World*, 19 (May, 1970), 5–9f.

Harvey, James C. and Charles H. Holmes. "Busing and School Desegregation," *Phi Delta Kappan*, 53 (May, 1972), 540–42.

"HEW Calls for Full Desegregation by 1967." *Southern School News*, 11 (May, 1965), 1.

Hindell, Keith, "Civil Rights Breaks the Cloture Barrier." *Political Quarterly*, 36 (April–June, 1965), 142–53.

"House Passes Voting Rights Bill." *Congressional Quarterly Weekly Report*, 23 (July 16, 1965), 1361–63.

"House Passes Comprehensive Civil Rights Bill." *Congressional Quarterly Weekly Report*, 22 (February 28,1964), 385.

Hudgins, H. C. "Desegregation: Where Schools Stand with the Courts as the New Year Begins." *American School Board Journal*, 156 (January, 1969), 21–25.

"The Issue Is Conduct." *Newsweek*, 68 (September 26, 1966), 32.

"It Looks Like a 'Hot Summer' with Selma the Beginning." *U.S. News & World Report*, 58 (March 22, 1965), 32–33.

Janowitz, Morris, "American Democracy and Military Service." *Trans-Action*, 4 (March, 1967), 5–7, 57–59.

Jenkins, Timothy Lionel. "A Study of the Federal Effort to End Job Bias: A History, A Status Report, and a Prognosis." *Howard Law Journal*, 14 (Summer, 1968), 259–329.

"Jobs and Minorities." *New Republic*, 158 (February 17, 1968), 12.

"Johnson Defeats Goldwater by 15 Million: GOP Loses 38 House Seats, State Legislatures." *Congressional Quarterly Weekly Report*, 22 (November 6, 1964), 2625–64.

Kain, John F. "Housing Segregation, Negro Employment and Metropolitan Decentralization." *Quarterly Journal of Economics*, 82 (May, 1968), 175–197.

Kempton, Murray. "Senator Goldwater Dissents." *The Spectator*, 212 (June 26, 1964), 843.

Killingsworth, Mark. "Desegregating Public Housing." *The New Leader*, 51 (October 7, 1968), 13–14.

Kinoy, Arthur. "Jones v. Mayer Co.: An Historic Step Forward." *Vanderbilt Law Review*, 22 (April, 1969), 475–83.

Knoll, Erwin. "There's Room for Negotiations." *Southern Education Report*, 1 (May–June, 1966), 4.

Kovarsky, Ivor. "The Negro and Fair Employment." *Kentucky Law Journal*, 56 (Summer, 1967–68), 757–829.

"Leaning on HEW." *Newsweek*, 66 (October 18, 1965), 98.

Lee, Ulysses. "The Draft and the Negro." *Current History*, 55 (July, 1968), 28–33, 47–48.

Leesen, Jim. "A Popular and Precise Phrase." *Southern Education Report*, 3 (June, 1968), 13–15.

————. "The Crumbling Legal Barriers to Desegregation." *Southern Education Report*, 2 (October, 1966), 11.

————. "Desegregation: A New Approach, A New Deadline." *Southern Education Report*, 3 (January–February, 1968), 14.

————. "Desegregating Faculties." *Southern Education Report*, 3 (May, 1968), 27.

————. "Few Statistics—No Summary." *Southern Education Report*, 4 (December, 1968), 11.

————. "Guidelines, A Repeat Performance." *Southern Education Report*, 2 (October, 1966), 28–30.

————. "Guidelines and a New Count." *Southern Education Report*, 2 (January–February, 1967), 31.

————. "Reprieve for Freedom of Choice." *Southern Education Report*, 2 (March, 1967), 30–31.

————. "The Attention Now Turns to Balance." *Southern Education Report*, 2 (March, 1967), 12.

————. "Time and Variations." *Southern Education Report*, 4 (July–August, 1968), 5.

Lodge, Claire C. "The Negro Job Situation: Has It Improved?" *Monthly Labor Review*, 92 (January, 1969), 20–28.

Lytle, Clifford M. "The History of the Civil Rights Bill of 1964." *Journal of Negro History*, 51 (October, 1966), 275–96.

Manley, John T. "The United States Civil Rights Act of 1964." *Contemporary Review*, 206 (January, 1965), 10–13.

Marshall, Ray. "Prospects for Equal Employment: Conflicting Portents." *Labor Law Journal*, 16 (August, 1965), 453–68.

Marshall, Ray and Vernon Briggs, Jr. "Remedies for Discrimination in Apprenticeship Programs." *Industrial Relations*, 6 (May, 1967), 303–20.

McCarty, L. Thorne and Russell B. Stevenson. "The Voting Rights Act of 1965: An Evaluation." *Harvard Civil Rights-Civil Liberties Review*, 3 (Spring, 1968), 357–411.

McLemore, Leslie Burl. "The Effects of Political Participation Upon a Closed Society. A State in Transition: The Changing Political Climate in Mississippi." *Negro Educational Review*, 23 (January, 1972), 5–12.

Meier, Deborah. "The Coleman Report." *Integrated Education*, 5 (December, 1967–January, 1968), 37–45.

"Moderate Forces Defeated in Disputes Over Party Platform." *Congressional Quarterly Weekly Report*, 22 (July 17, 1964), 1485.

Mooney, Joseph D. "Housing Segregation, Negro Employment and Metropolitan Decentralization." *Quarterly Journal of Economics*, 83 (May, 1969), 299–311.

Morsell, John. "Racial Desegregation and Integration in Public Education." *Journal of Negro Education*, 38 (Summer, 1969), 276–84.

Moskas, Charles C. "Racial Integration in the Armed Forces." *American Journal of Sociology*, 72 (September, 1966), 132–48.

Muse, Benjamin. "Climax of a Revolution." *New South*, 23 (Summer, 1968), 2–13.

"NAACP Official Says Regulations Are Weak." *Southern School News*, 11 (June, 1965), 3.

"National Guard and Negroes." *America*, 117 (September 2, 1967), 213.

"Negroes Double Enrollment with Whites." *Southern School News*, 11 (December, 1964), 1.

"Negroes in the Army." *Trans-Action*, 4 (December, 1966), 5.

"Negroes Move Up in Government." *U.S. News & World Report*, 63 (July 3, 1967), 57–58.

"1964 Platform Turns GOP Sharply to the Right." *Congressional Quarterly Weekly Report*, 22 (July 17, 1964), 1488.

"Notes: Desegregation of Public School Faculties." *Iowa Law Review*, 51 (Spring, 1966), 681–96.

"Only Nine Percent of Southern, Border Negroes in School with Whites." *Congressional Quarterly Weekly Report*, 22 (January 3, 1964), 2.

"Opening the Door." *Time*, 91 (April 19, 1968), 20.

"Opening the Record on Jobs for Negroes." *Business Week*, August 12, 1967, 130.

"President Proposes New Civil Rights Legislation." *Congressional Quarterly Report*, 25 (February 17, 1967), 239.

Prothro, James W. "Stateways Versus Folkways Revisited." *Journal of Politics*, 34 (May, 1972), 352–64.

Pyle, Christopher and Richard Morgan. "Johnson's Civil Rights Shake-Up." *The New Leader*, 48 (October 11, 1965), 3–6.

Rachel, Anthony M. "EEO: We Must Not Settle for Less." *Civil Service Journal*, 7 (July–September, 1966), 1–5.

"Racism Arrested?" *Christian Century*, 85 (April 24, 1968), 507–08.

Rasmussen, David. "A Note on the Relative Income of Nonwhite Men, 1948–1968." *Quarterly Journal of Economics*, 84 (February, 1970), 168–72.

"Revised Figures Show More Negroes in Biracial Schools." *Southern School News*, 10 (January, 1964), pt. 1, 14.

Rutledge, Edward and Jack E. Wood, Jr. "Government and the Ghettos." *Social Action*, 33 (May, 1967), 15–21.

Ryan, William. "Uncle Sam's Betrayal." *The Progressive*, 32 (May, 1968), 25–28.

"Senate Bypasses Judiciary on Civil Rights." *Congressional Quarterly Weekly Report*, 22 (February 28, 1964), 385.

"Senate Kills Civil Rights Bill." *Congressional Quarterly Weekly Report,* 24 (September 23, 1966), 2199.

"Senate Passes Voting Rights Bill, 77–19." *Congressional Quarterly Weekly Report,* 23 (May 28, 1965), 1007–09.

"Senate Rejects Limit on Civil Rights Debate." *Congresional Quarterly Weekly Report,* 24 (September 16, 1966), 2141.

"Senate Wraps Up Final Version of the Civil Rights Act." *Congressional Quarterly Weekly Report,* 22 (June 19, 1964), 1199–1204.

Smith, Donald Hugh. "Civil Rights: A Problem of Communications." *Phylon,* 27 (Winter, 1966), 379–87.

Sorkin, Alan L. "Education, Migration and Negro Employment." *Social Forces,* 47 (March, 1969), 265–74.

"Southern Negro Voter Statistics by State." *Congressional Quarterly Weekly Report,* 23 (March 23, 1965), 557.

"State of the Union Message, January 10, 1967." *Congressional Quarterly Weekly Report,* 25 (January 13, 1967), 45.

Steif, William. "The New Look in Civil Rights Enforcement." *Southern Education Report,* 3 (September, 1967), 4–5.

Stillman, Richard III. "Negroes in the Armed Forces." *Phylon,* 30 (Summer, 1969), 139–59.

"Sweeping Civil Rights Bill Introduced in Congress." *Congressional Quarterly Weekly Report,* 23 (March 19, 1965), 427–28.

"Text of President Johnson's Civil Rights Message, February 15, 1967." *Congressional Quarterly Weekly Report,* 25 (February 17, 1967), 262–67.

"Text of President Johnson's March 13 News Conference." *Congressional Quarterly Weekly Report,* 23 (March 19, 1965), 449–51.

"Text of President Johnson's Message on Civil Rights, April 28, 1966." *Congressional Quarterly Weekly Report,* 24 (May 6, 1966), 943–46.

"Text of President Johnson's State of Union Message, January 4, 1965." *Congressional Quarterly Weekly Report,* 23 (January 8, 1965), 52.

"Text of the President's Voting Rights Speech to Congress, March 15, 1965." *Congressional Quarterly Weekly Report,* 23 (March 19, 1965), 445–47.

"The Time for Pretending is Past." *Christianity and Crisis,* 24 (June 26, 1964), 843.

Tyler, Harold R. "The Meaning of the Civil Rights Act." *New South,* 19 (May, 1964), 3–7.

Van Til, William. "The Great American Cop-Out." *Phi Delta Kappan,* 54 (October, 1972), 128.

"Voting Rights." *Congressional Quarterly Weekly Report,* 23 (August 13, 1965), 1595.

"Voting Rights Bill Sent to the President." *Congressional Quarterly Weekly Report,* 23 (August 6, 1965), 1539–40.

Walden, John C. and Allen D. Cleveland. "The South's New Segregation Academies." *Phi Delta Kappan,* 53 (December, 1971), 234–35f.

Walker, Alice. "Civil Rights Movement: What Good Was It?" *American Scholar*, 36 (Autumn, 1967), 550–54.

Weaver, Robert C. "Eleanor and LBJ and Black America." *Crisis*, 79 (June–July, 1972), 191–92.

Worsnop, Richard L. "Black Pride." *Editorial Research Reports*, 2 (September 11, 1968), 661–680.

Zangrando, Robert L. "From Civil Rights to Black Liberation: The Unsettled 1960's." *Current History*, 57 (November, 1969), 281–86f.

NEWSPAPERS

New York *Times*, 1963–69.